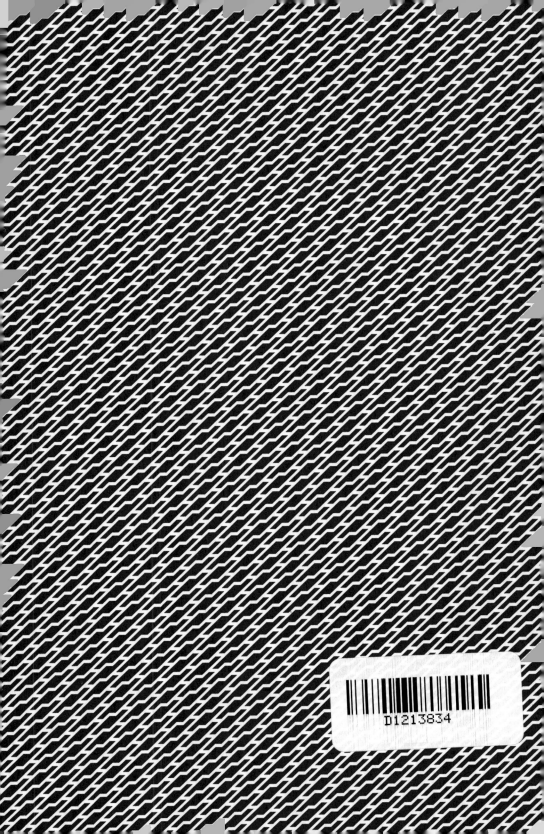

VORTEX ©2014 WILLIAM CARDINI
FIRST EDITION OCTOBER 2014
ISBN 9780985415037

PUBLISHED BY SPARKPLUG BOOKS,
PO BOX 10952, PORTLAND, OR, 972960952
PRINTED IN THE US BY
1984 PRINTING OF OAKLAND, CA

SPARKPLUGCOMICBOOKS.COM
HYPERCASTLE.COM

COVER BY GLADE HENSEL

VORTEX

WILLIAM CARDINI

SPARKPLUG BOOKS

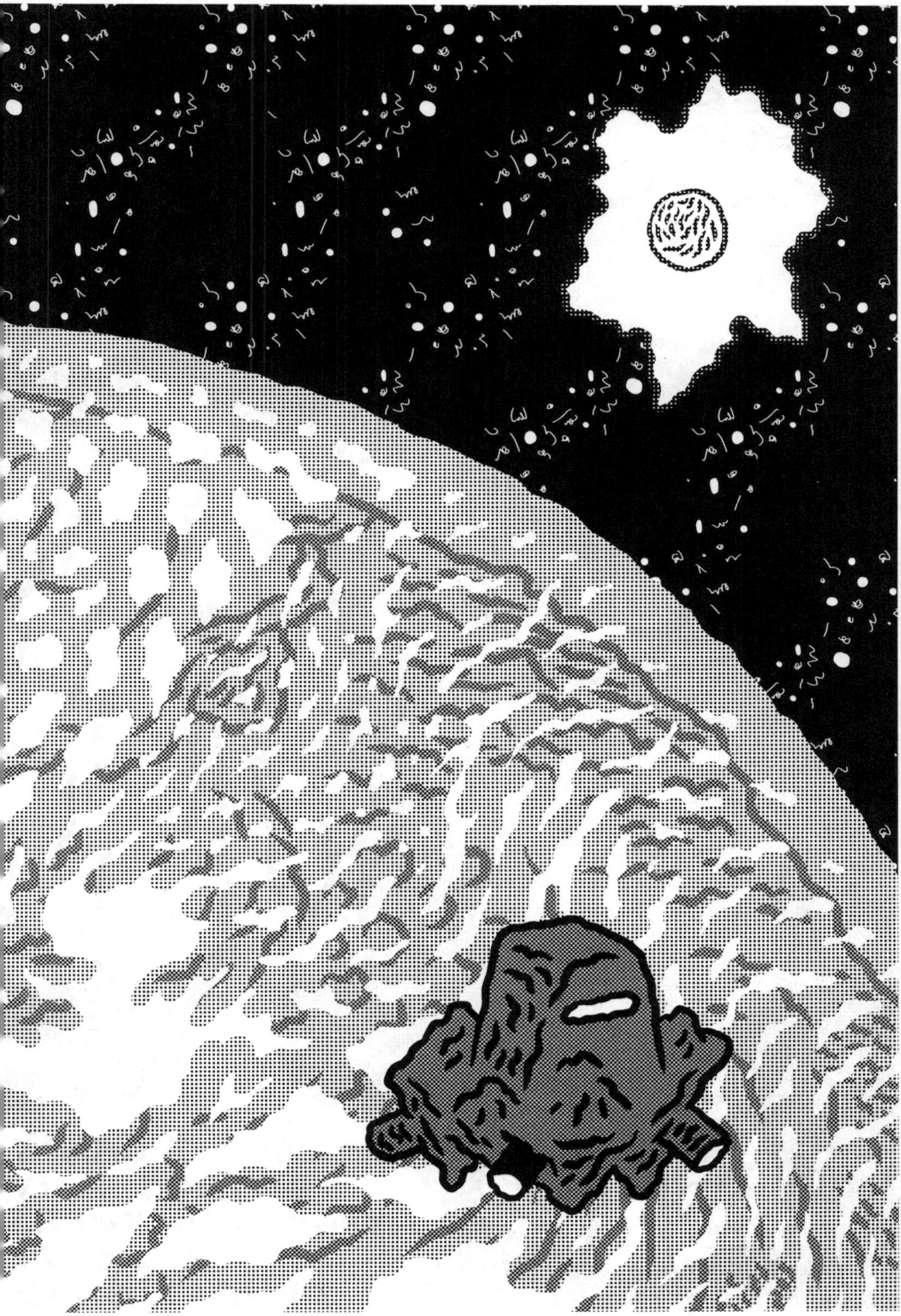

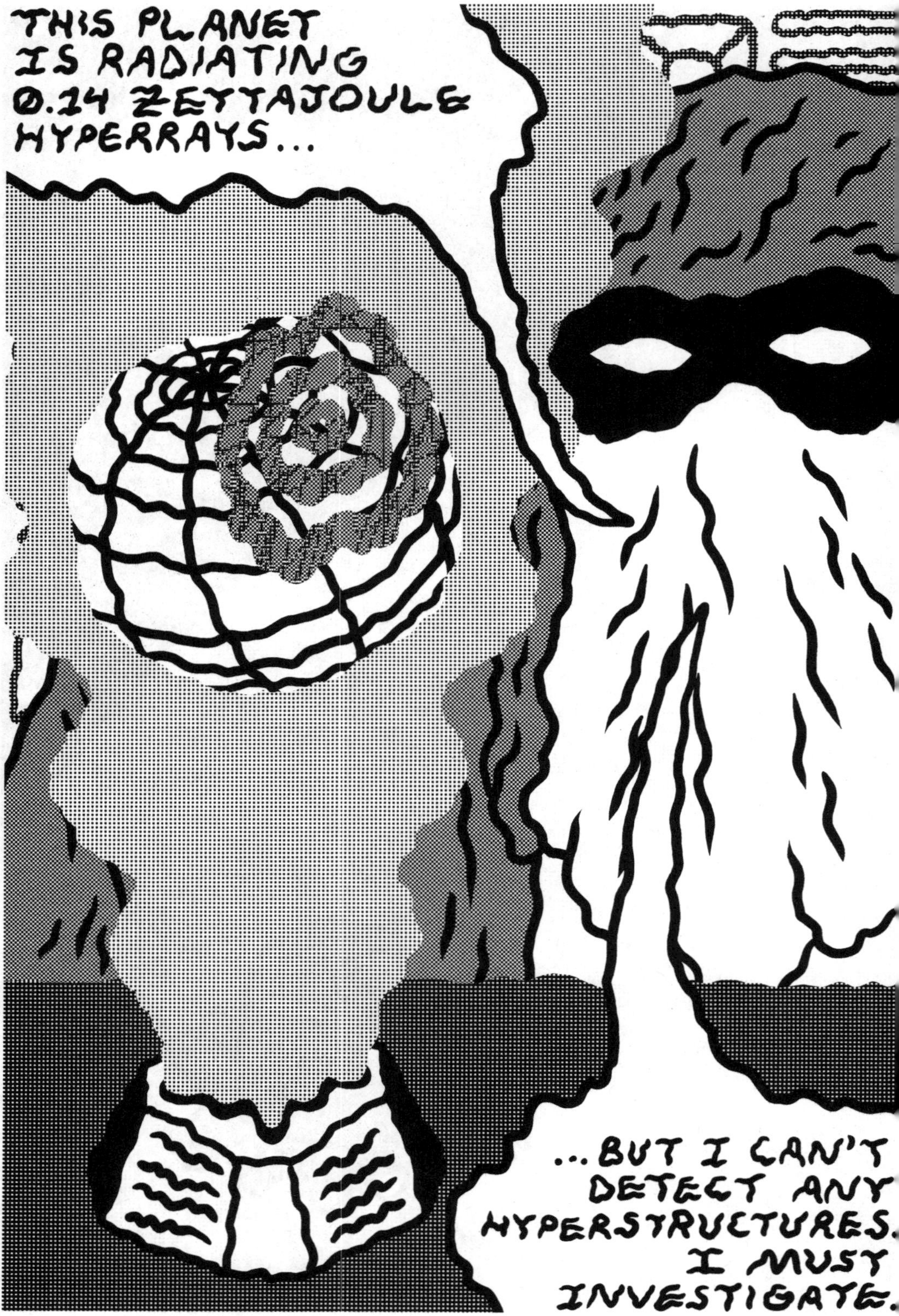
THIS PLANET IS RADIATING 0.14 ZETTAJOULE HYPERRAYS...
...BUT I CAN'T DETECT ANY HYPERSTRUCTURES. I MUST INVESTIGATE.

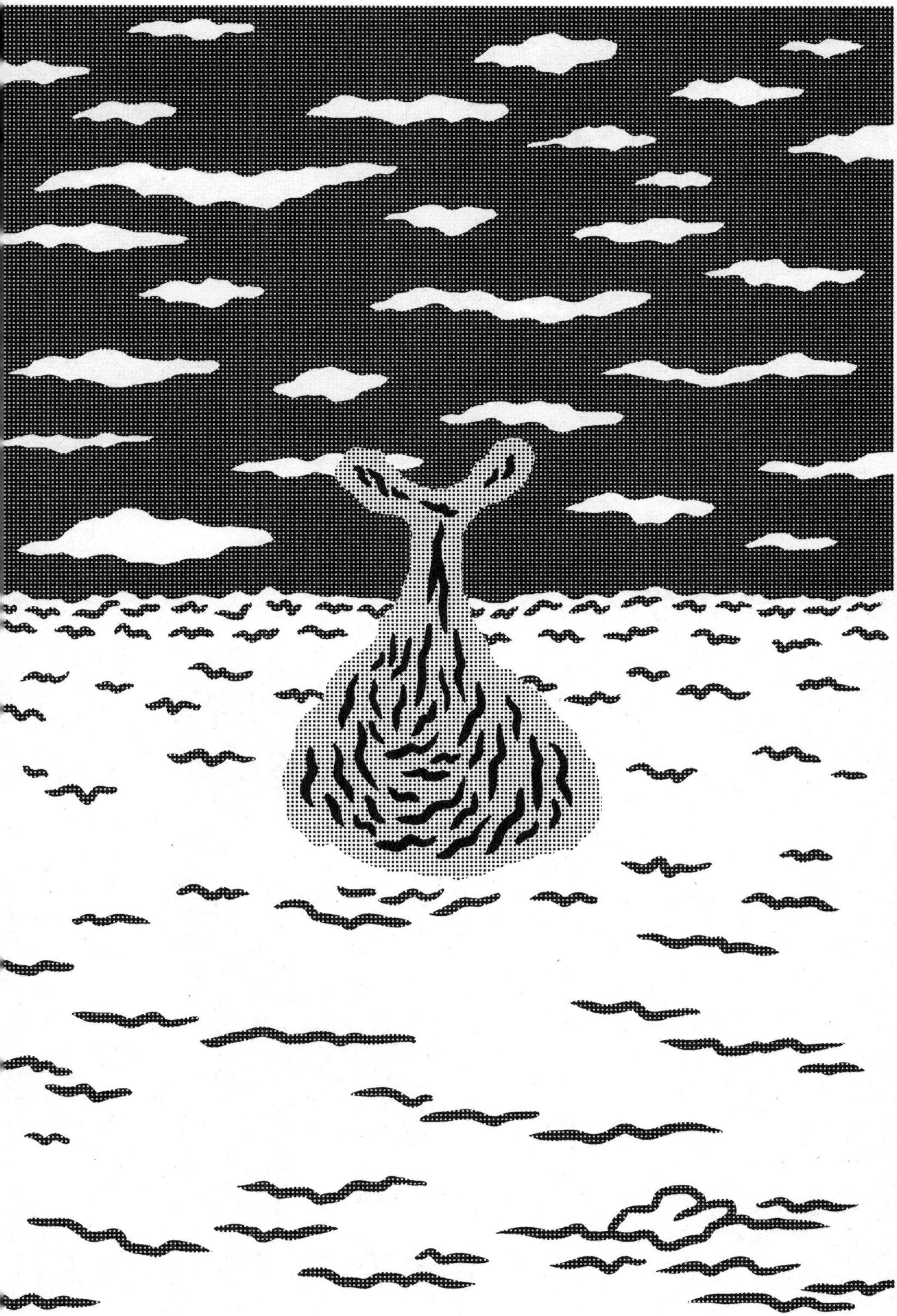

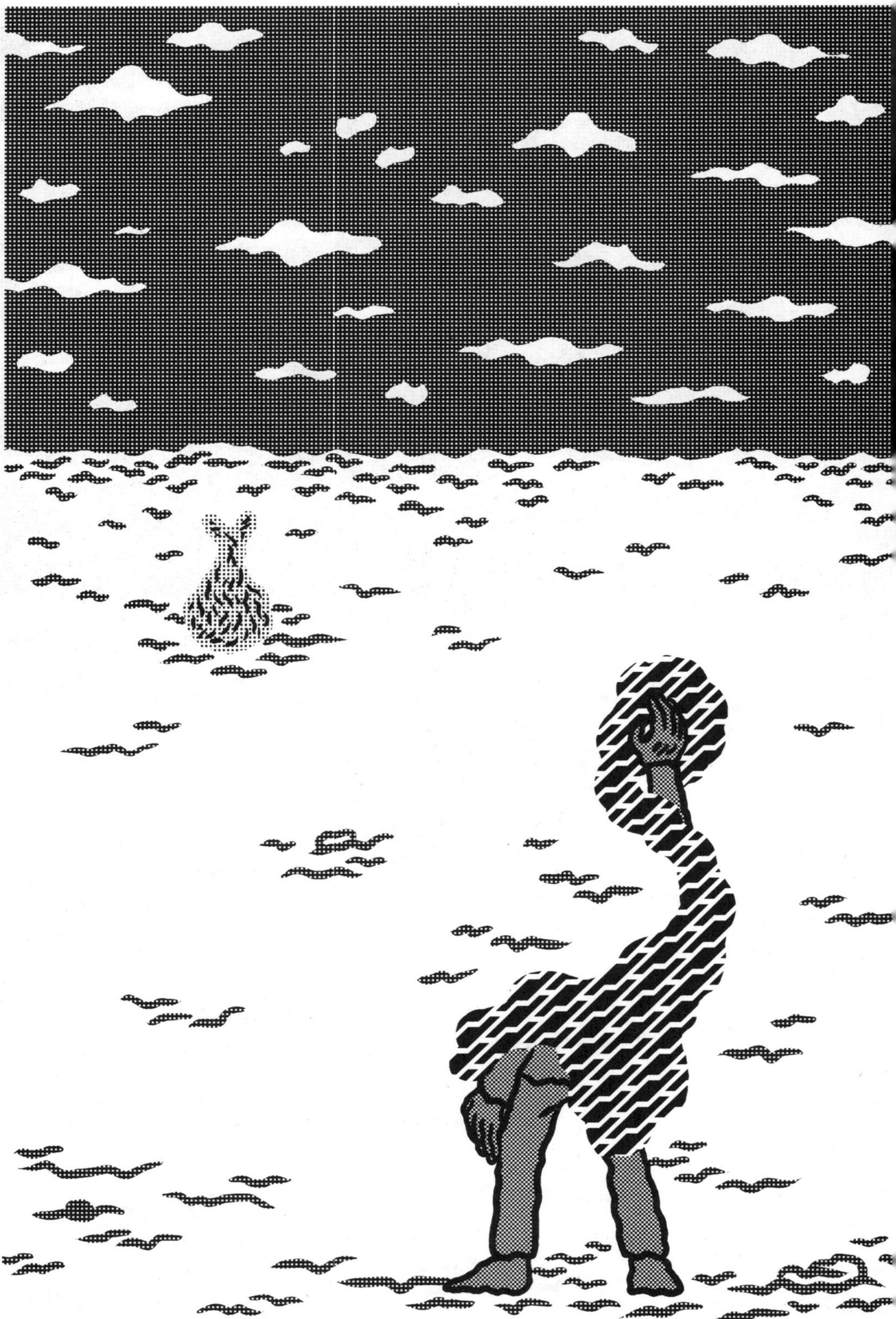

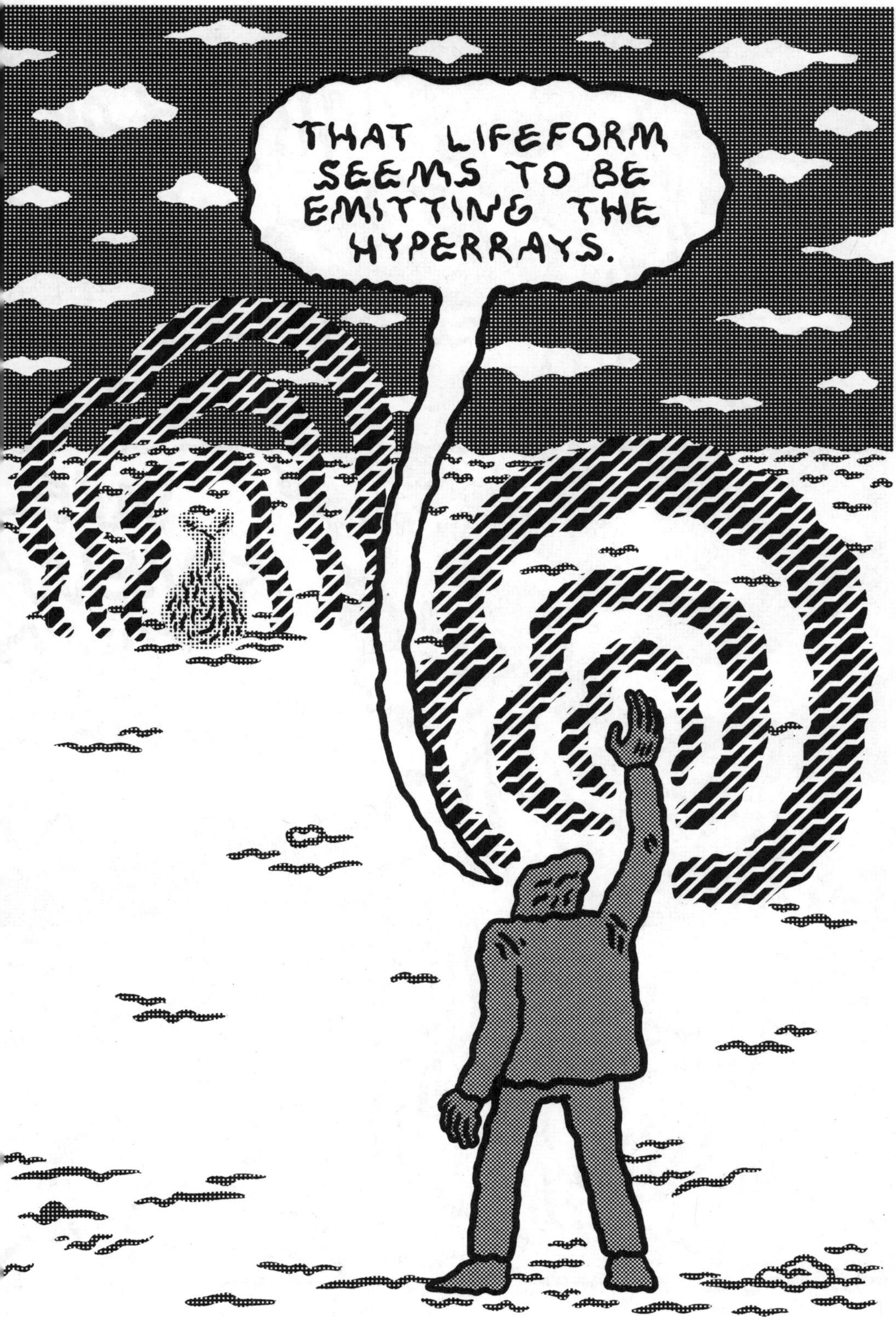
THAT LIFEFORM SEEMS TO BE EMITTING THE HYPERRAYS.

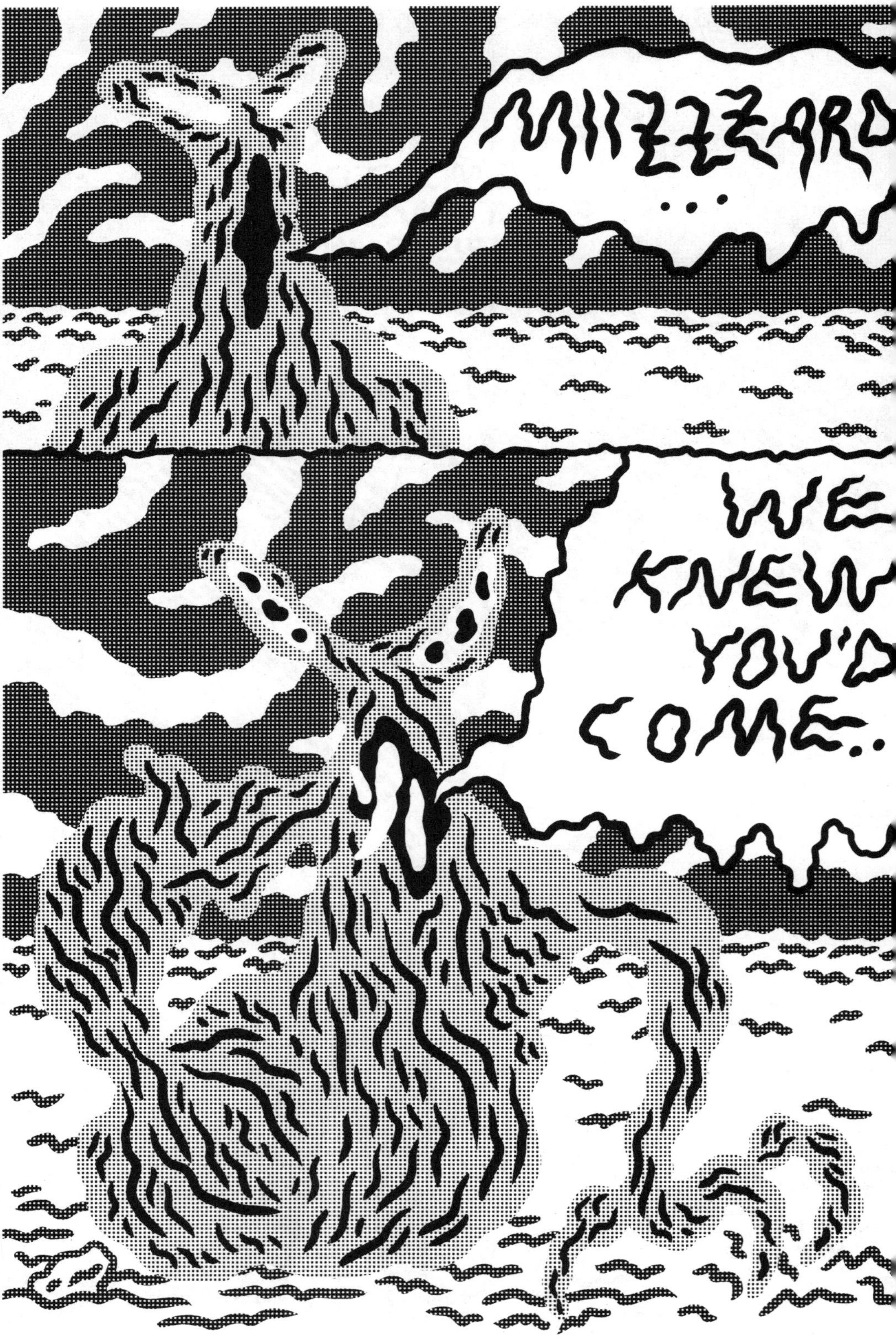
WIIZZZARD ...
WE KNEW YOU'D COME..

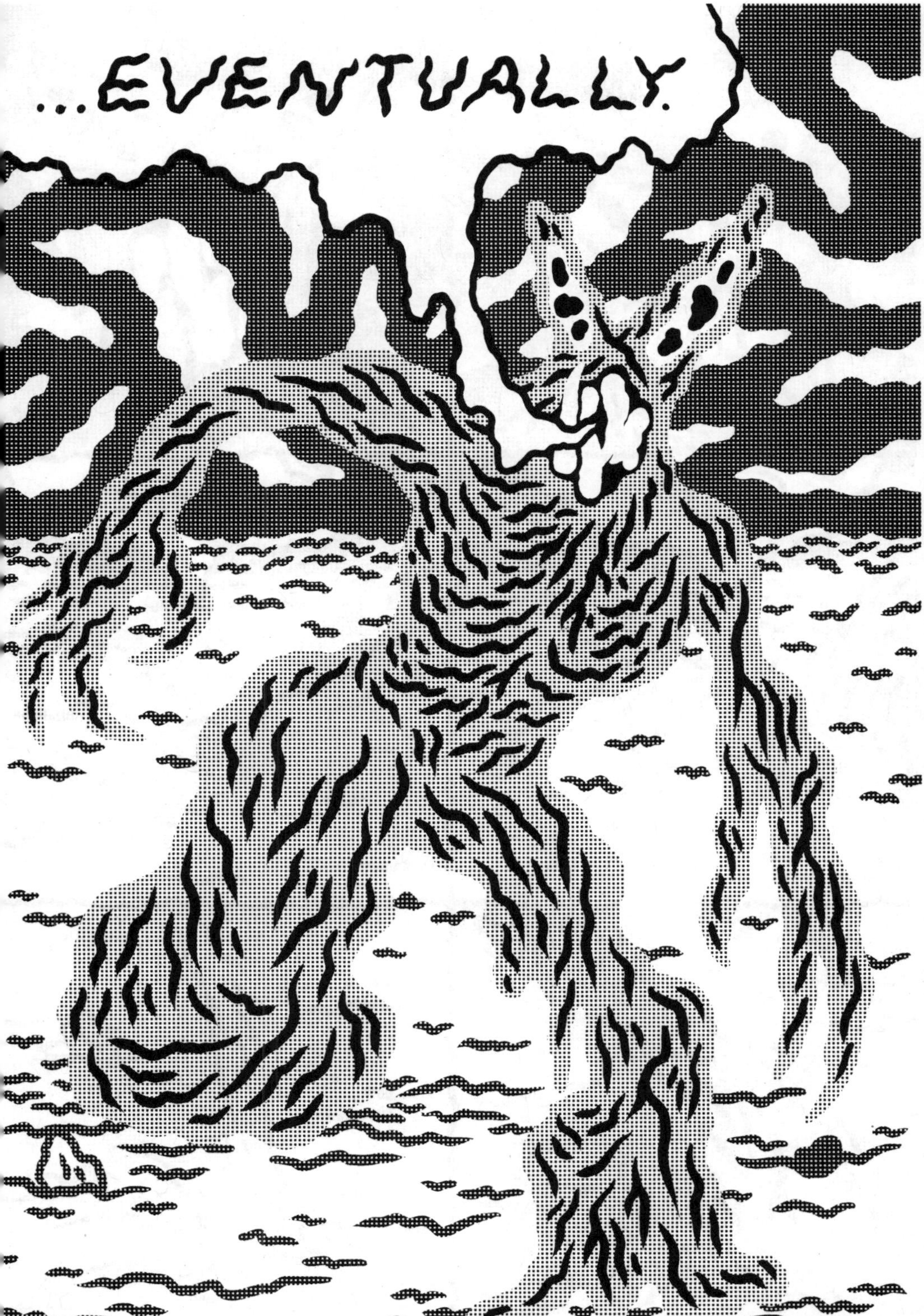
...EVENTUALLY.

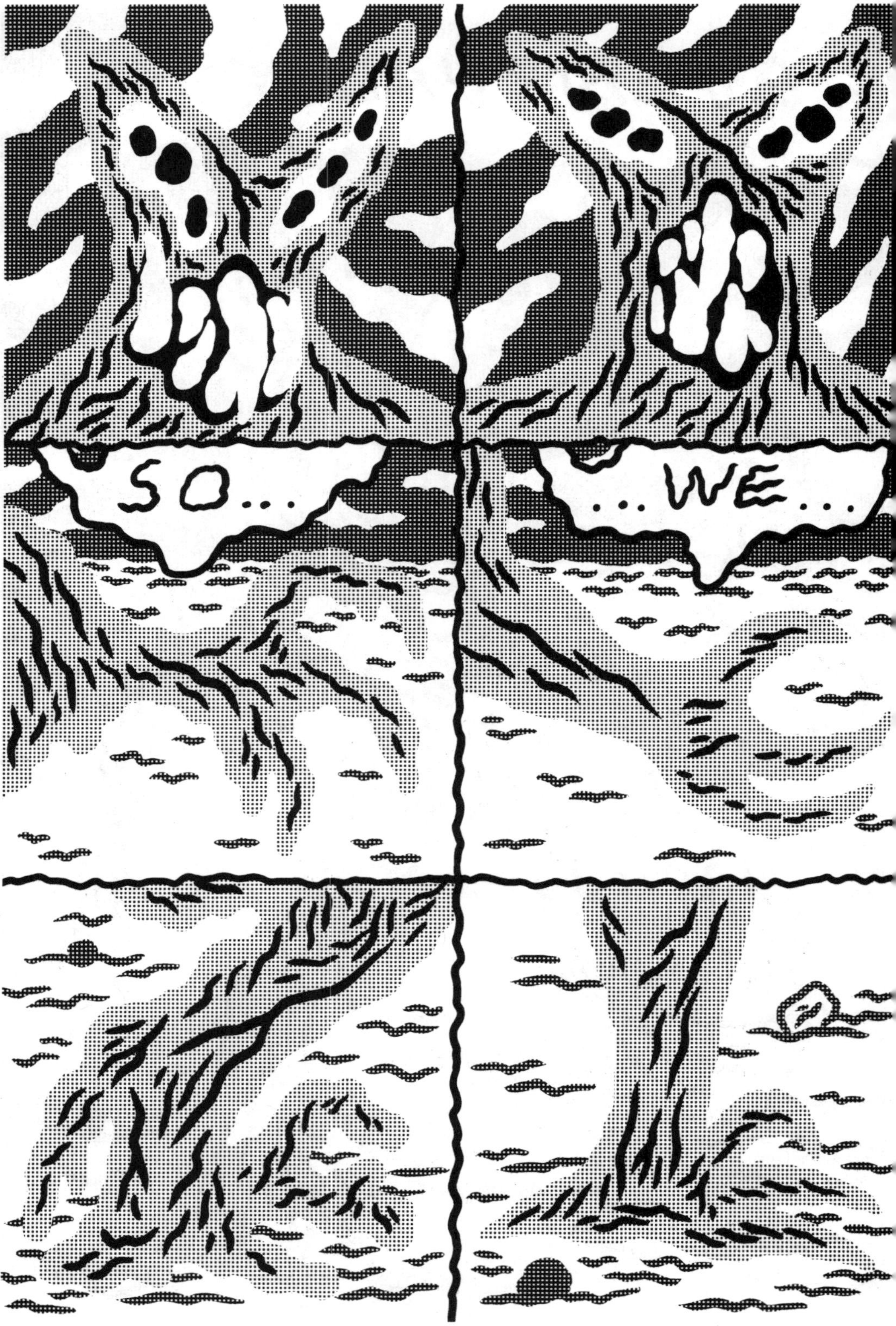
SO...
...WE...

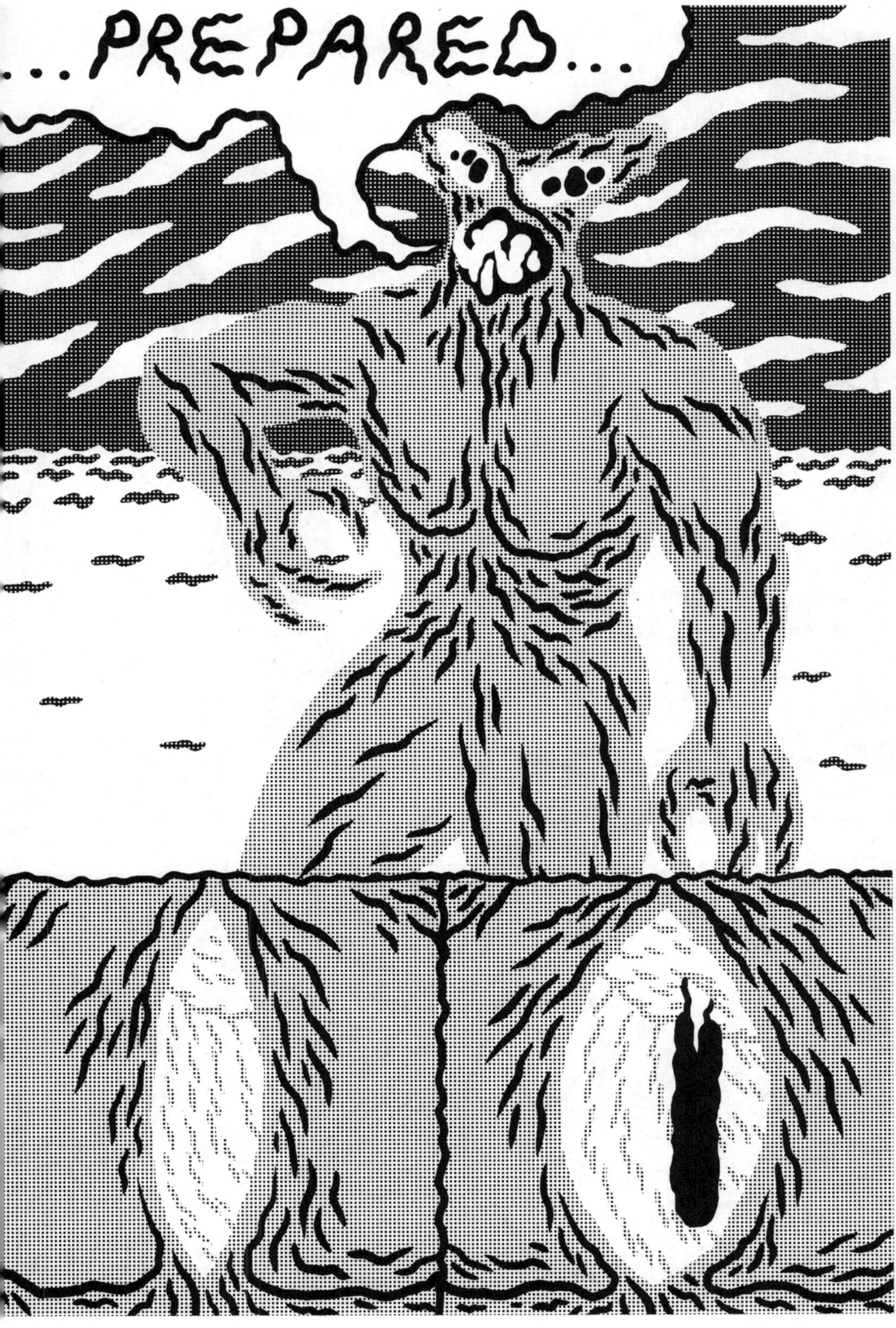
...PREPARED...

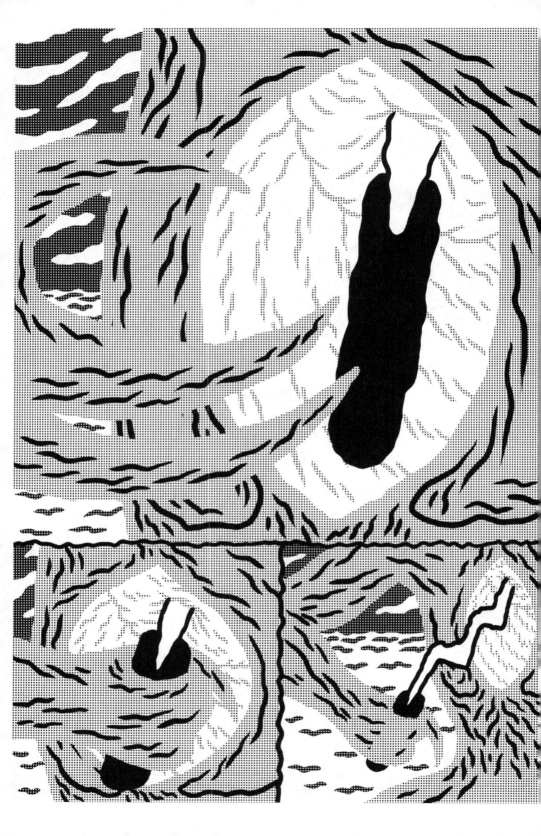

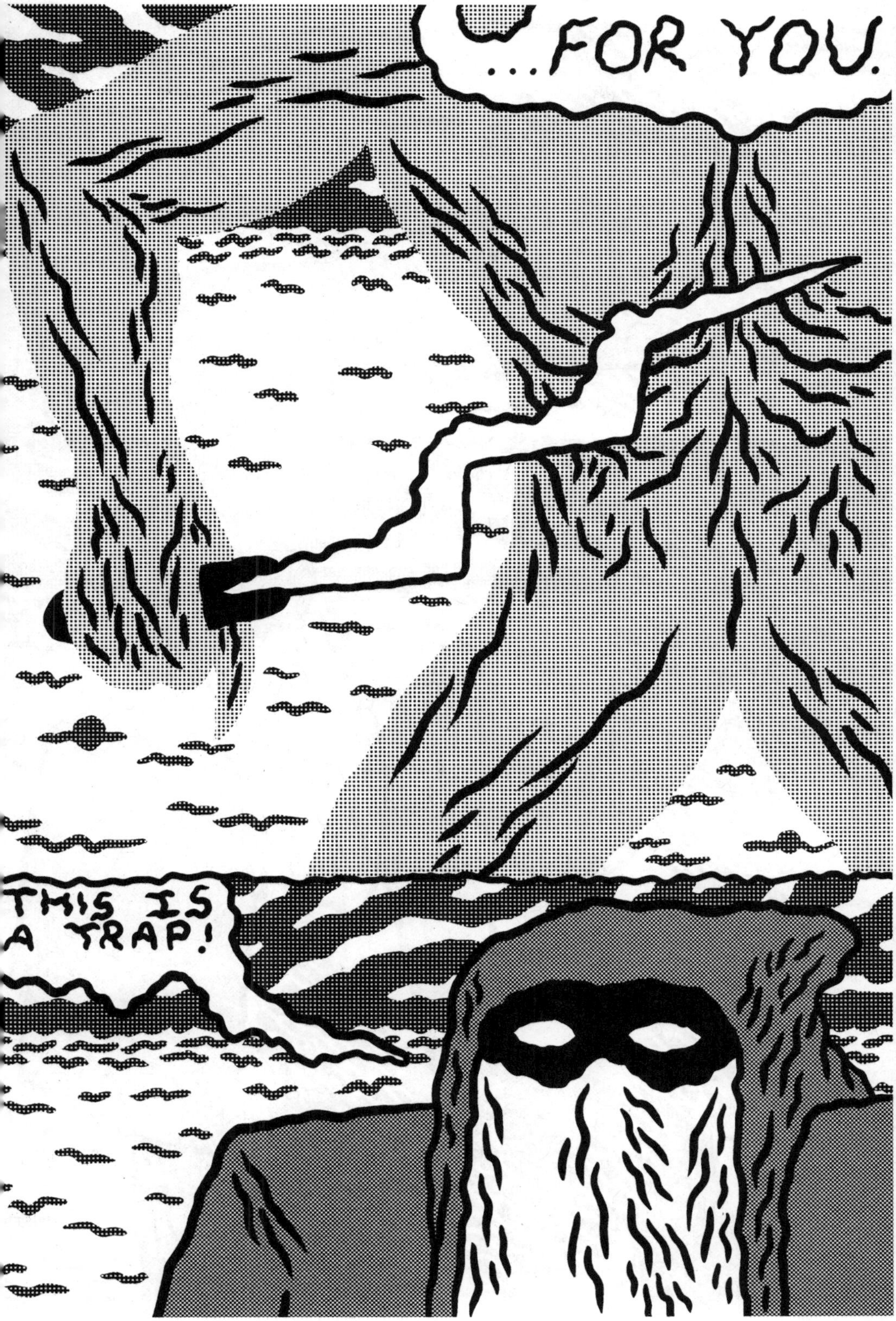
...FOR YOU.
THIS IS A TRAP!

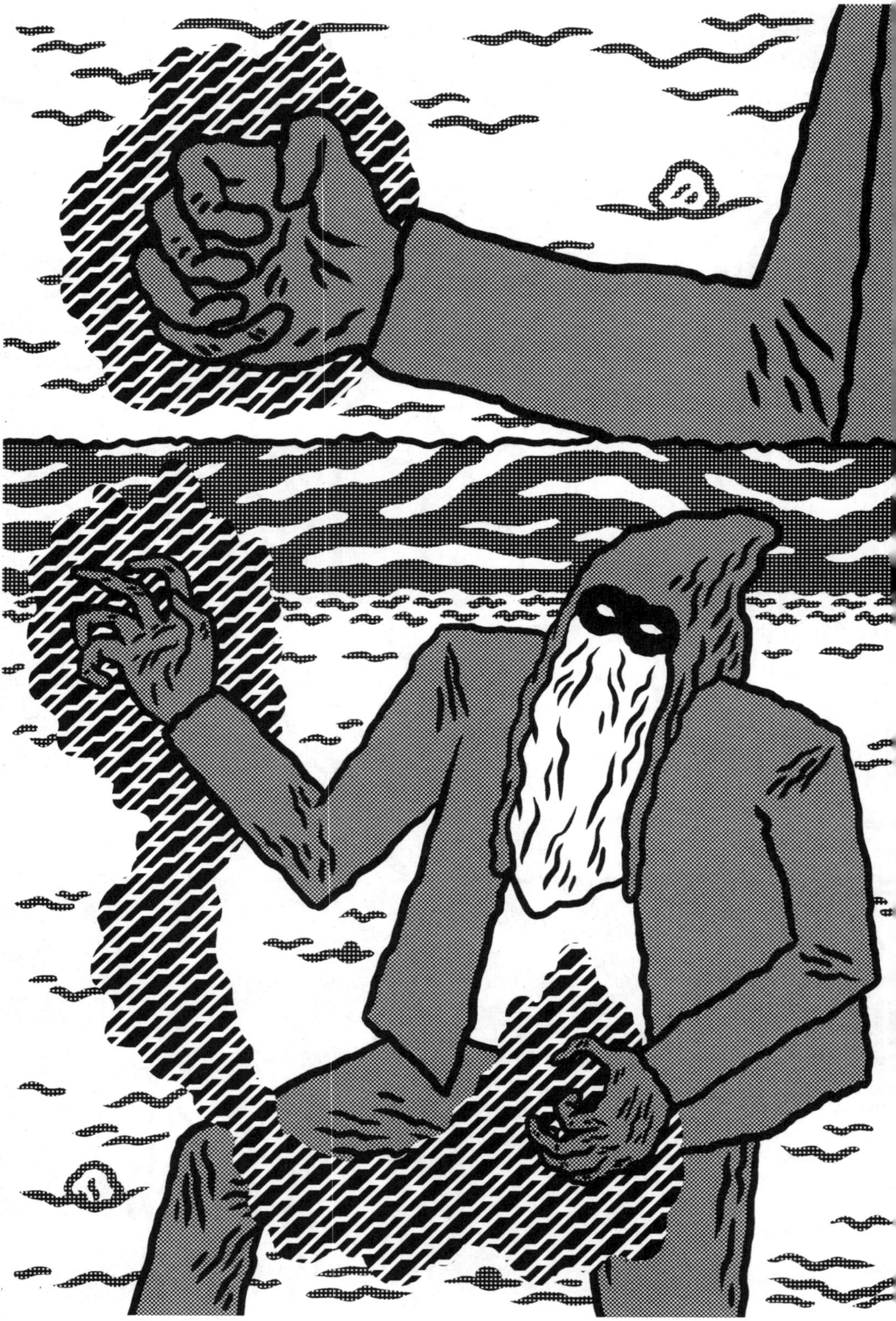

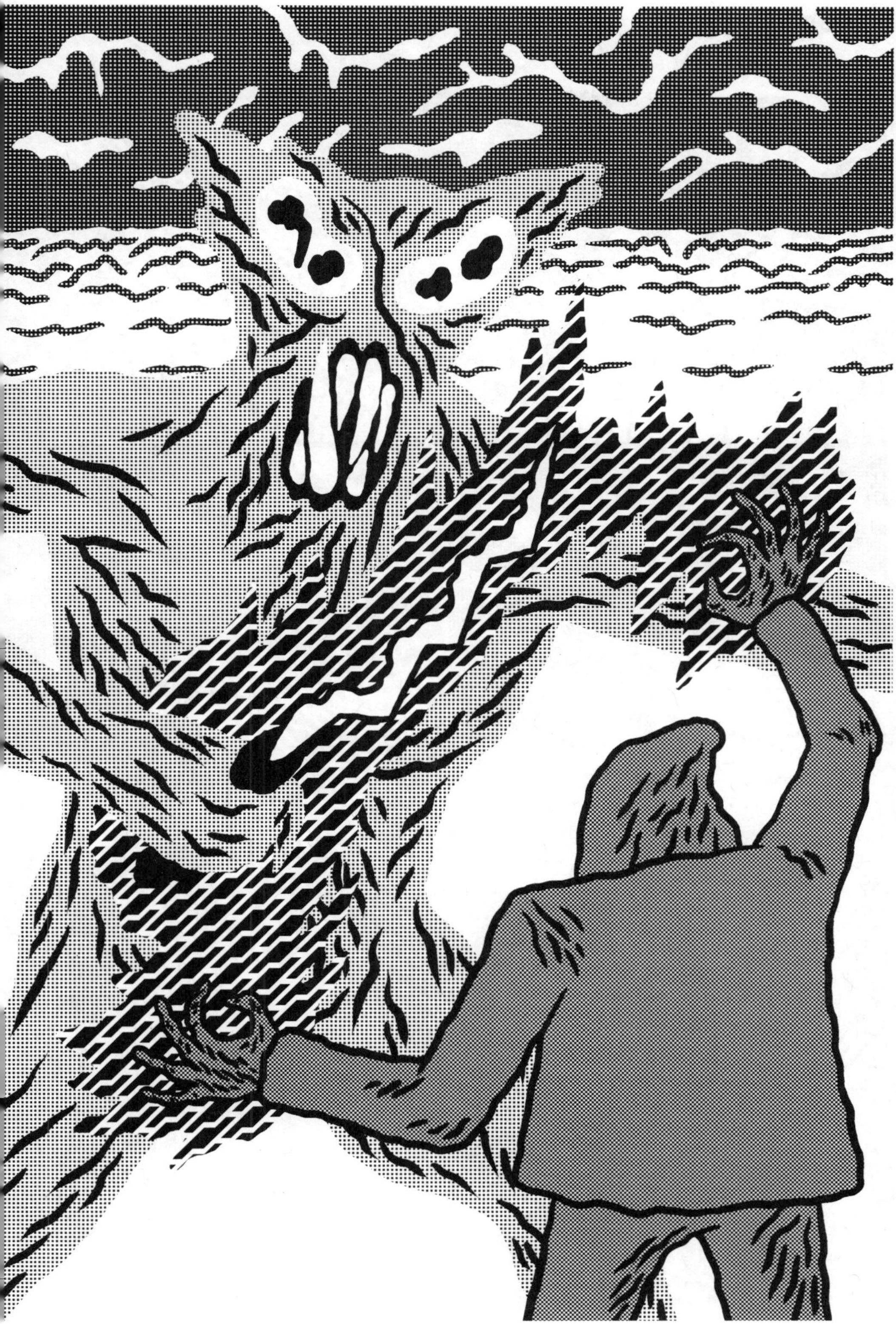

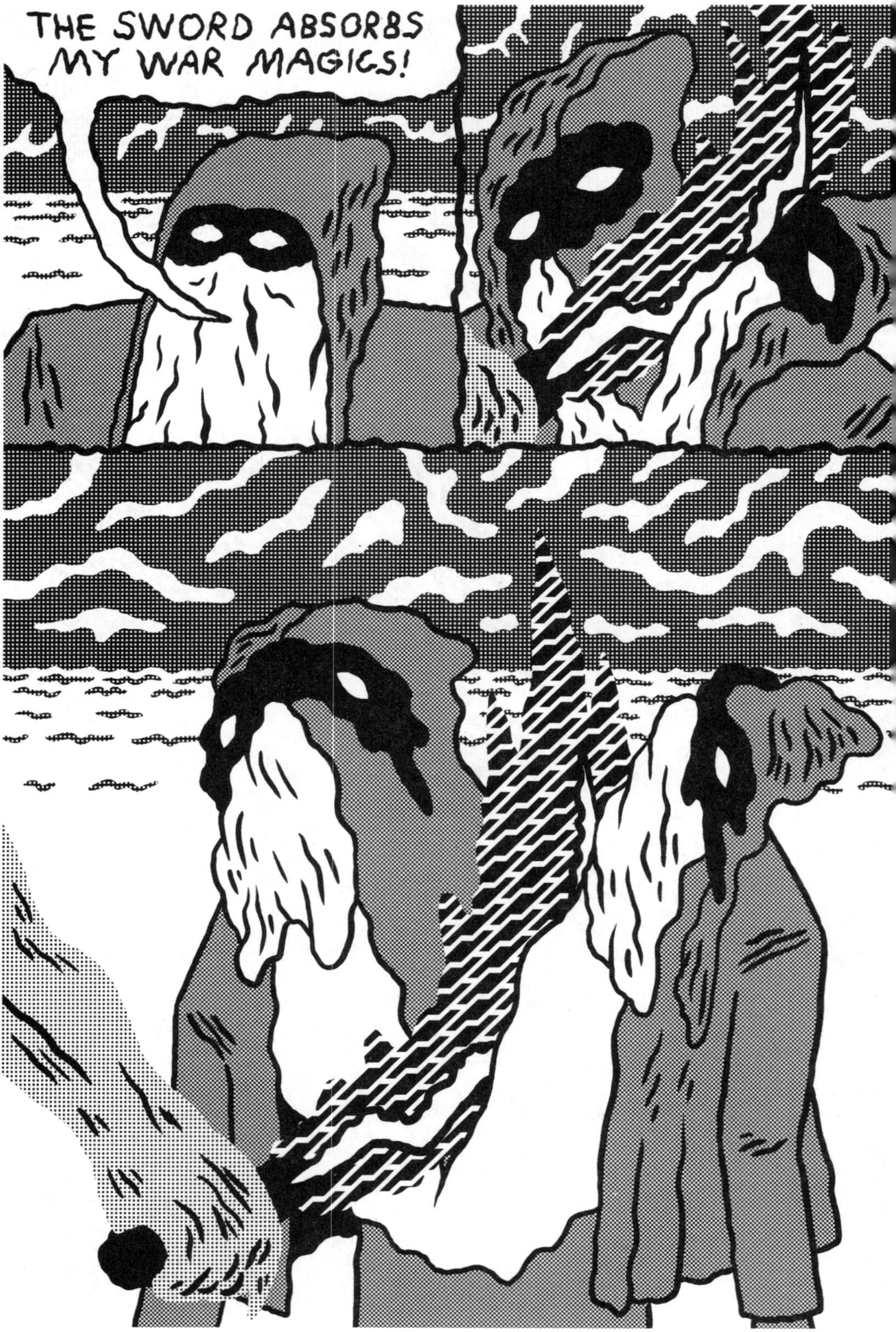
THE SWORD ABSORBS MY WAR MAGICS!

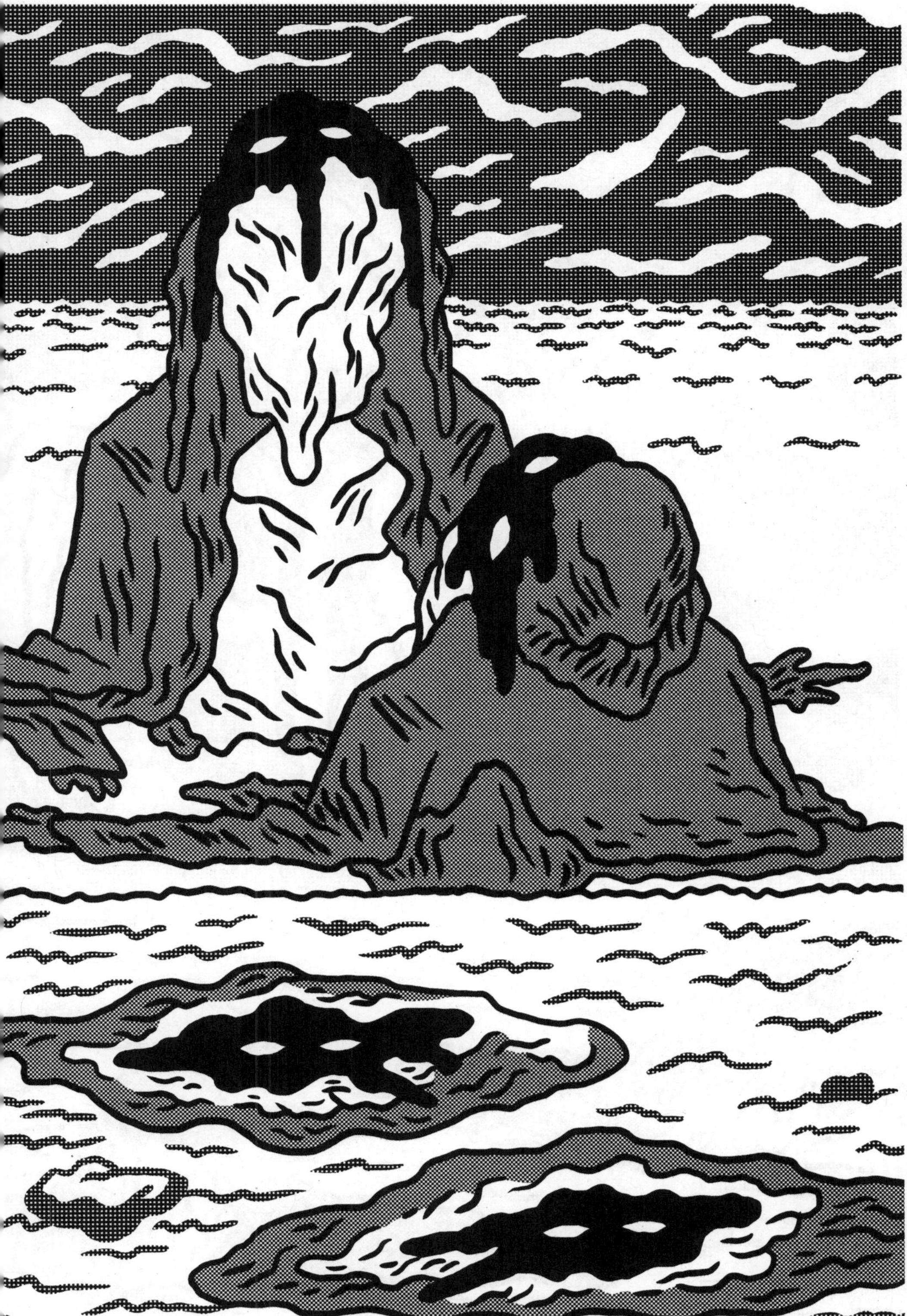

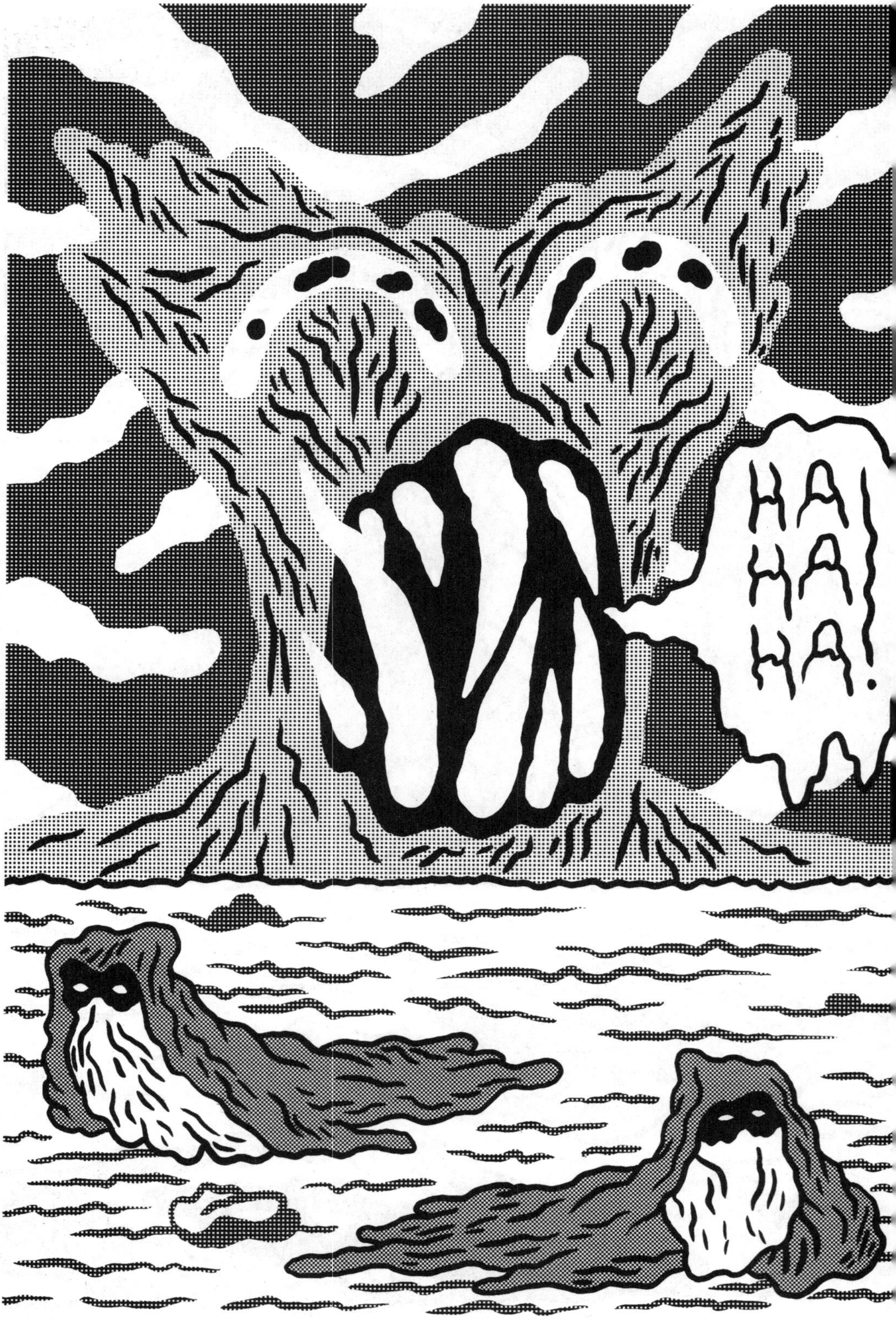
HA HA HA HA!

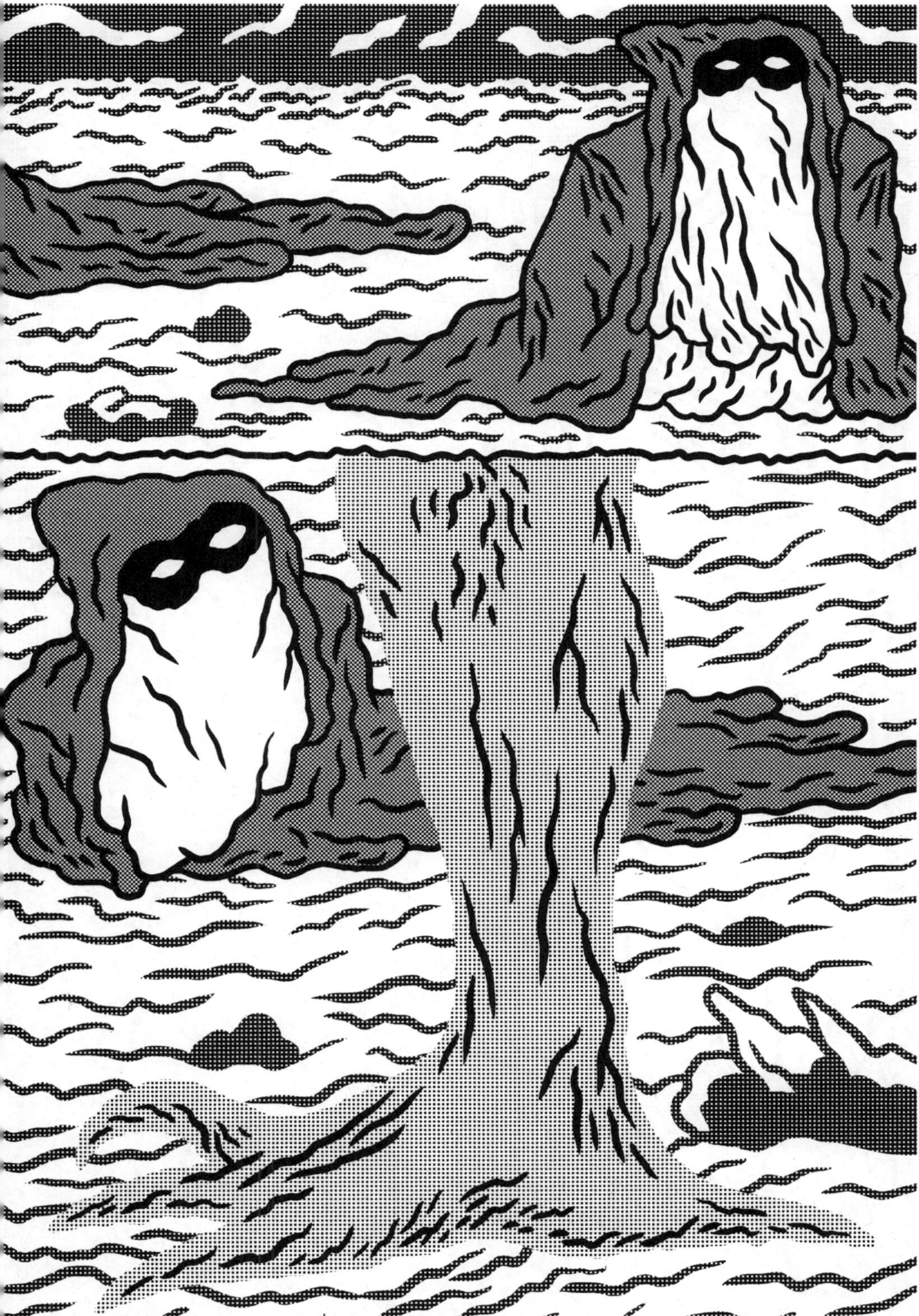

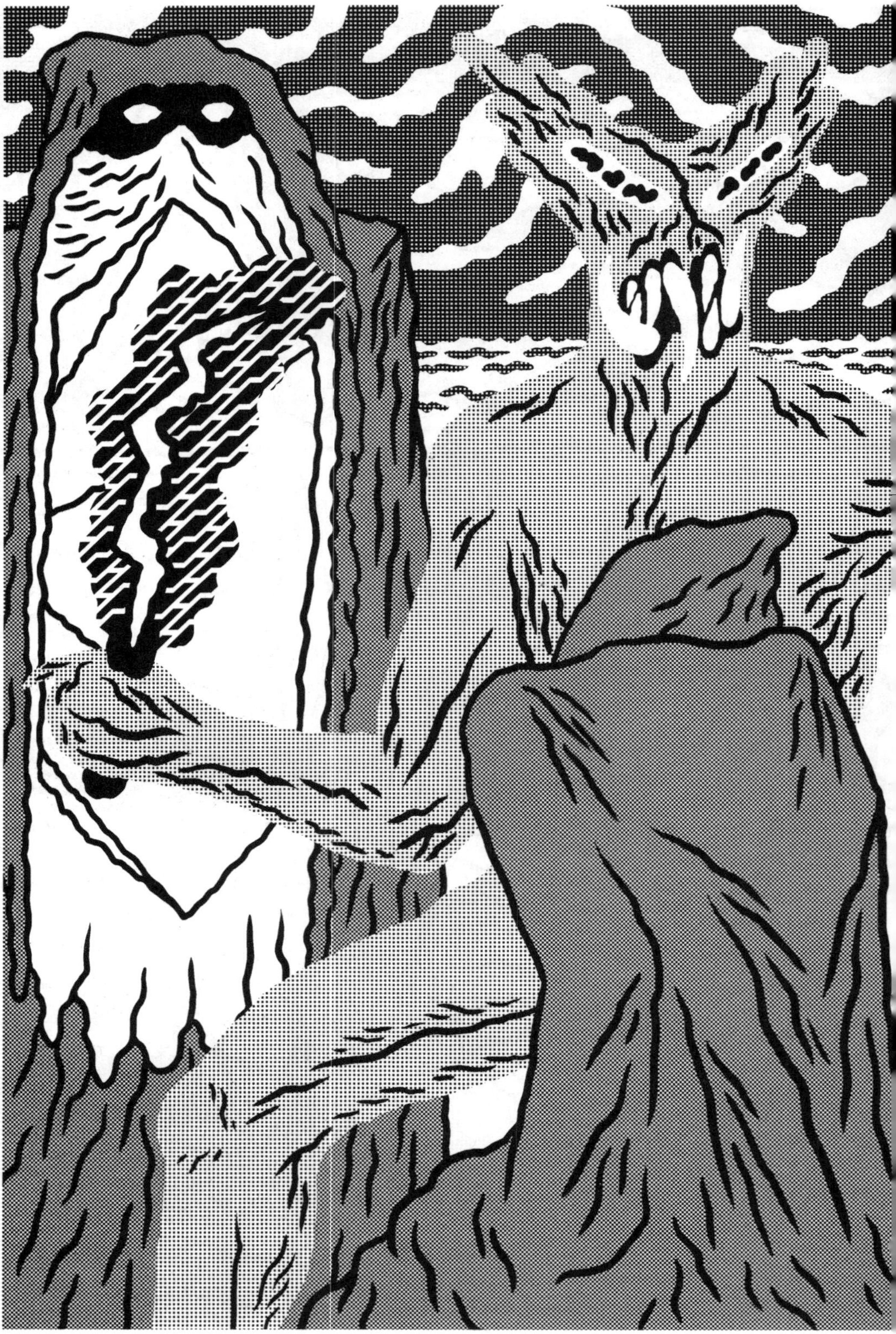

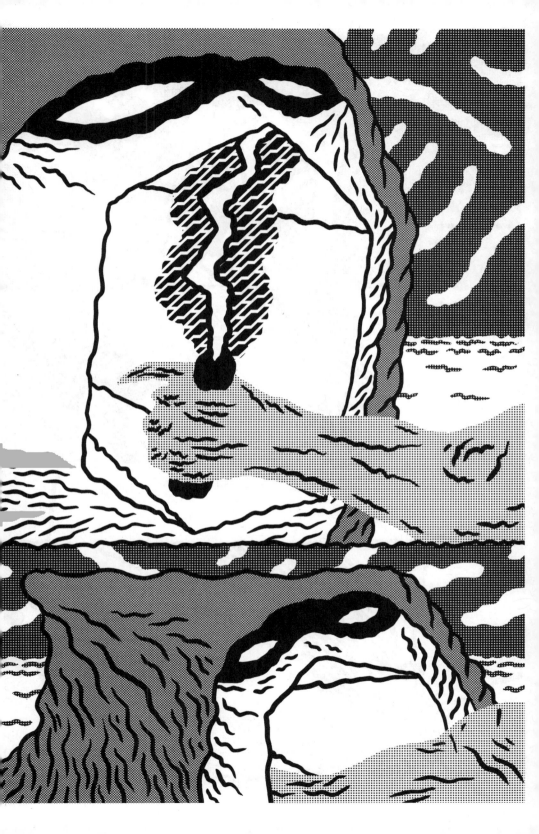

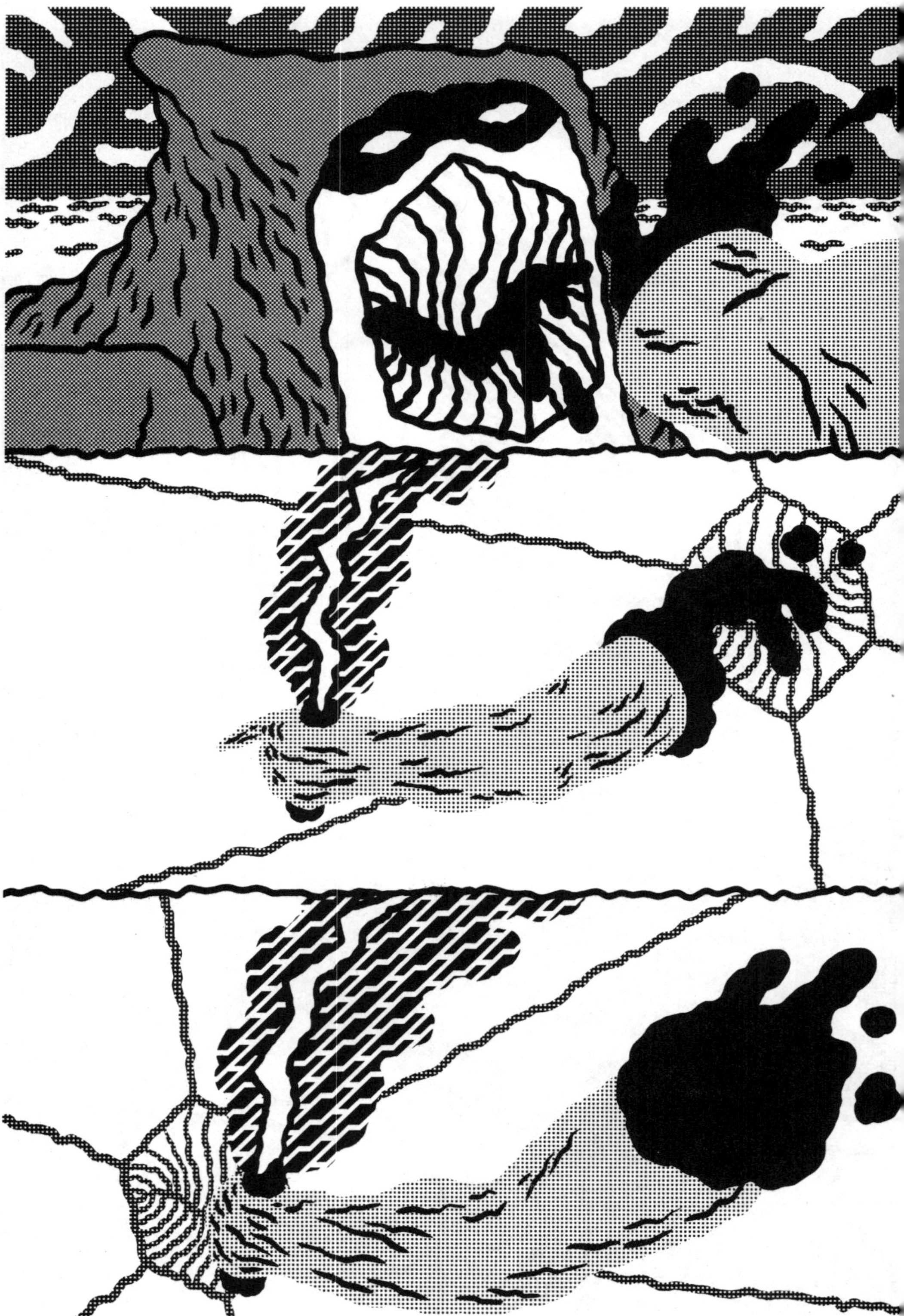

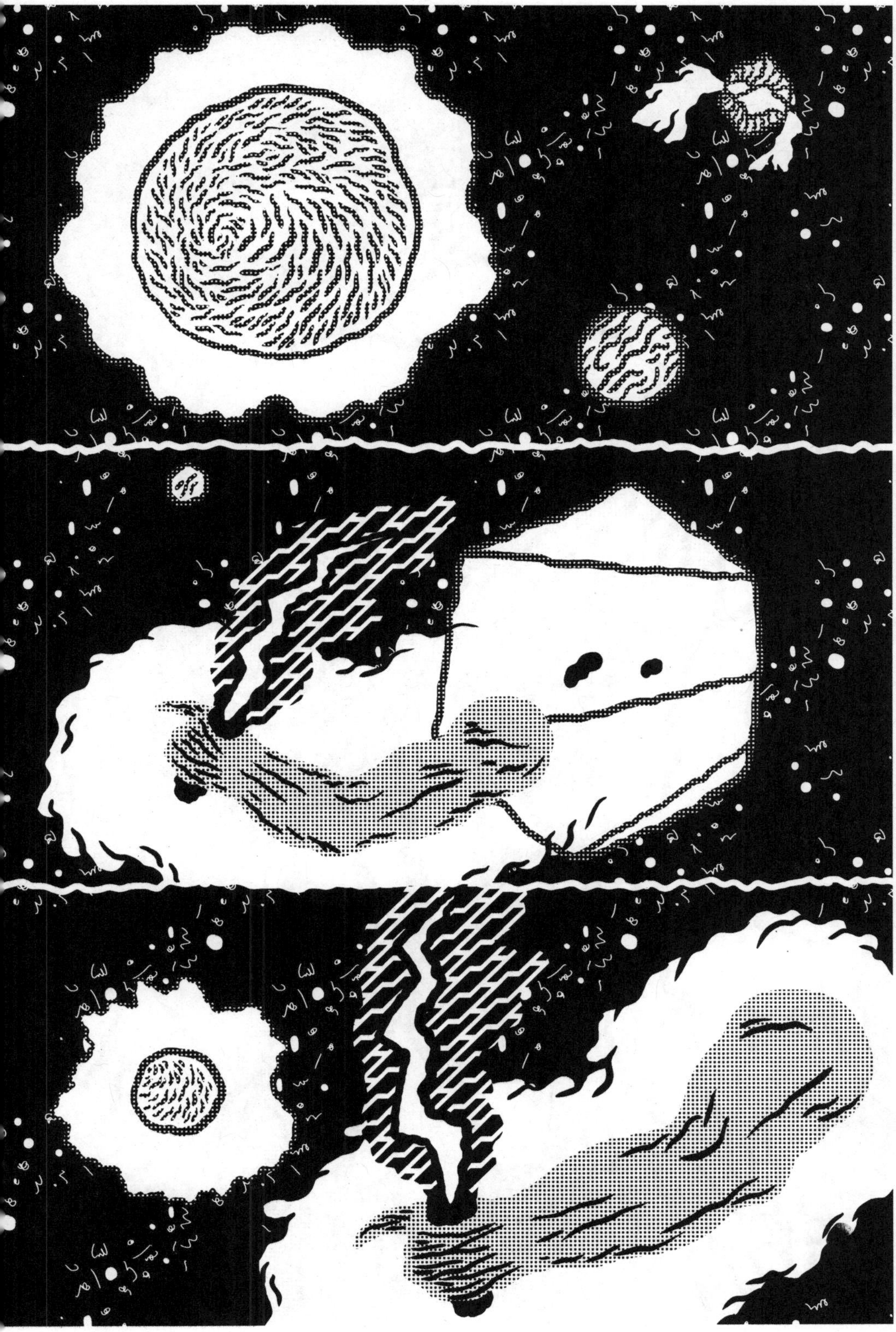

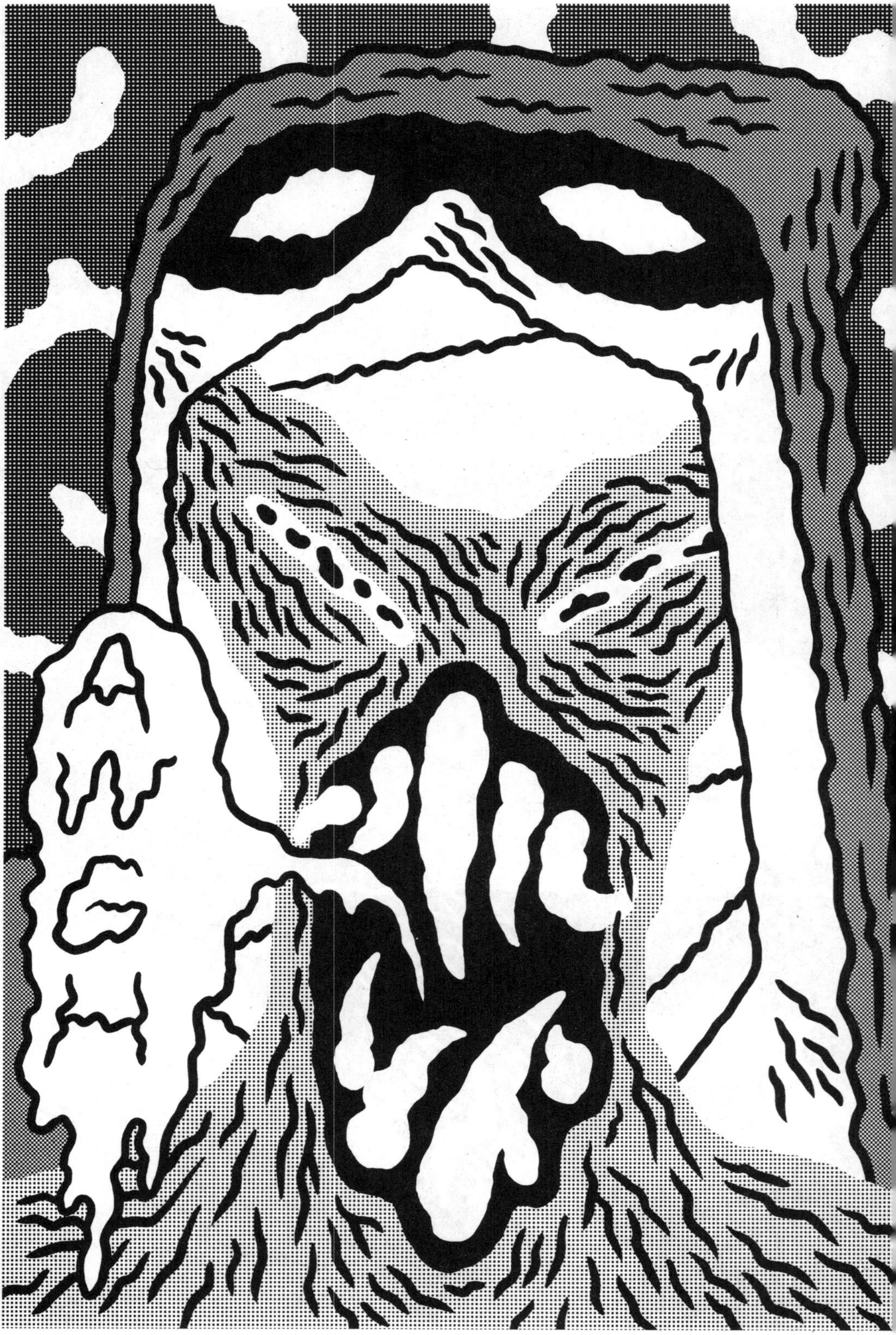
AAGH

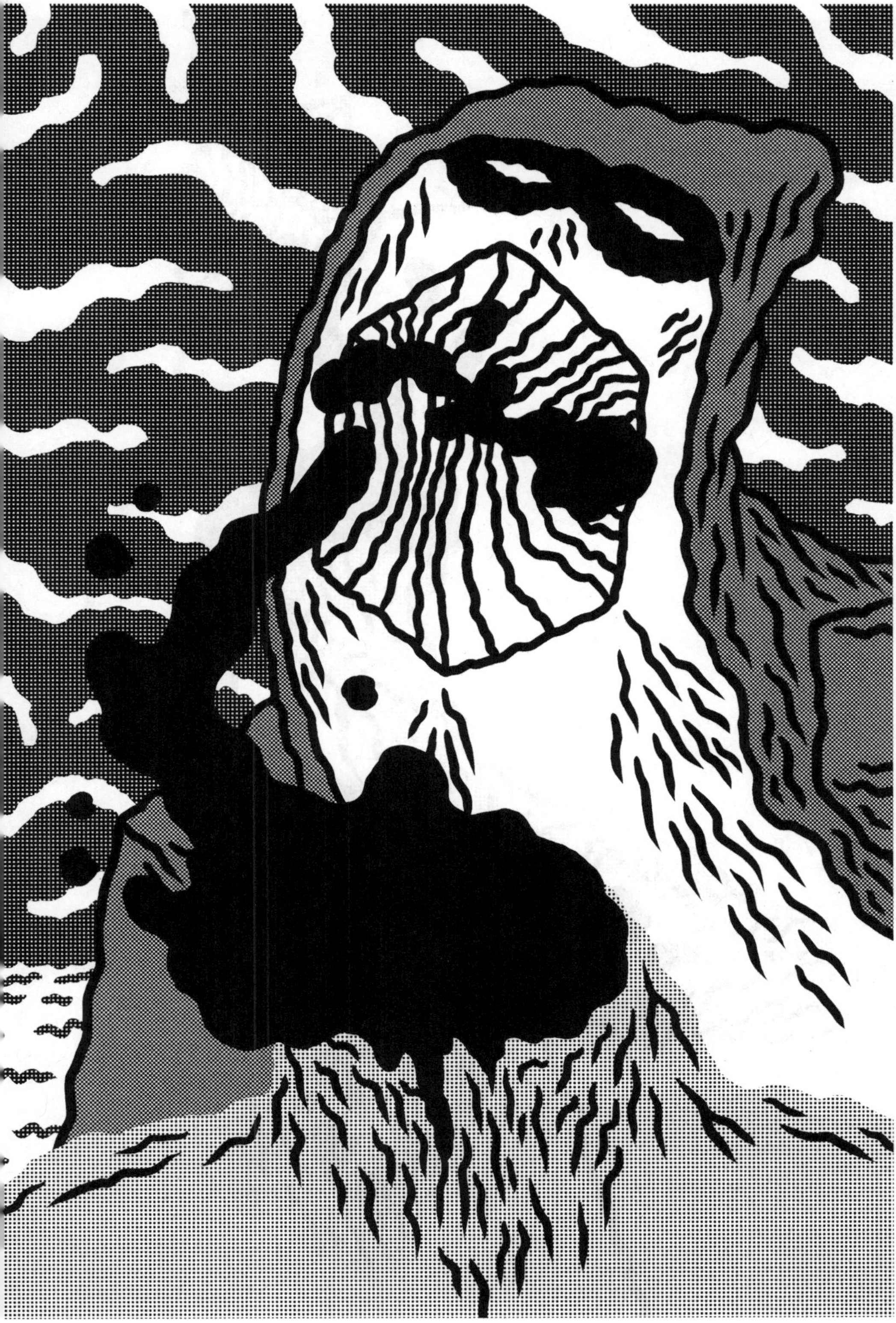

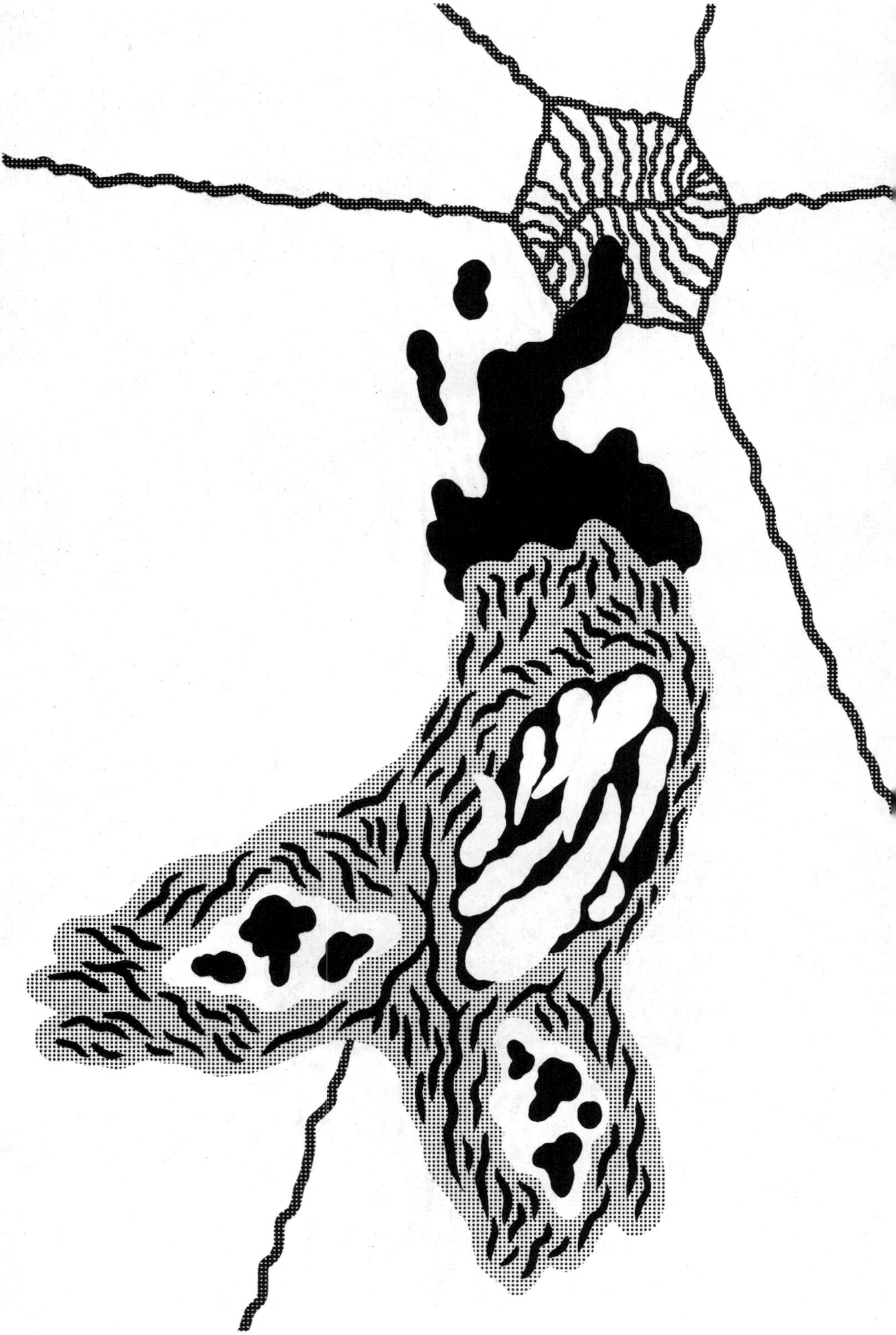

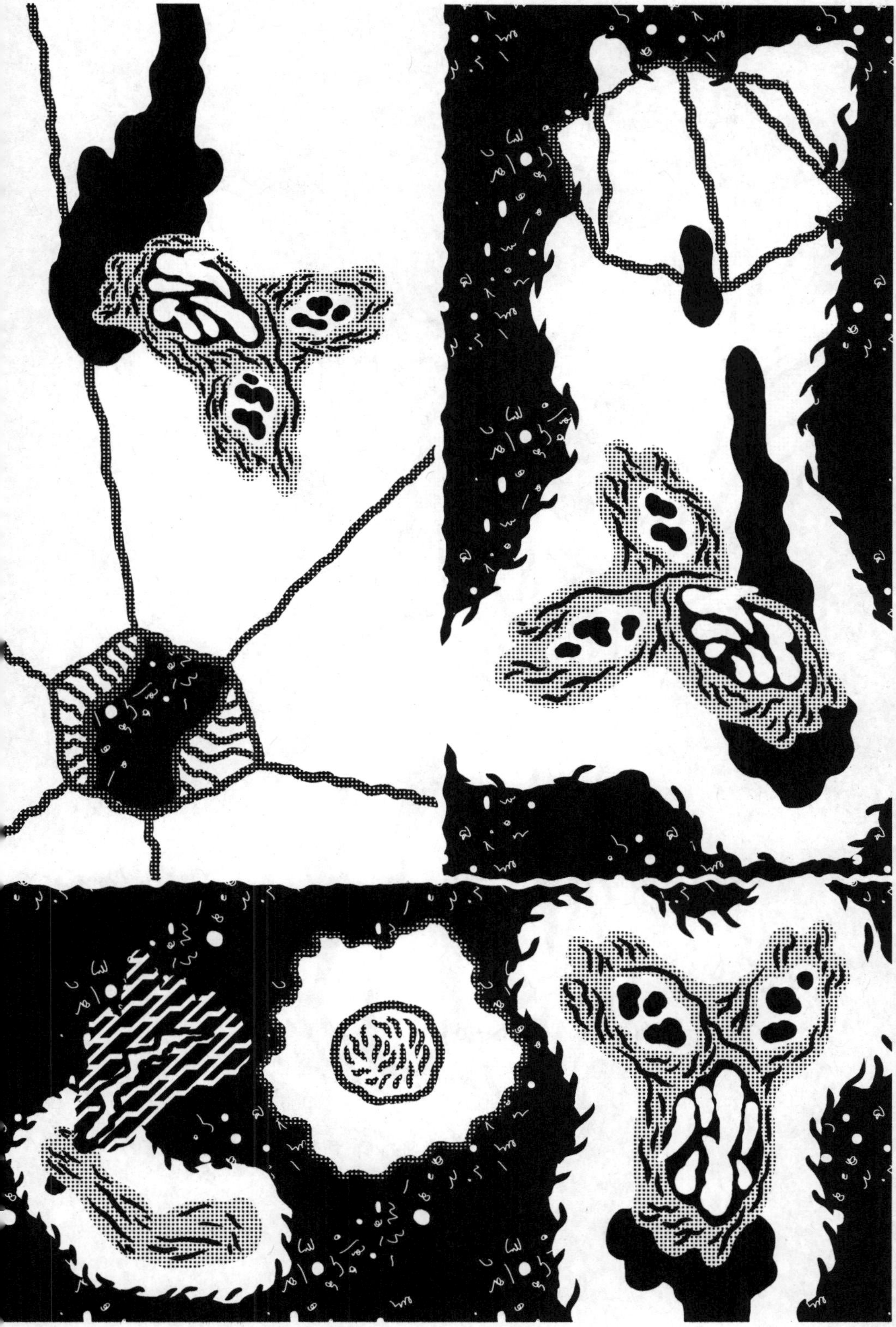

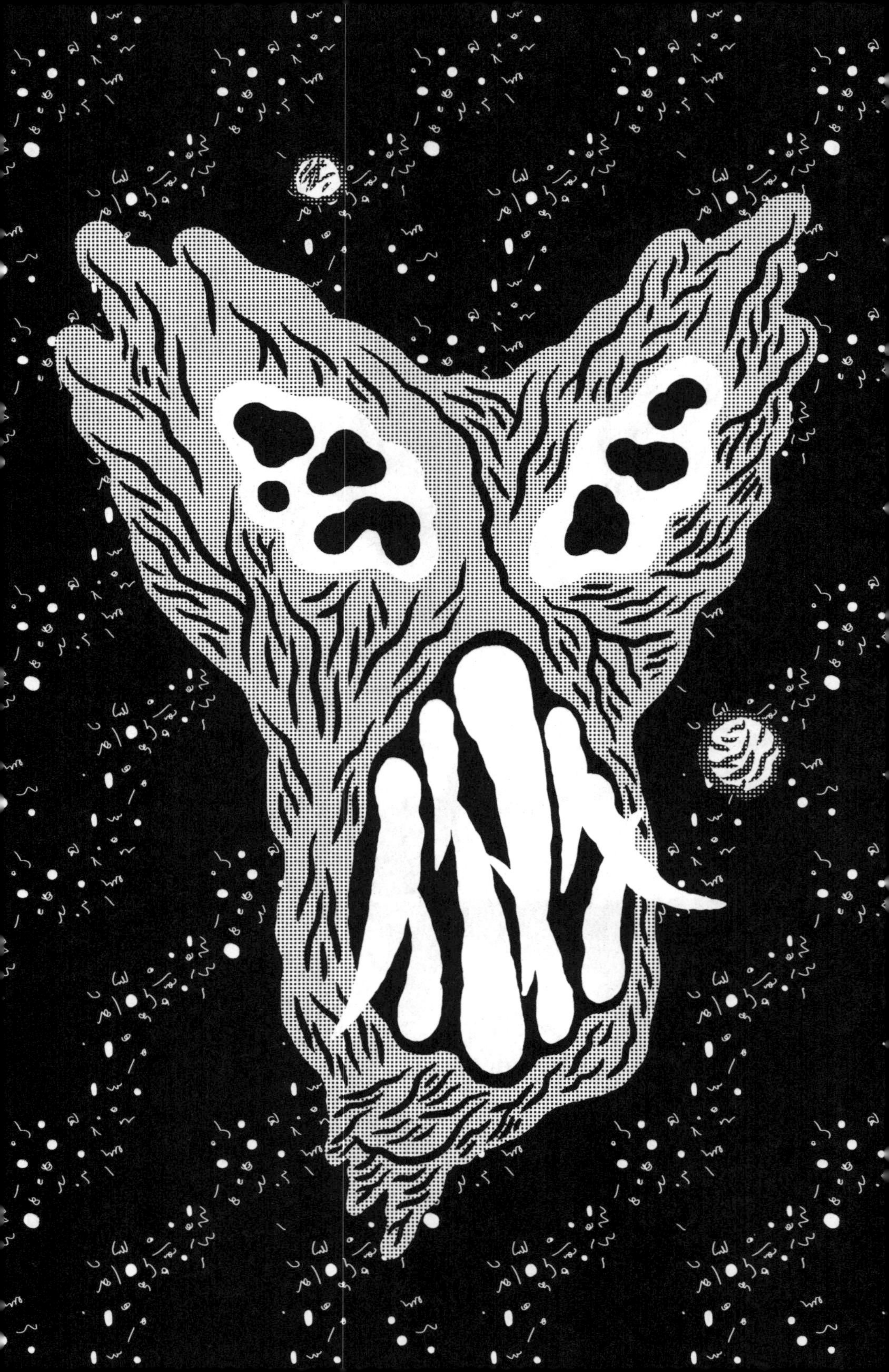

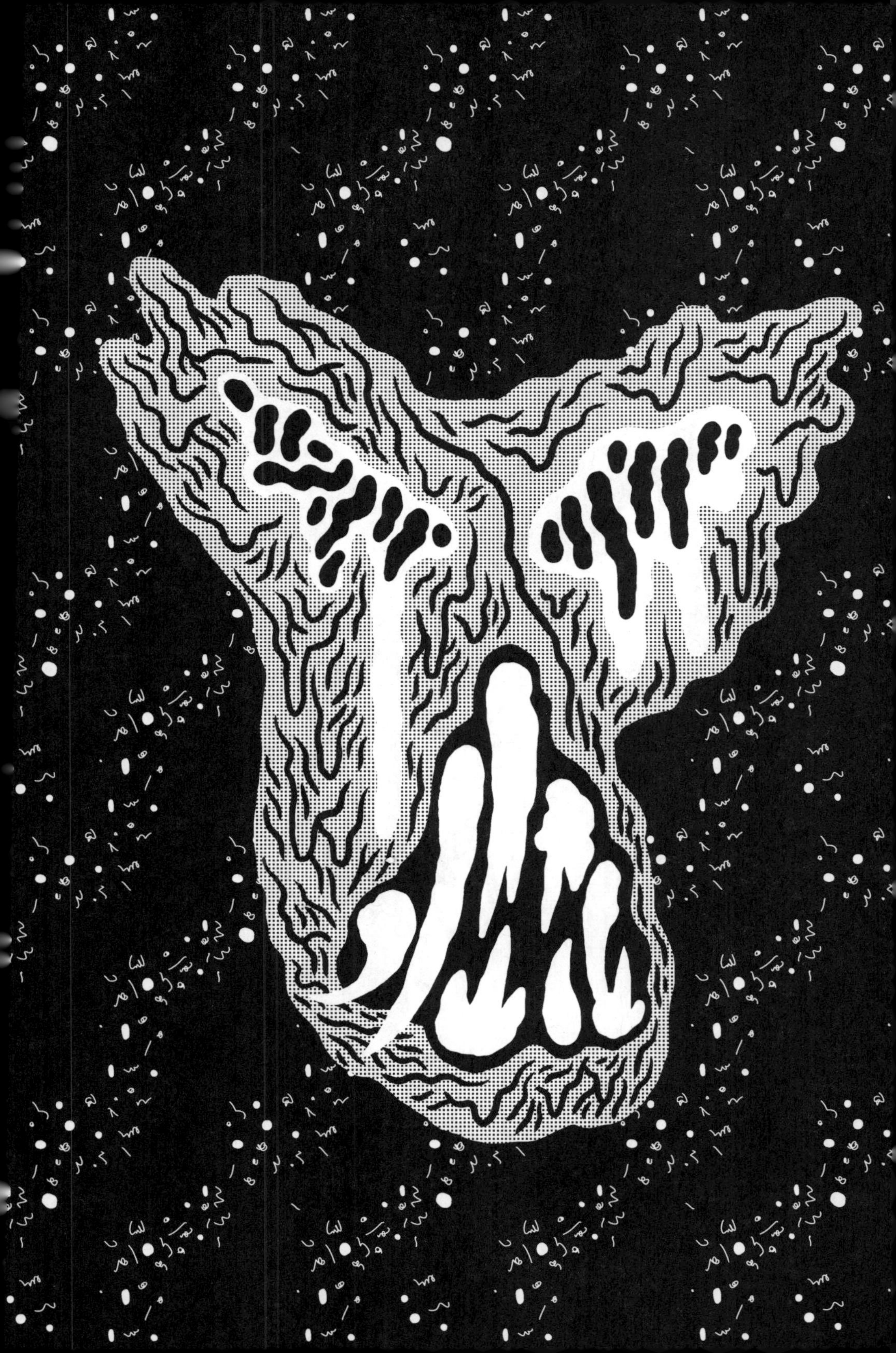

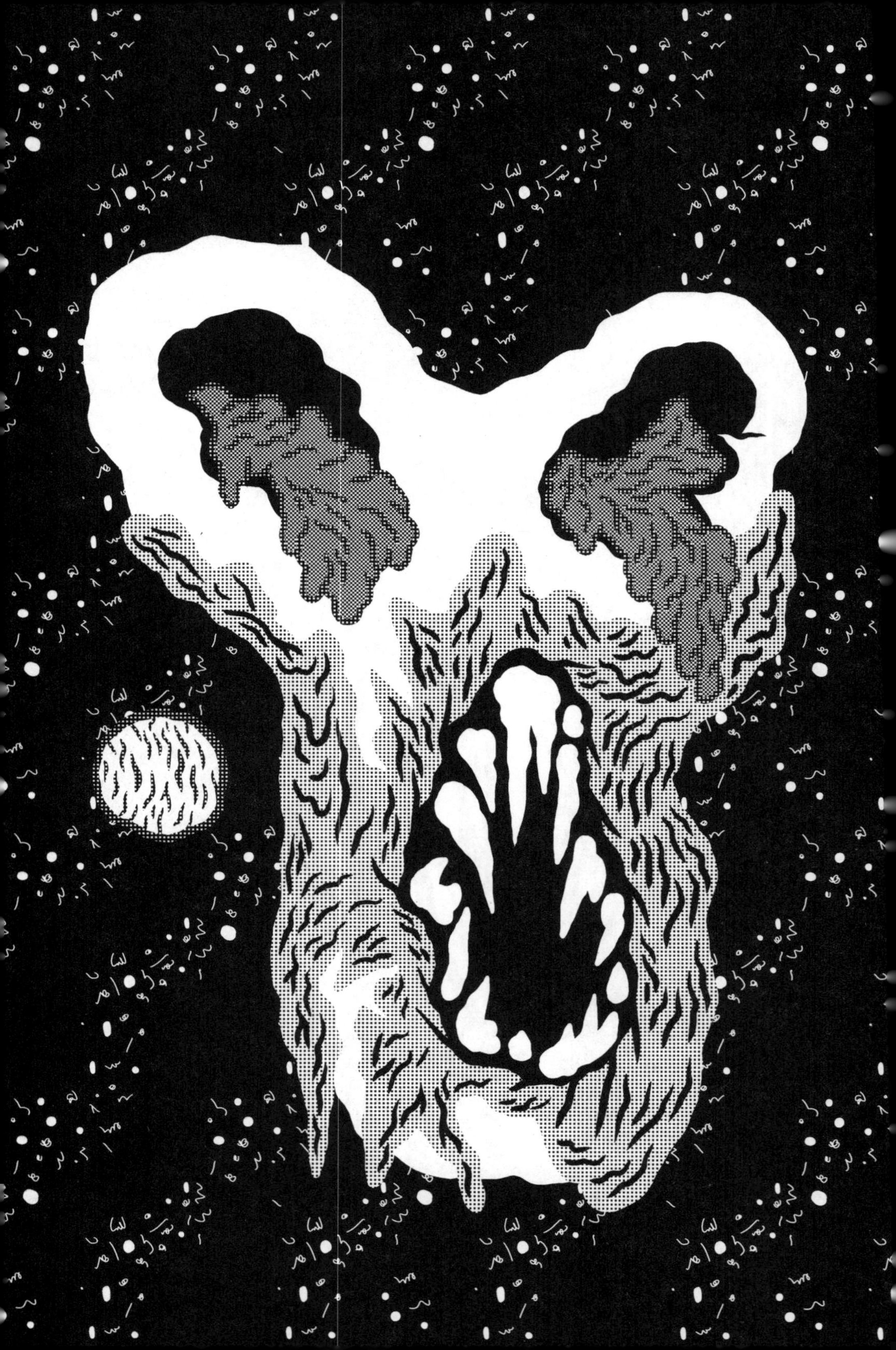

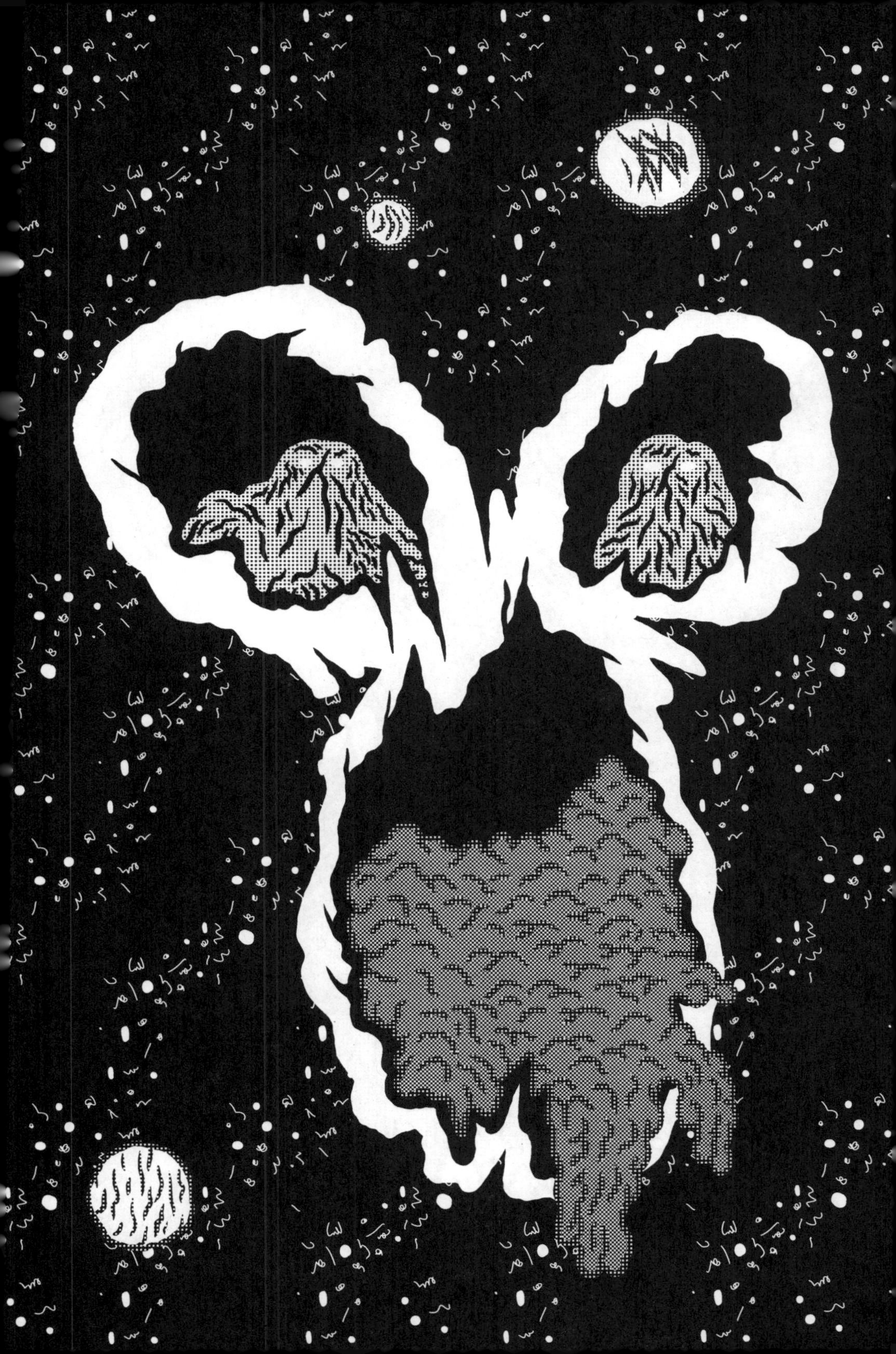

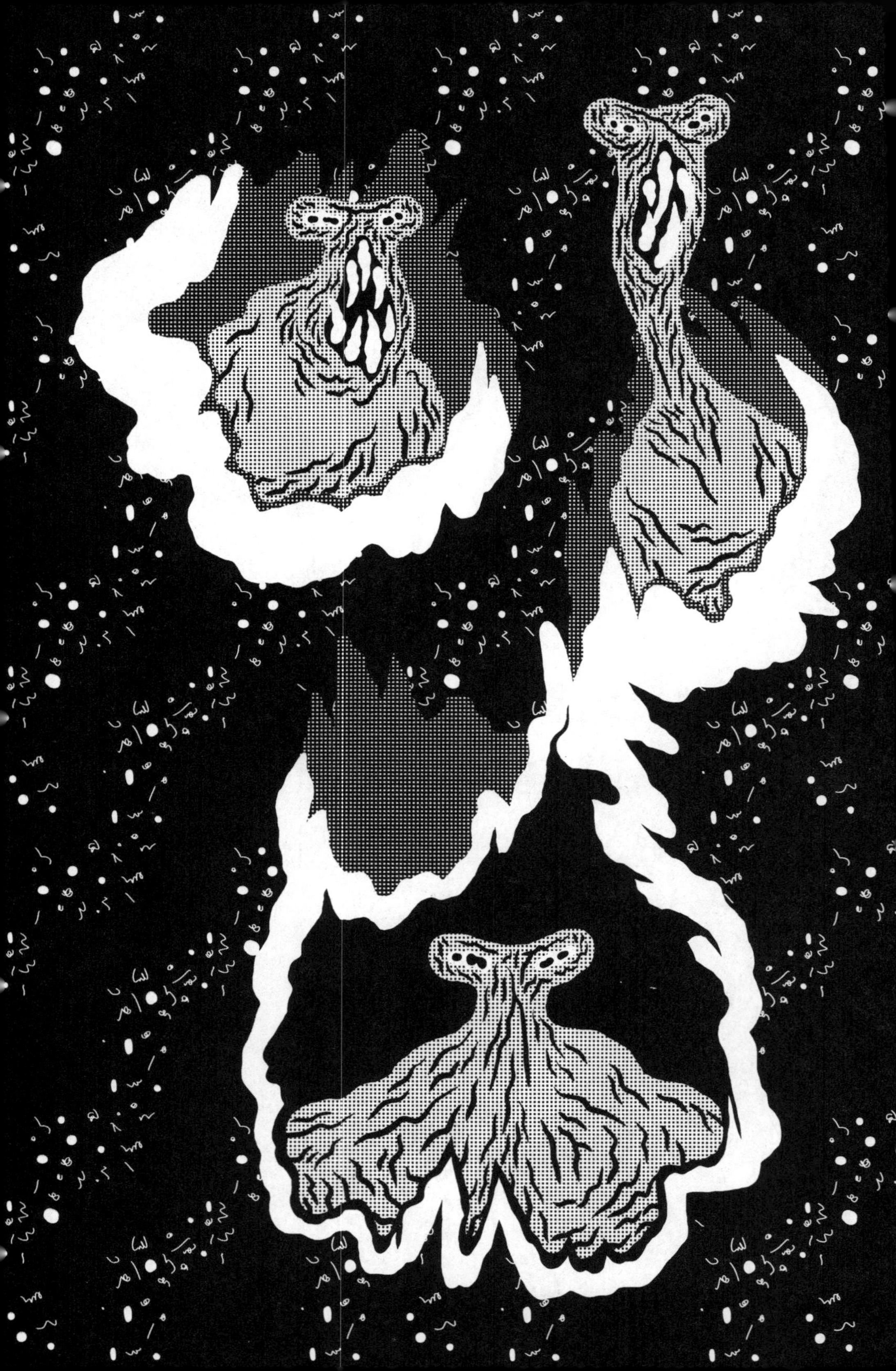

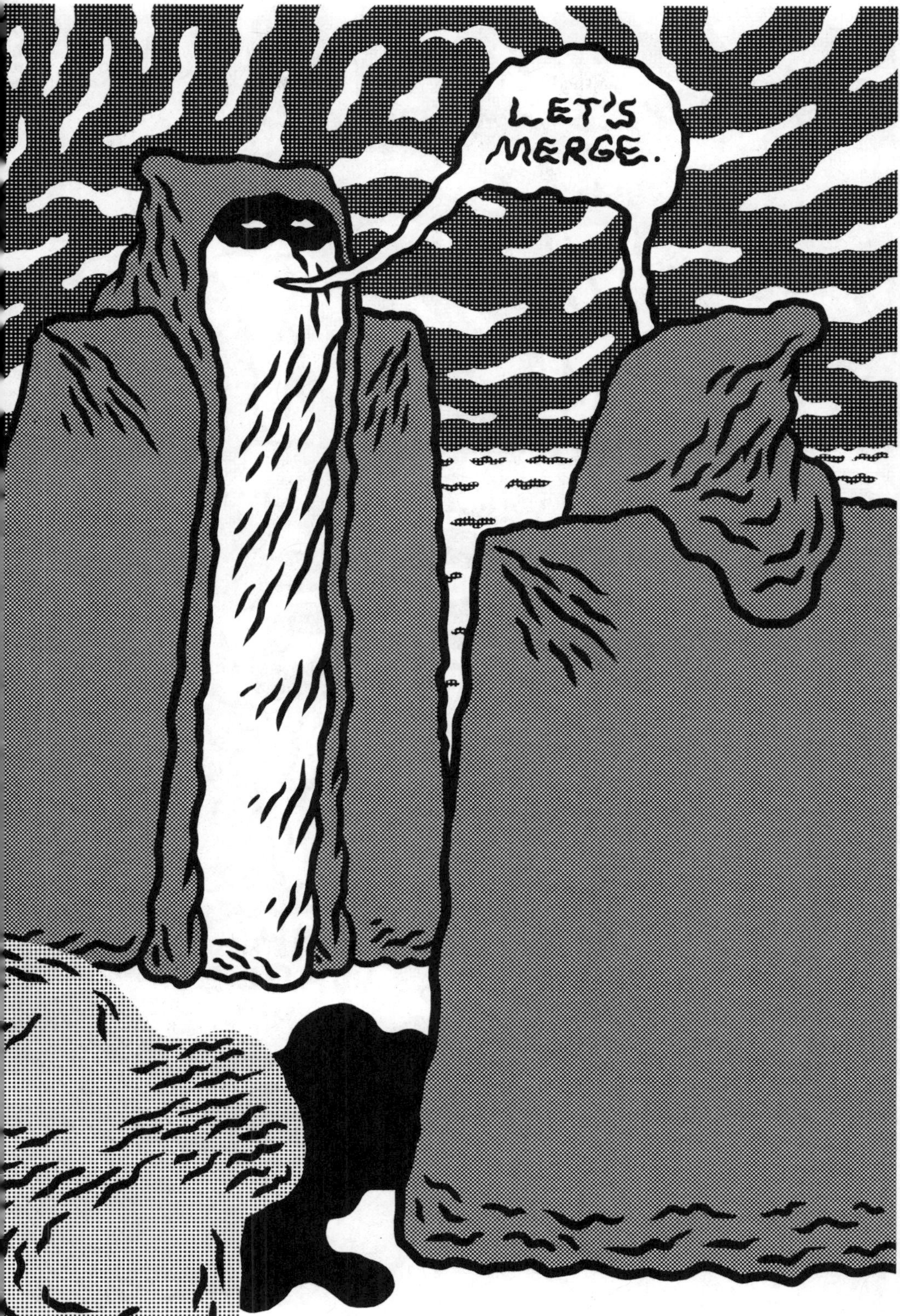
LET'S MERGE.

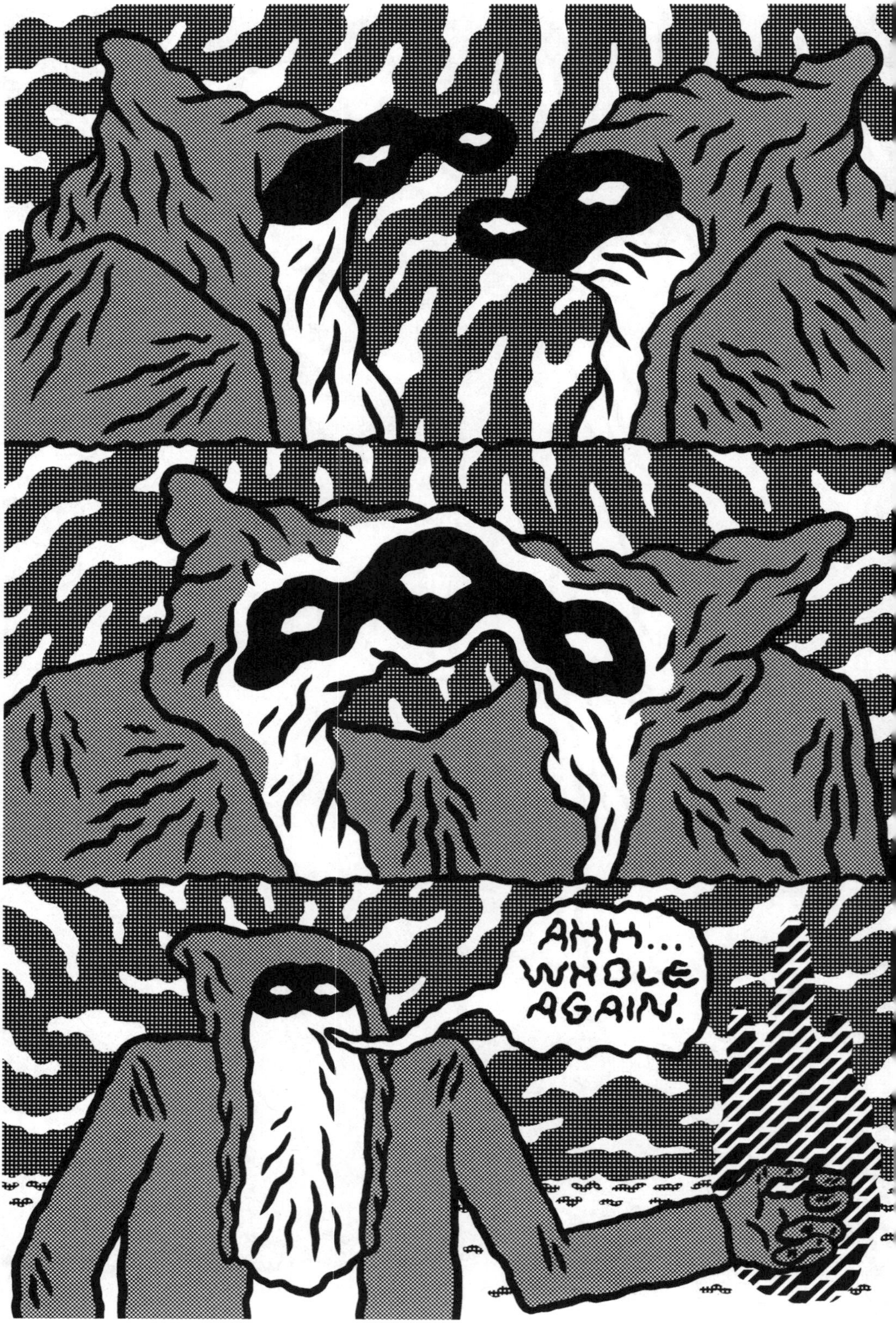
AHH... WHOLE AGAIN.

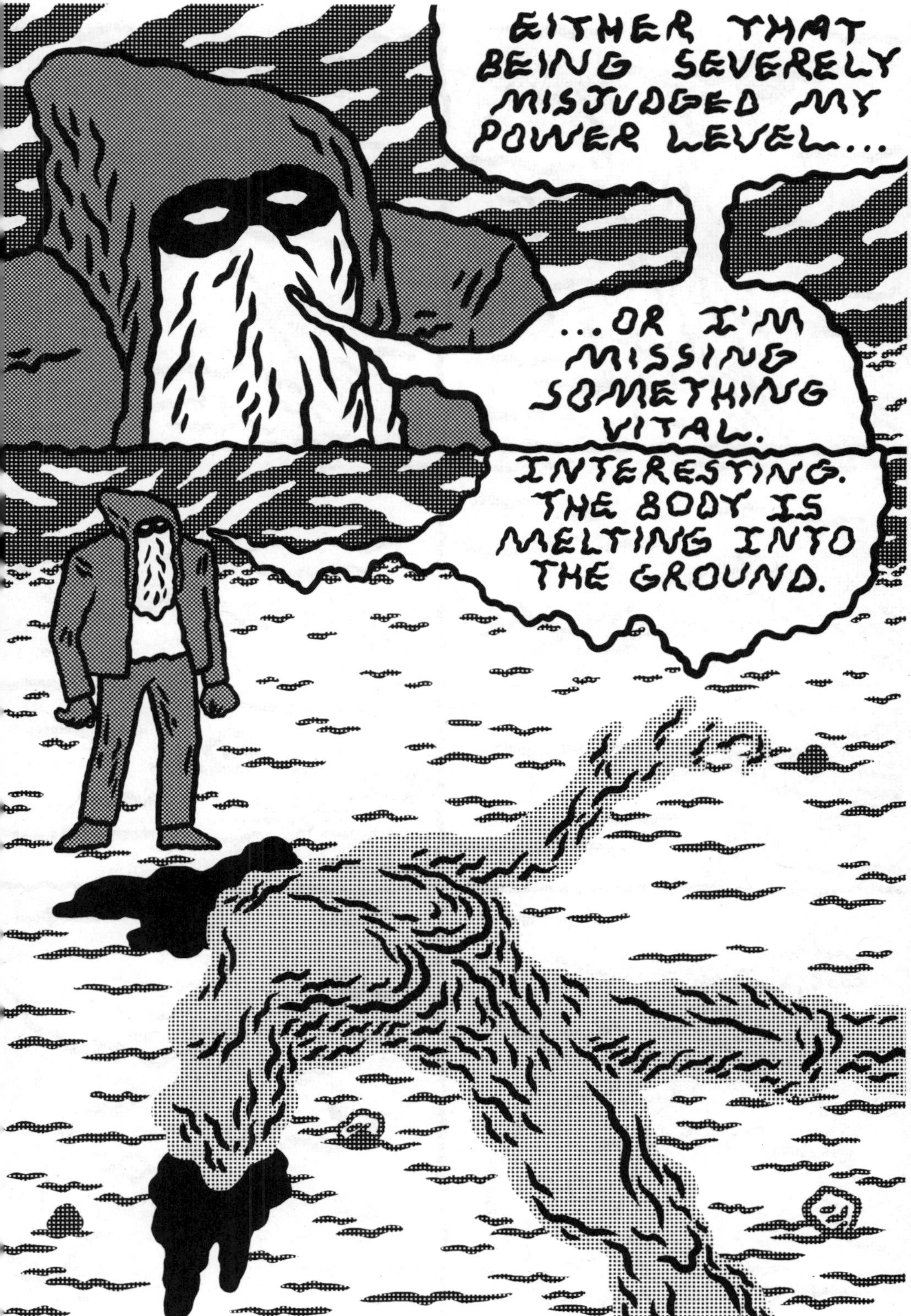
EITHER THAT BEING SEVERELY MISJUDGED MY POWER LEVEL...
...OR I'M MISSING SOMETHING VITAL.
INTERESTING. THE BODY IS MELTING INTO THE GROUND.

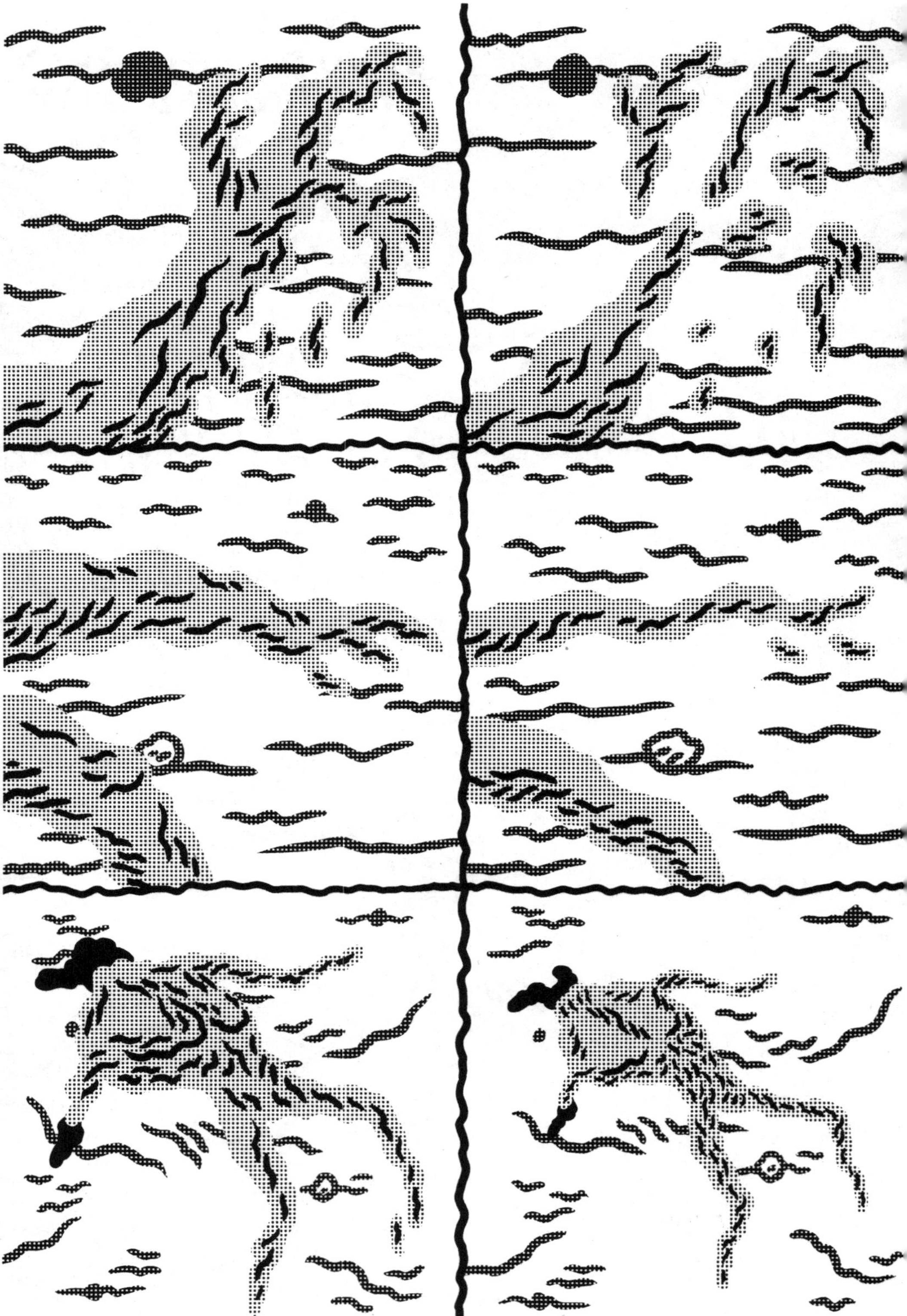

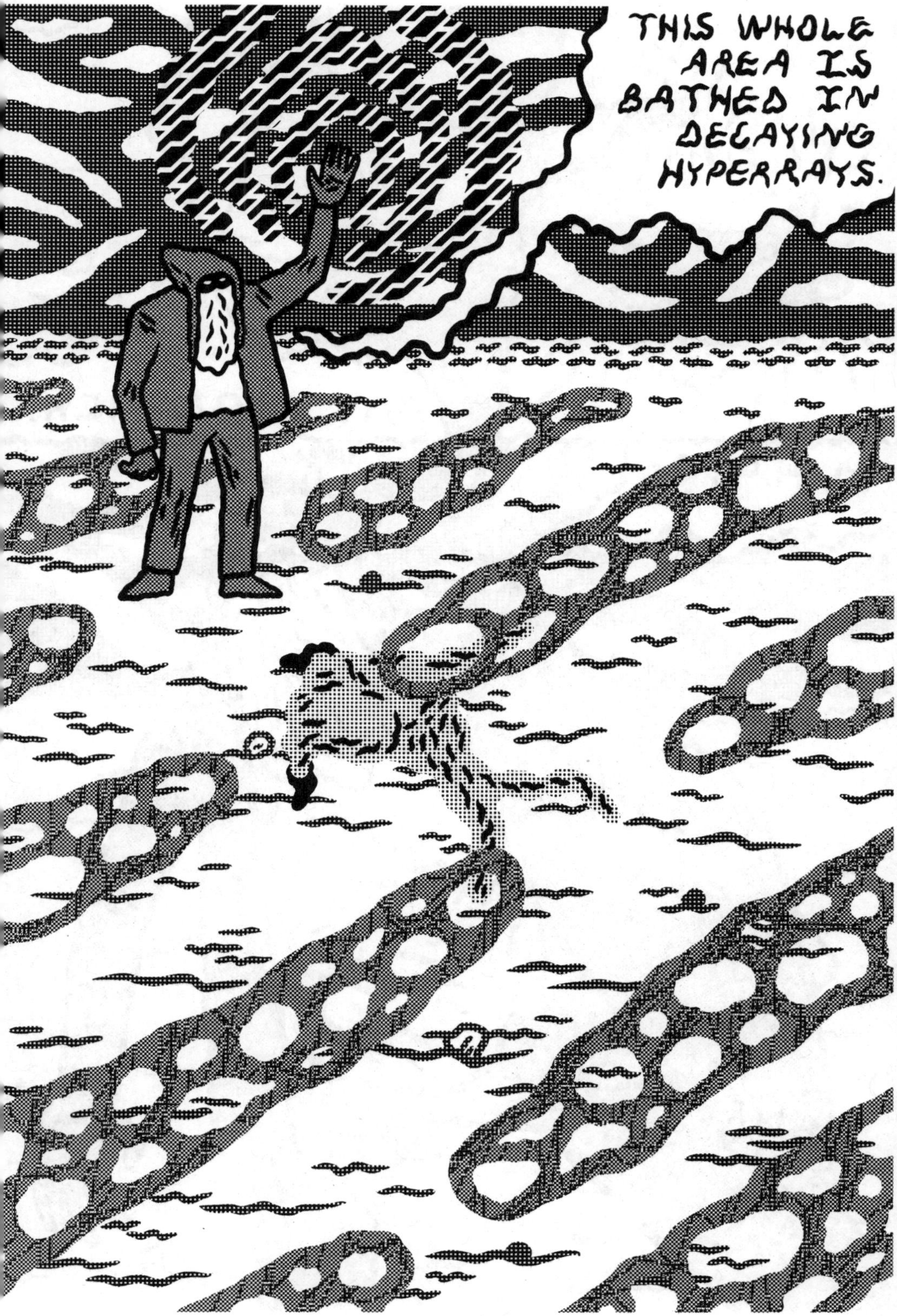
THIS WHOLE AREA IS BATHED IN DECAYING HYPERRAYS.

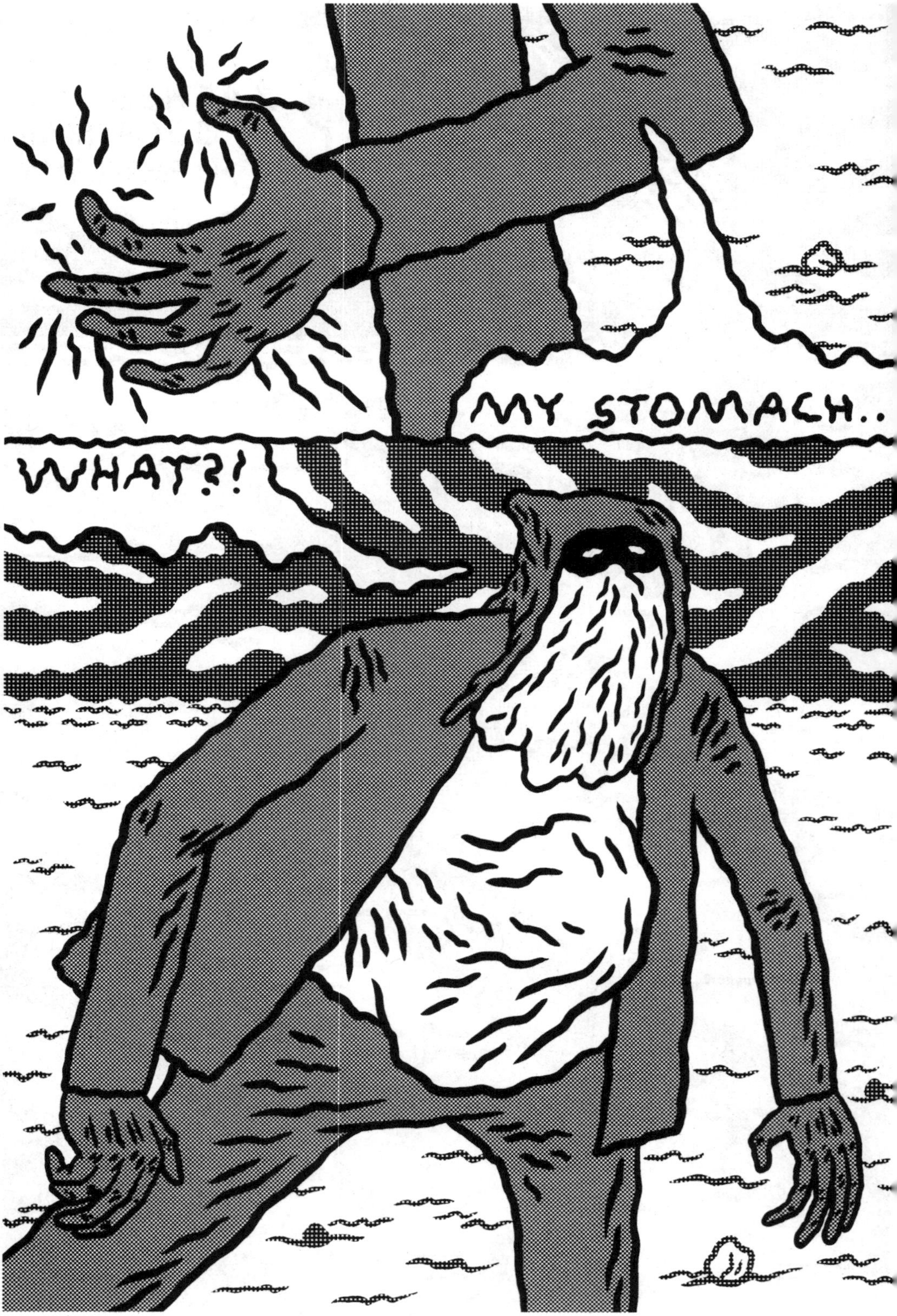
MY STOMACH..
WHAT?!

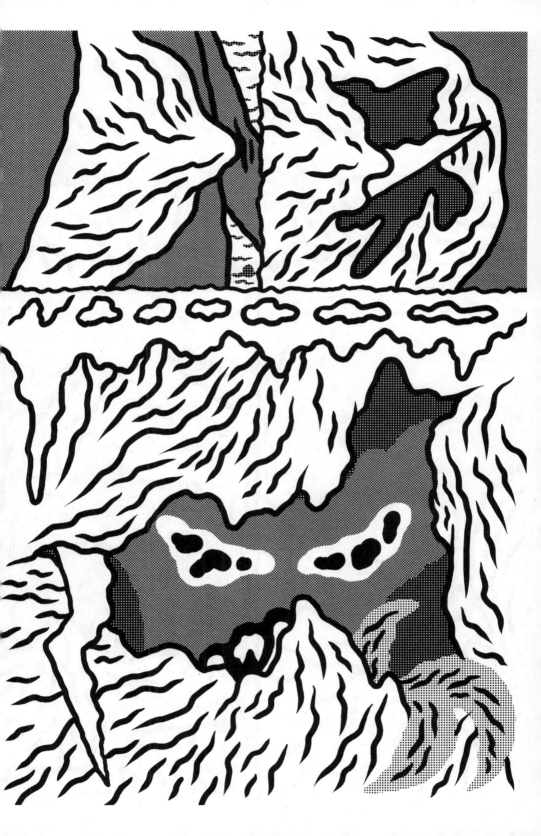

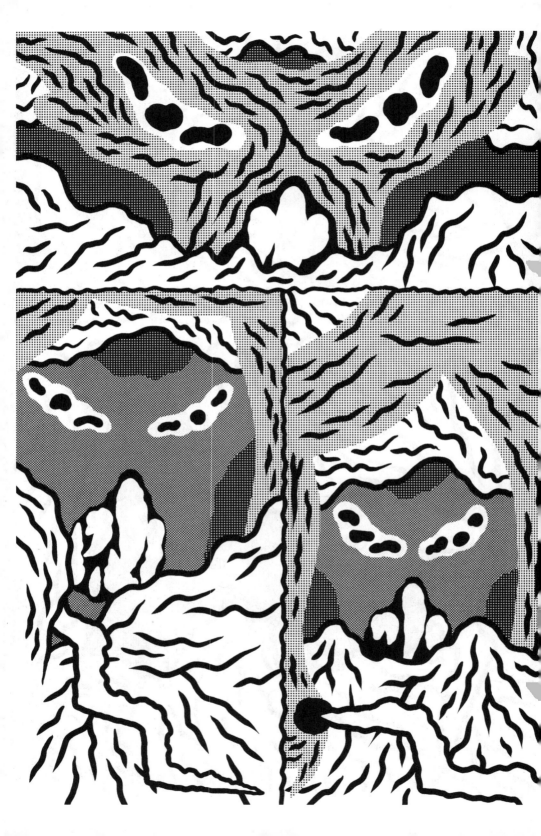

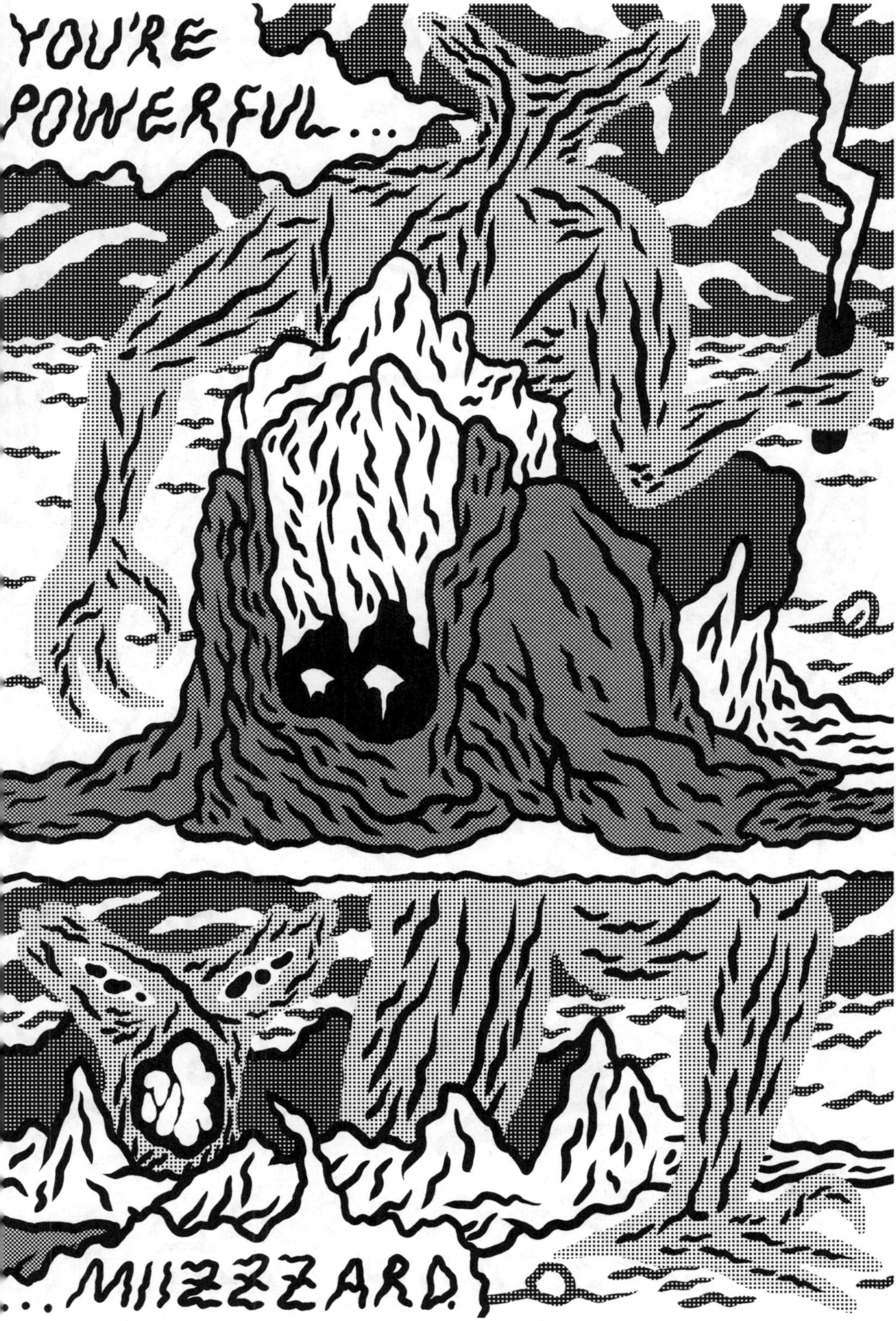
YOU'RE POWERFUL...
...MIIZZZARD.

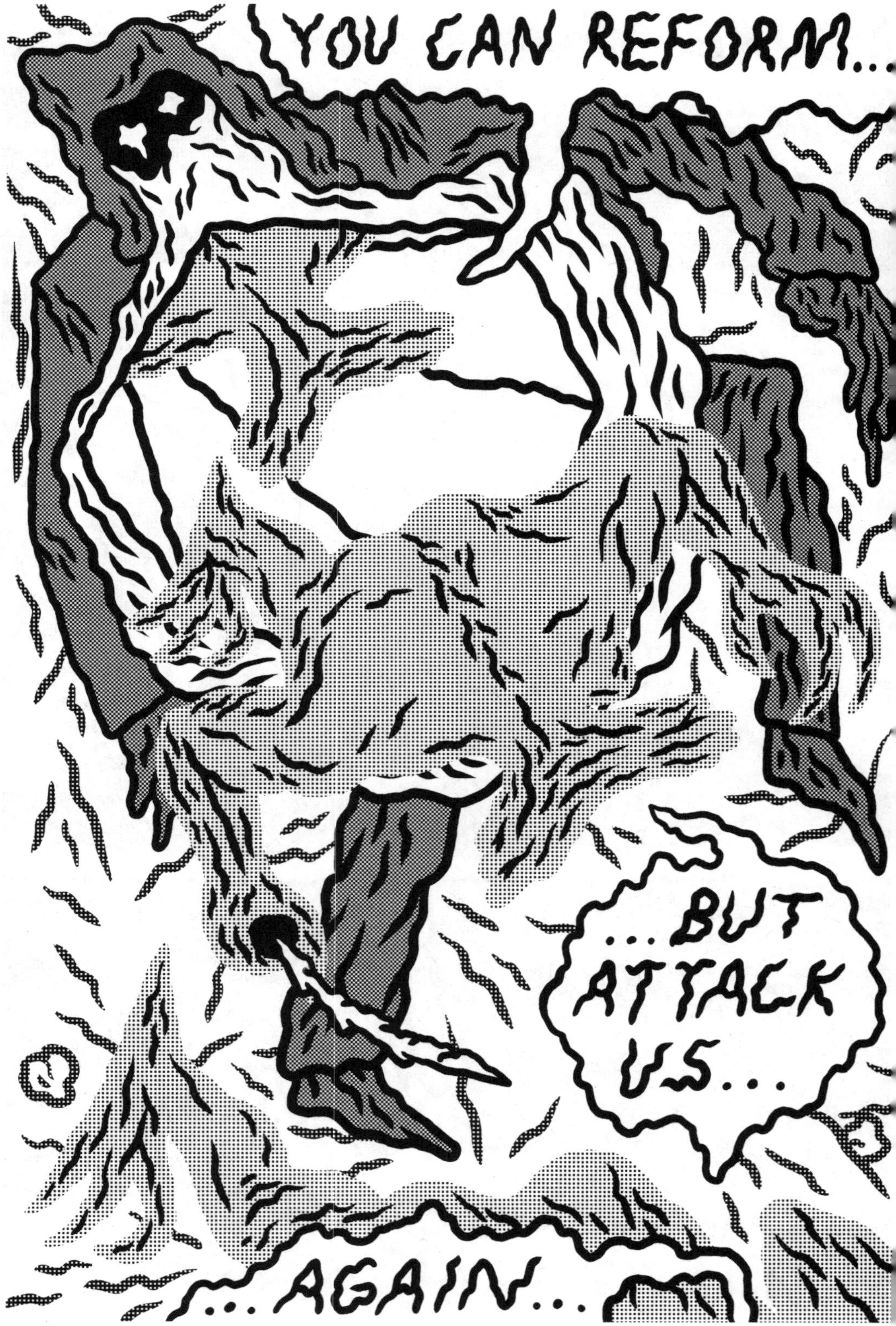
YOU CAN REFORM...
...BUT ATTACK US...
...AGAIN...

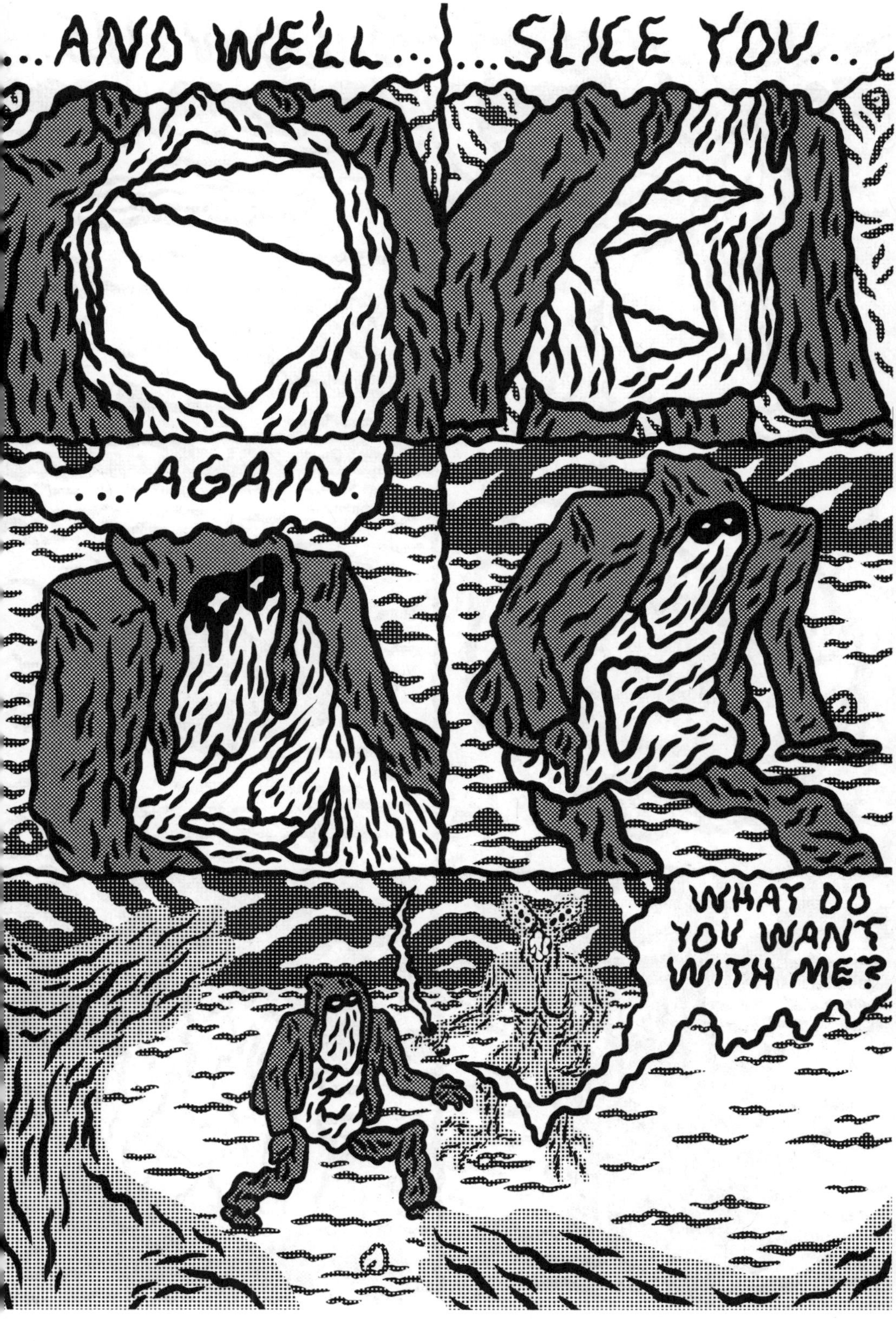
...AND WE'LL...
...SLICE YOU...
...AGAIN.
WHAT DO YOU WANT WITH ME?

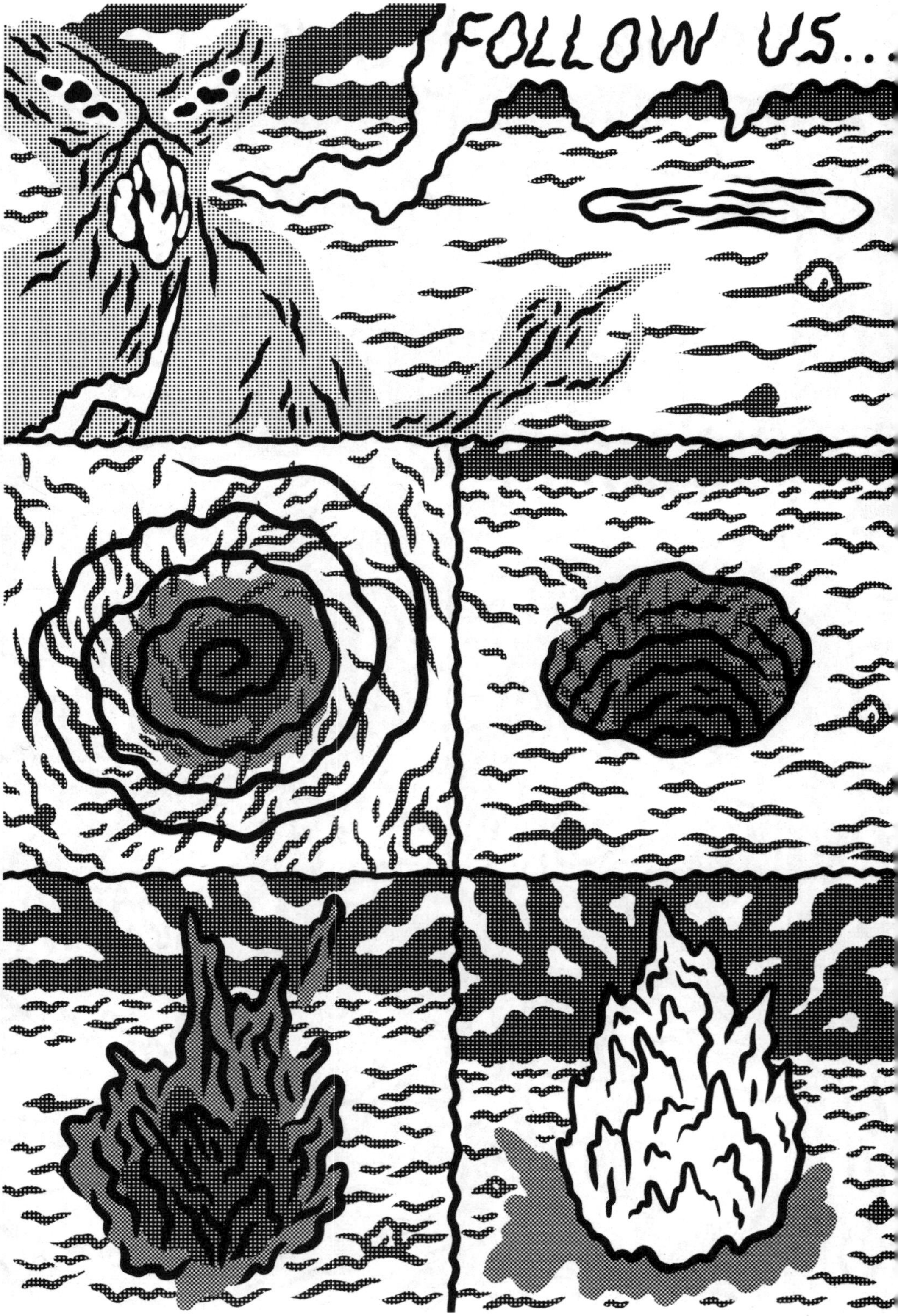
FOLLOW US...

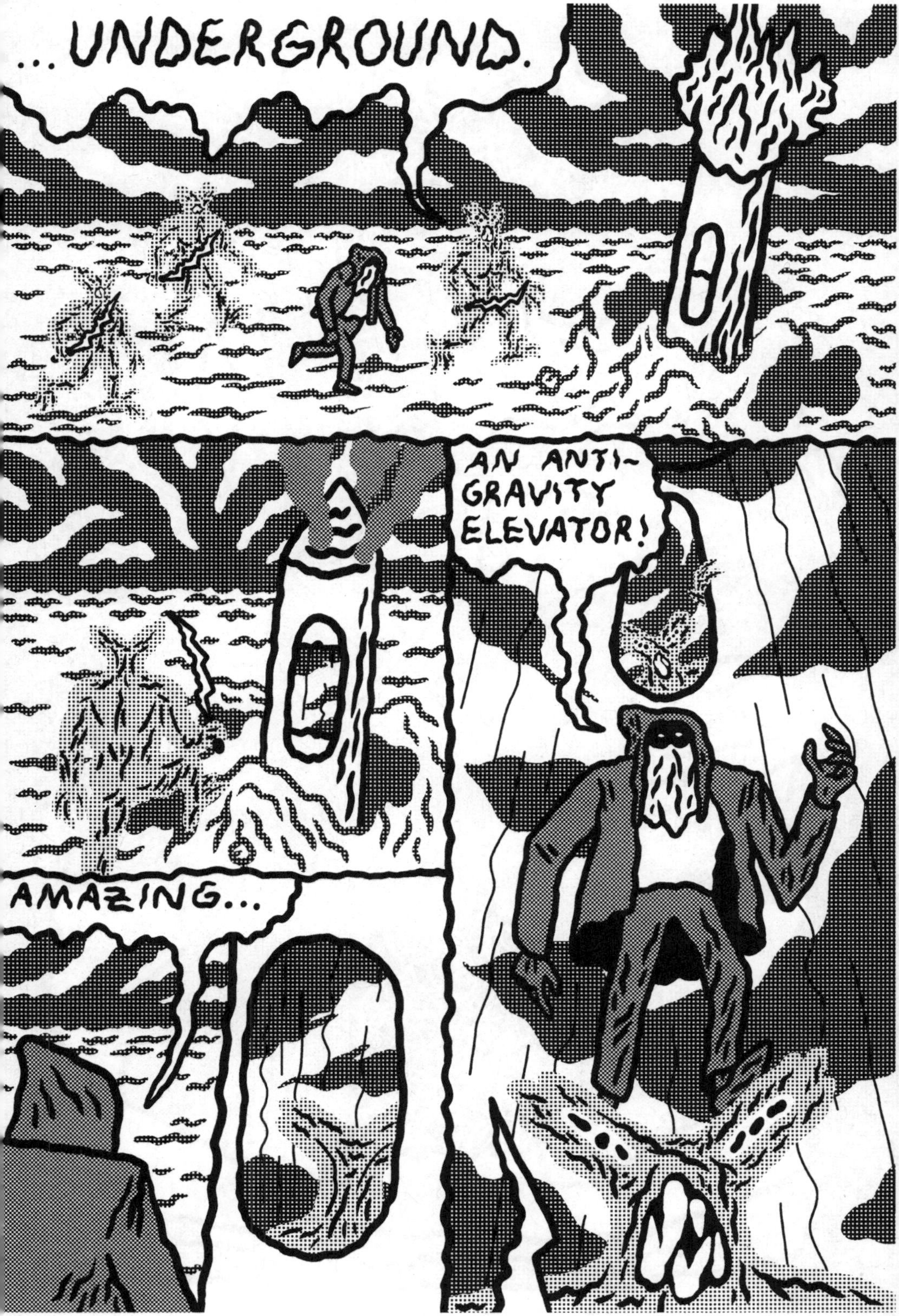
...UNDERGROUND.
AN ANTI-GRAVITY ELEVATOR!
AMAZING...

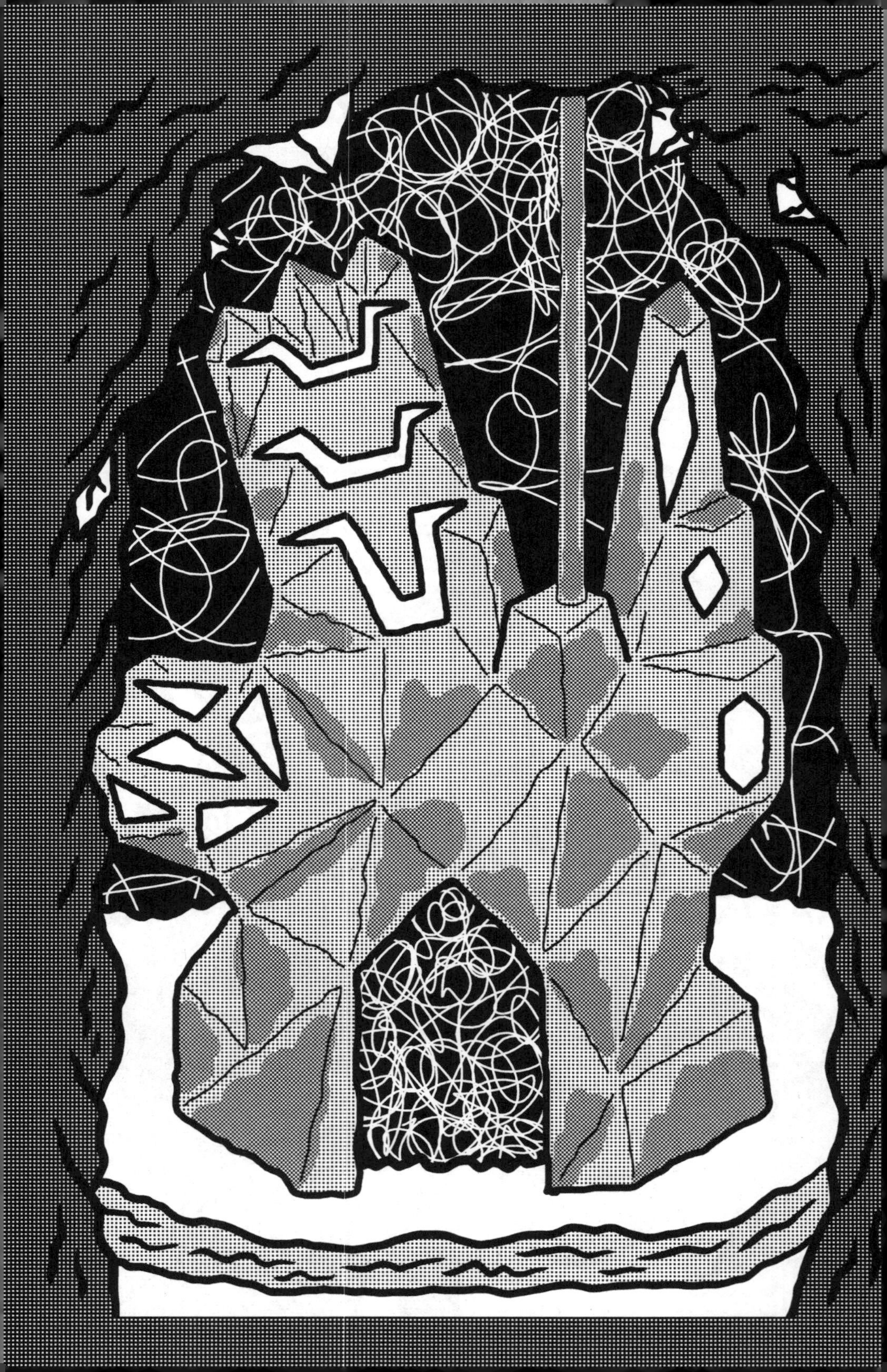

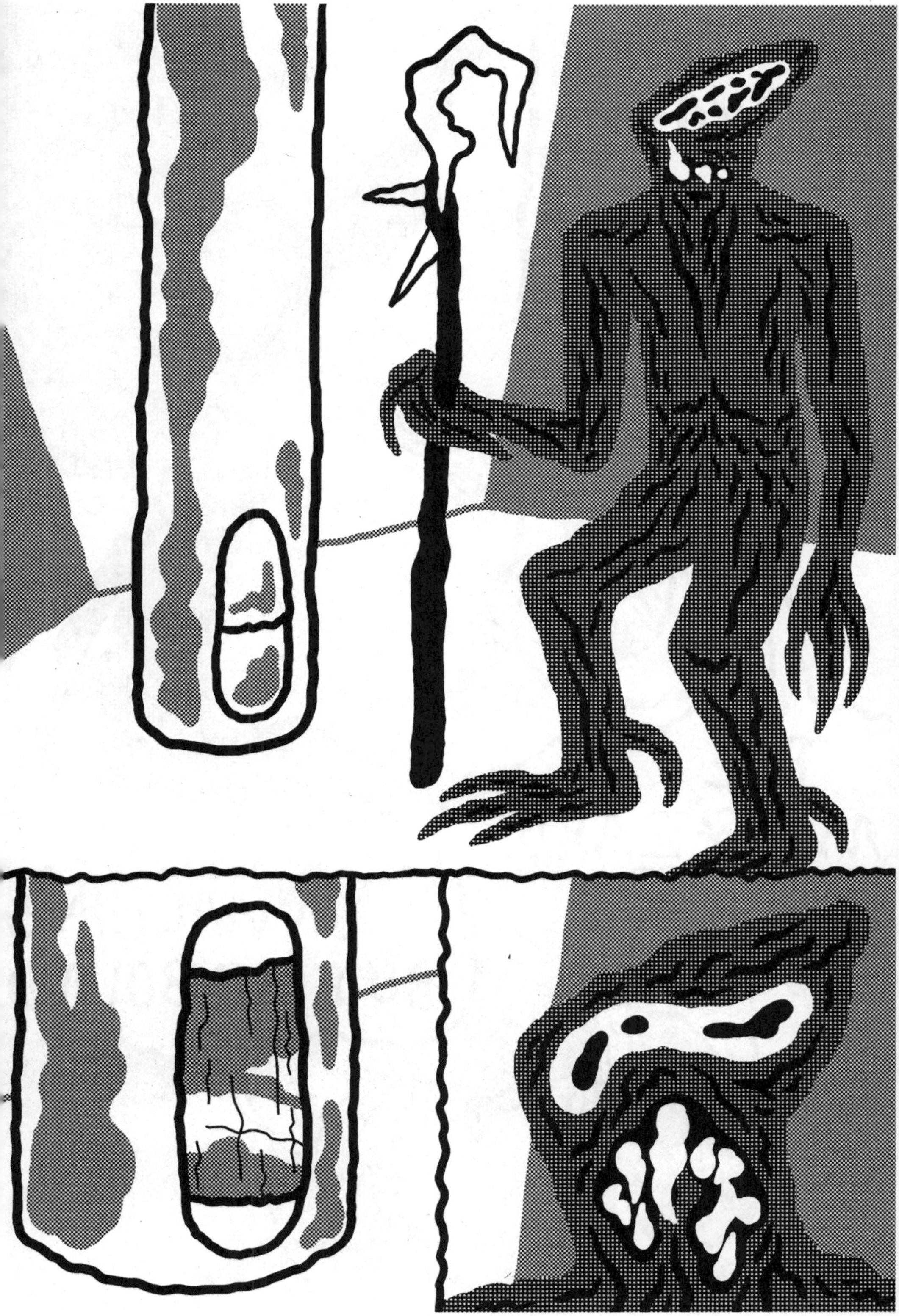

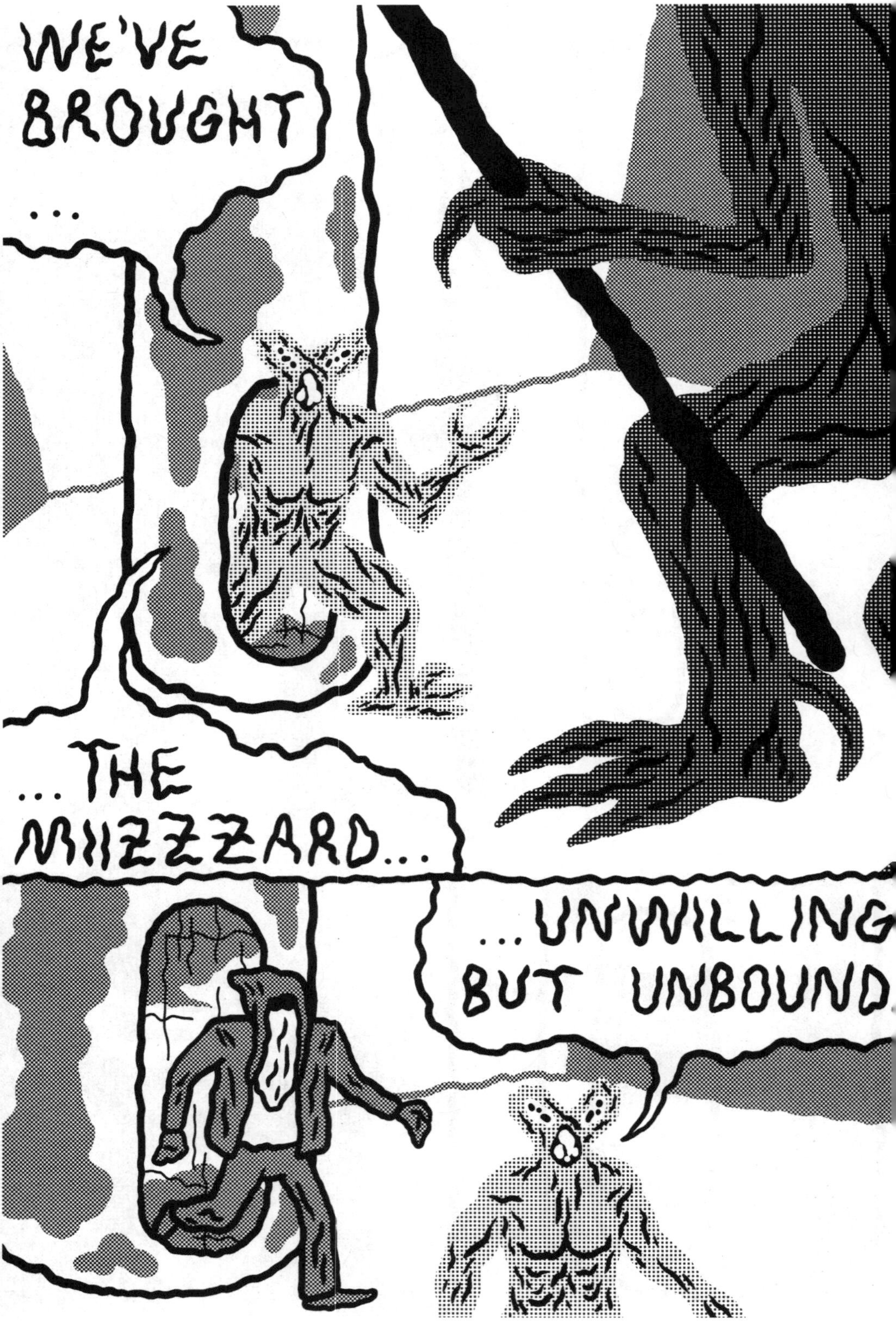
WE'VE BROUGHT ...
...THE MIIZZZARD...
...UNWILLING BUT UNBOUND

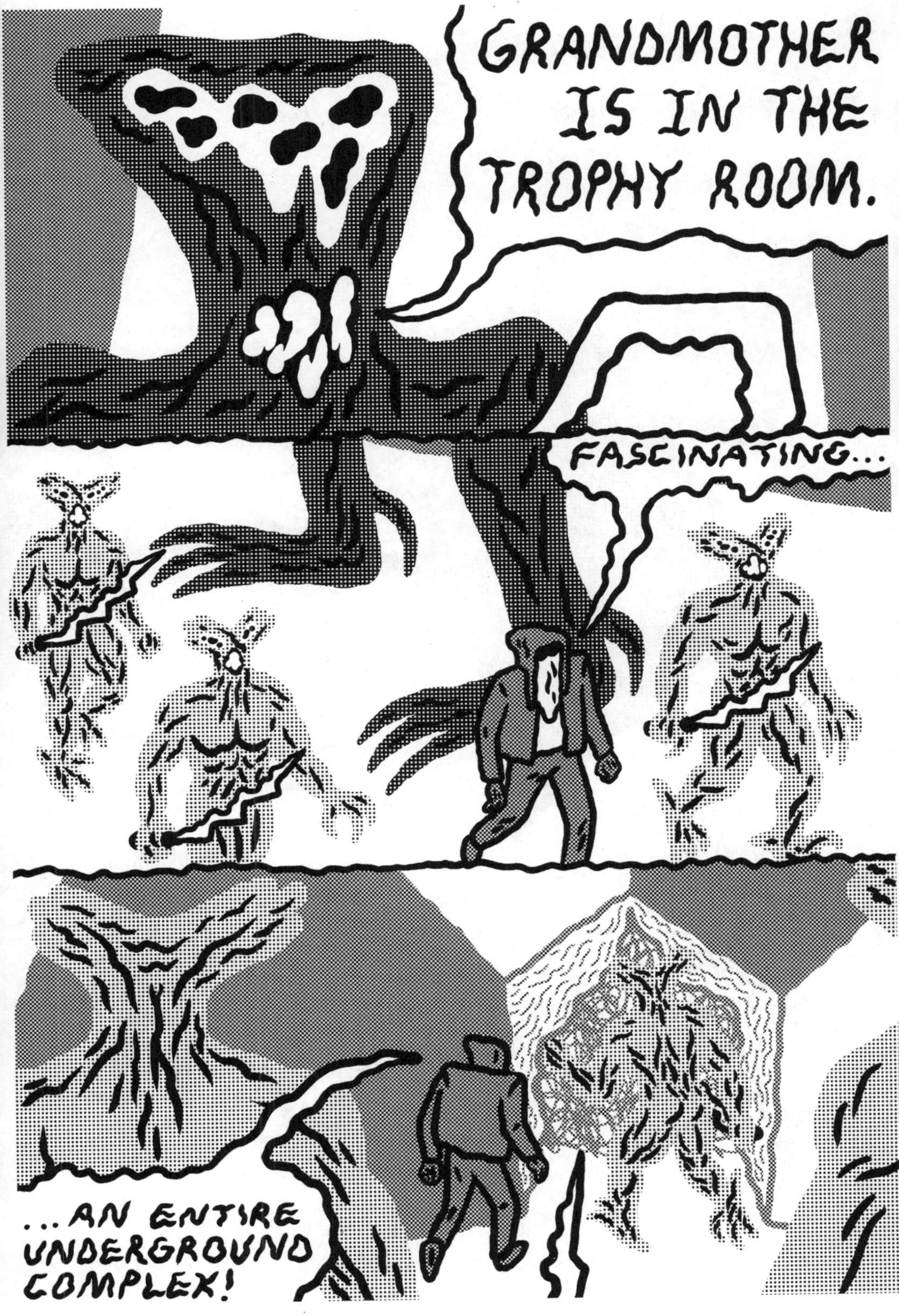
GRANDMOTHER IS IN THE TROPHY ROOM.
FASCINATING...
...AN ENTIRE UNDERGROUND COMPLEX!

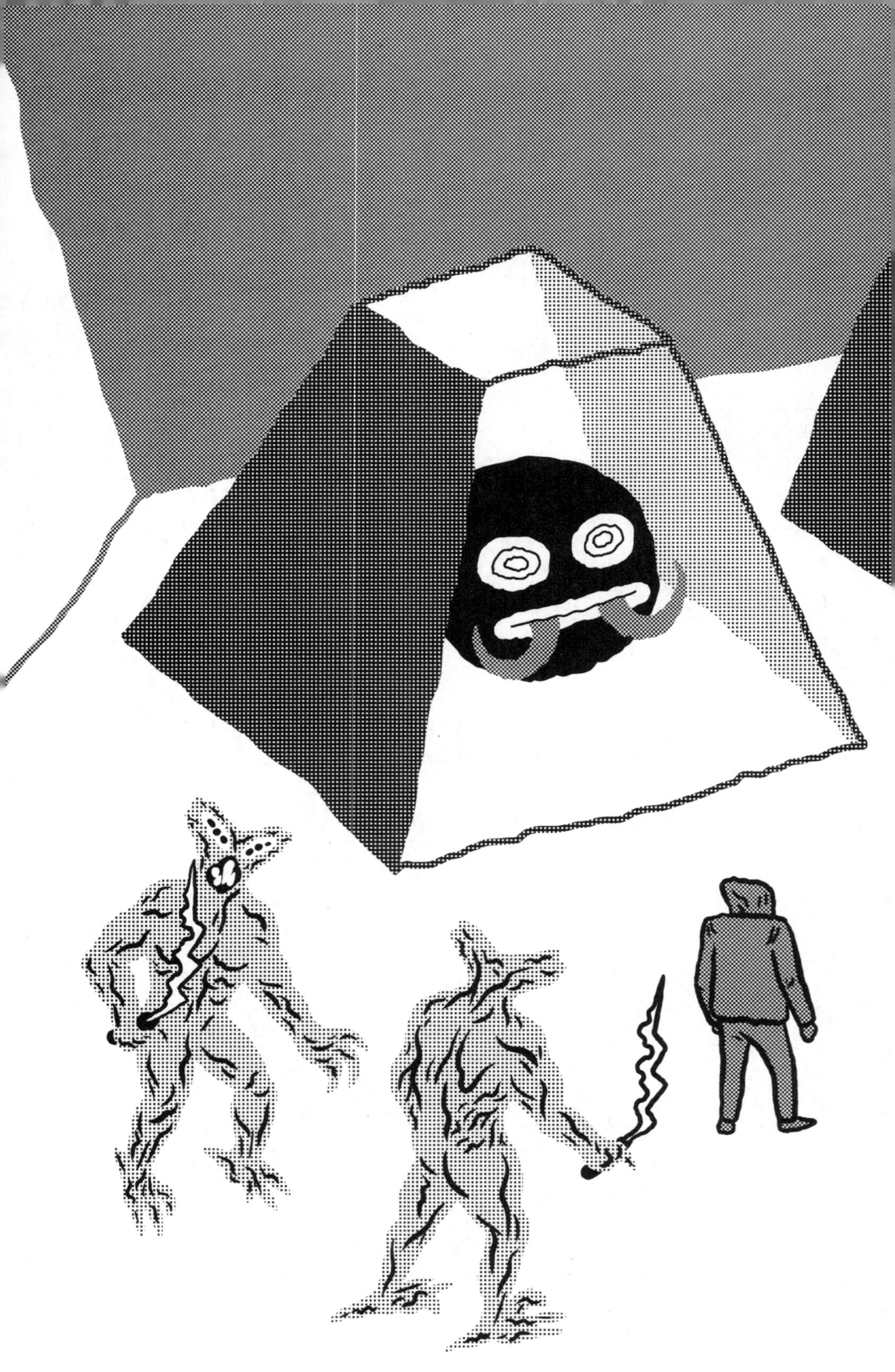

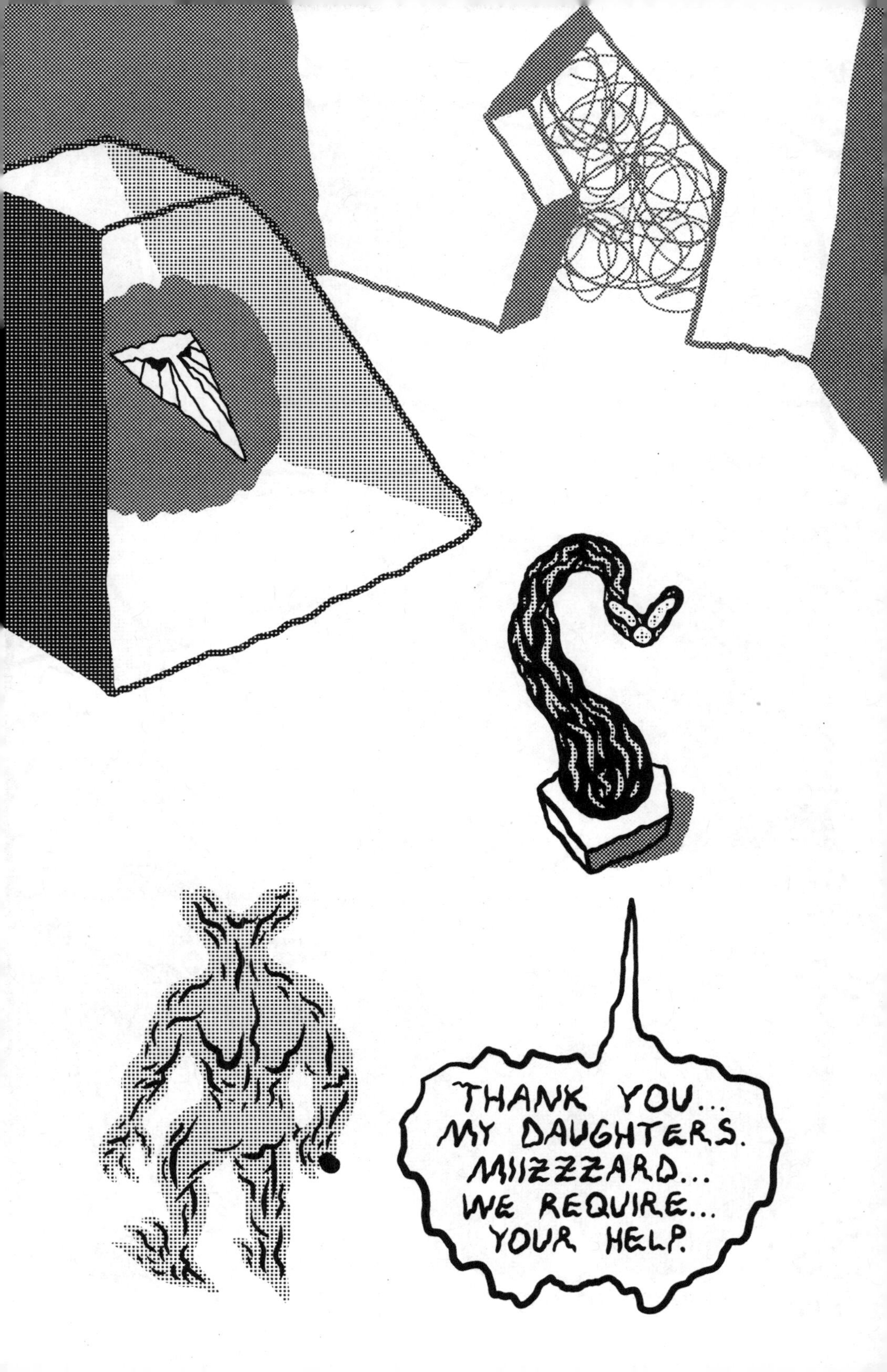
THANK YOU... MY DAUGHTERS. MIIZZZARD... WE REQUIRE... YOUR HELP.

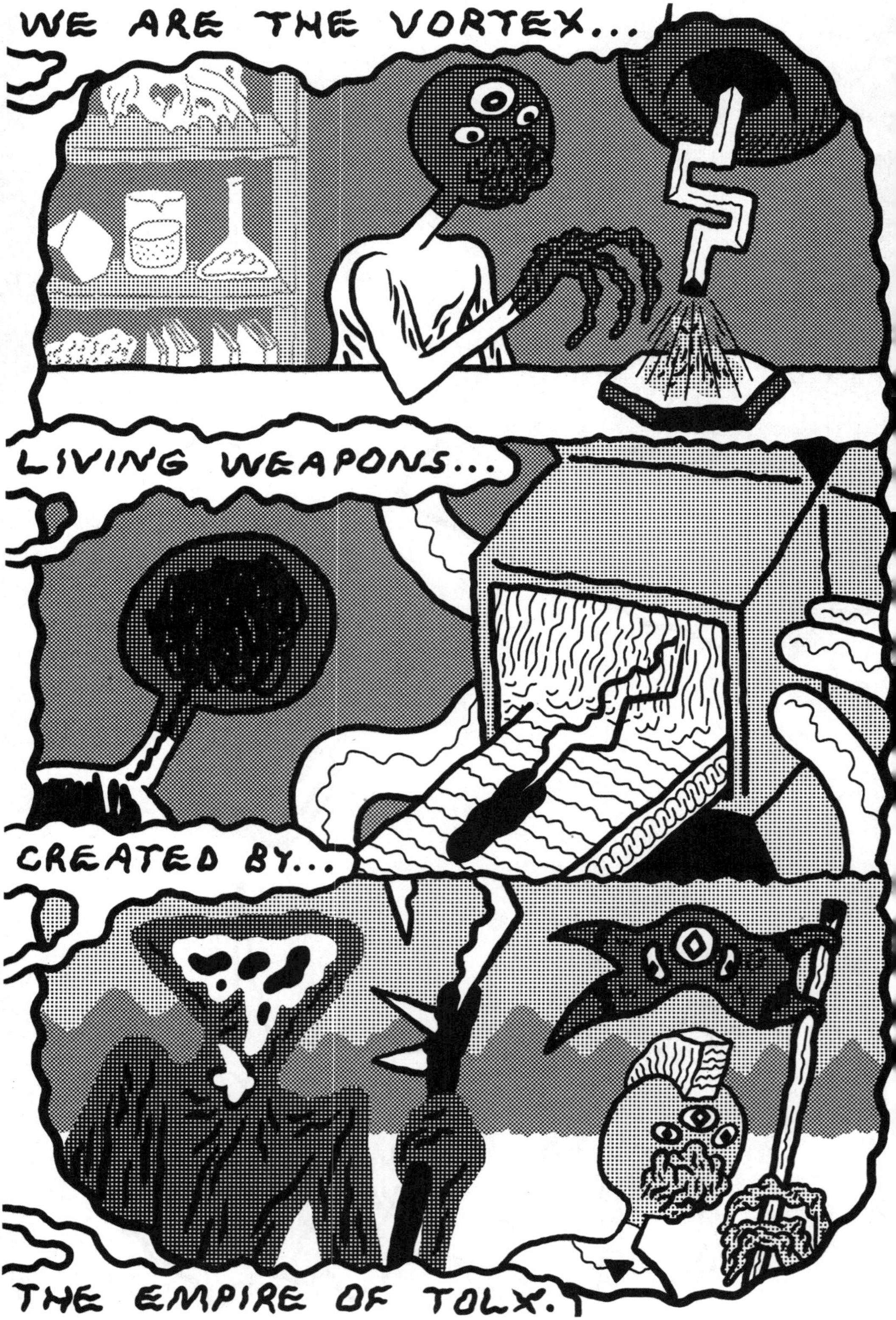
WE ARE THE VORTEX...
LIVING WEAPONS...
CREATED BY...
THE EMPIRE OF TOLX.

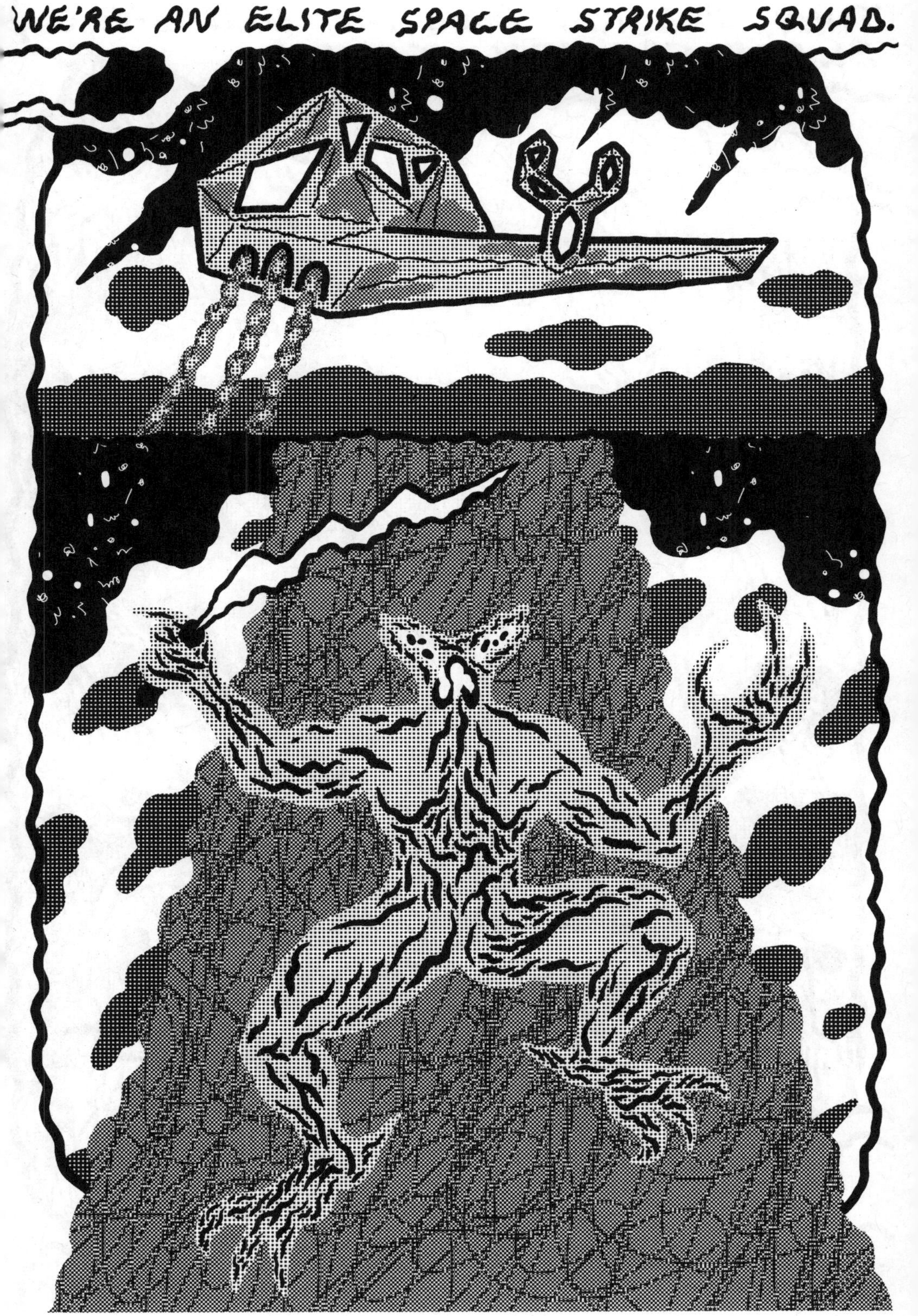
WE'RE AN ELITE SPACE STRIKE SQUAD.

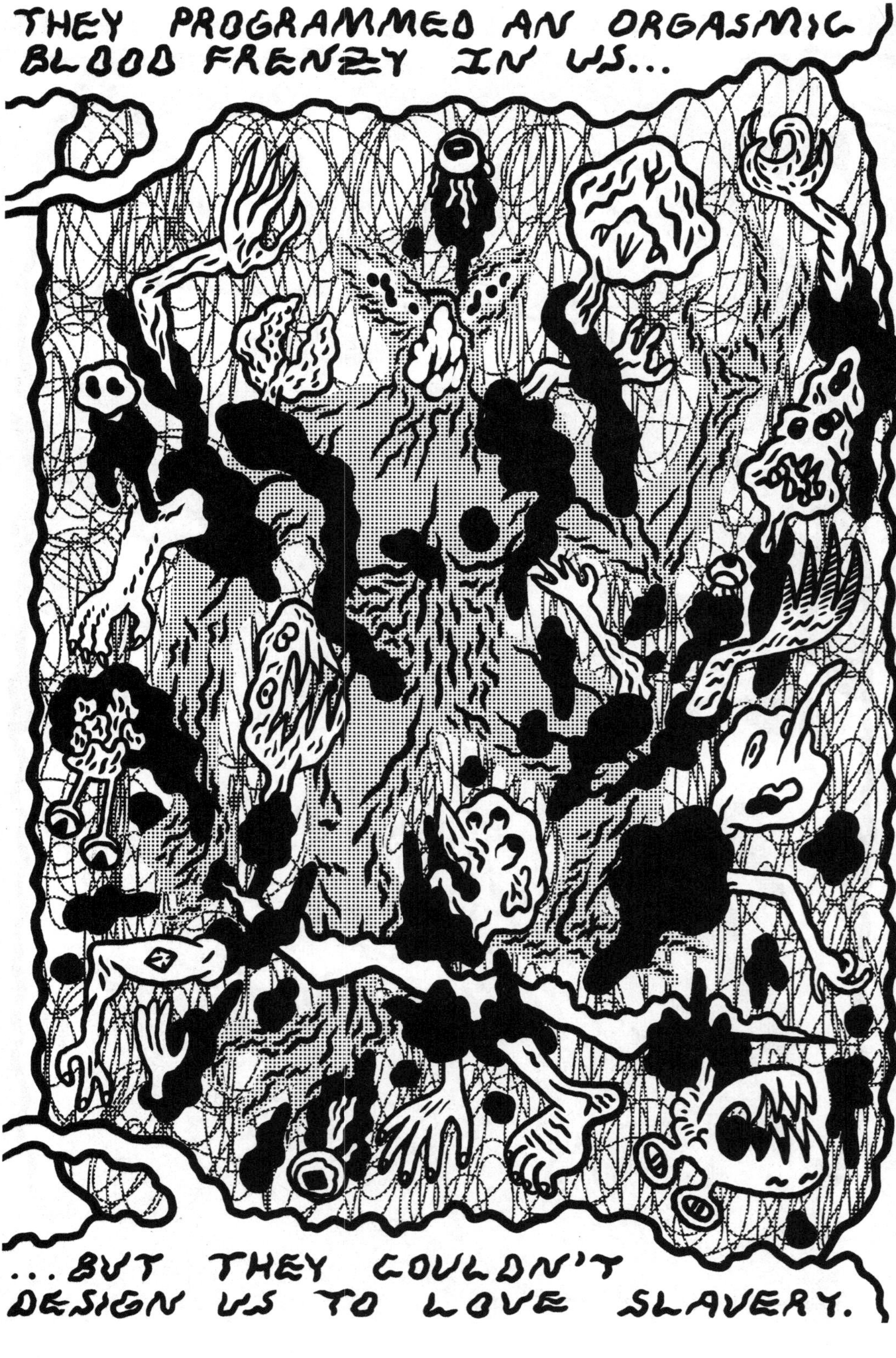
THEY PROGRAMMED AN ORGASMIC BLOOD FRENZY IN US...
...BUT THEY COULDN'T DESIGN US TO LOVE SLAVERY.

THERE'S A CONTROL DEVICE IN US.

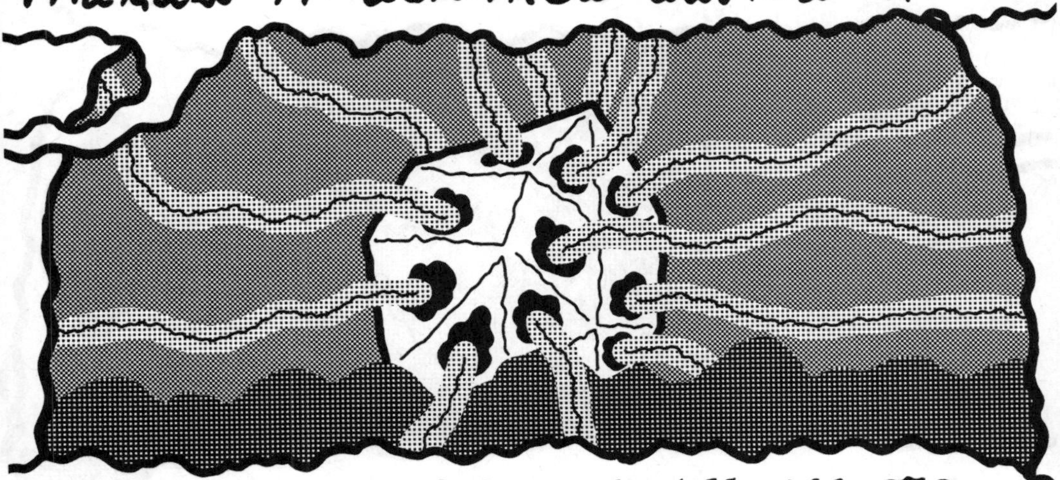

WHEN THE EMPIRE WANTS US TO ATTACK, THE DEVICE TAKES US OVER.

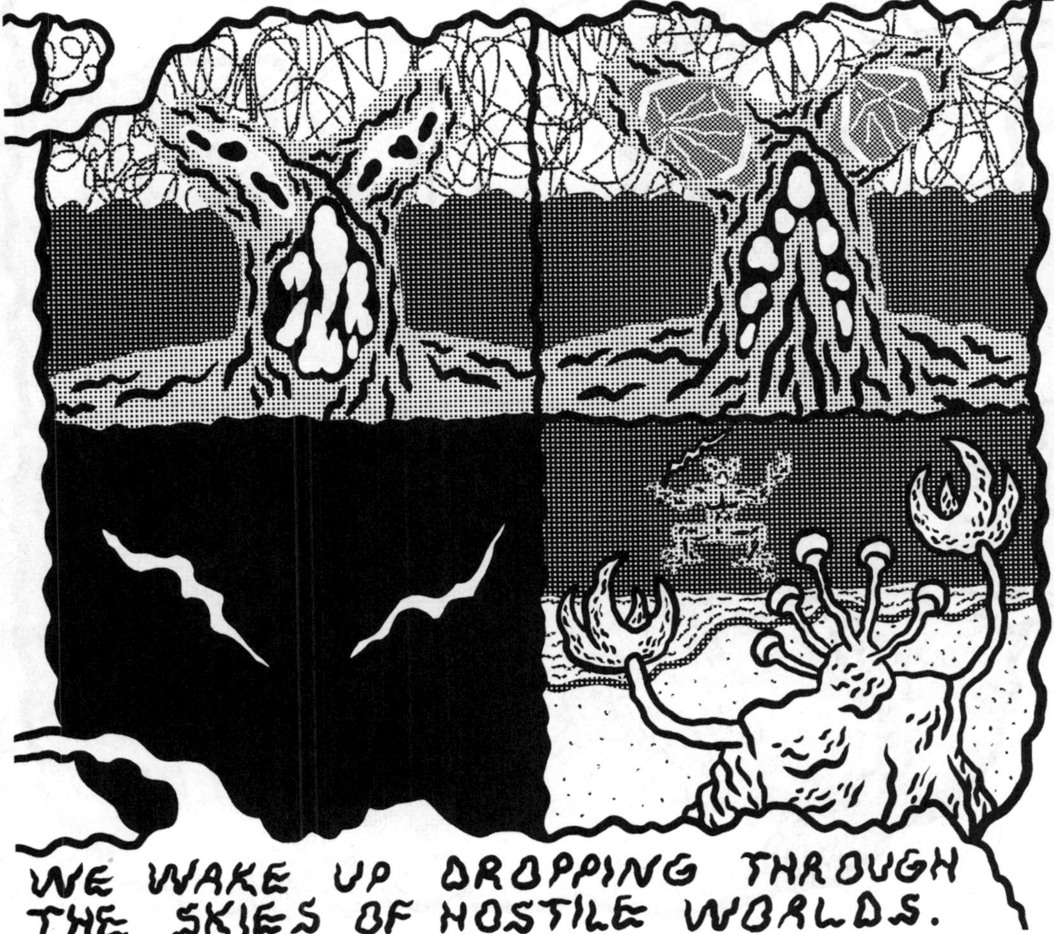

WE WAKE UP DROPPING THROUGH THE SKIES OF HOSTILE WORLDS.

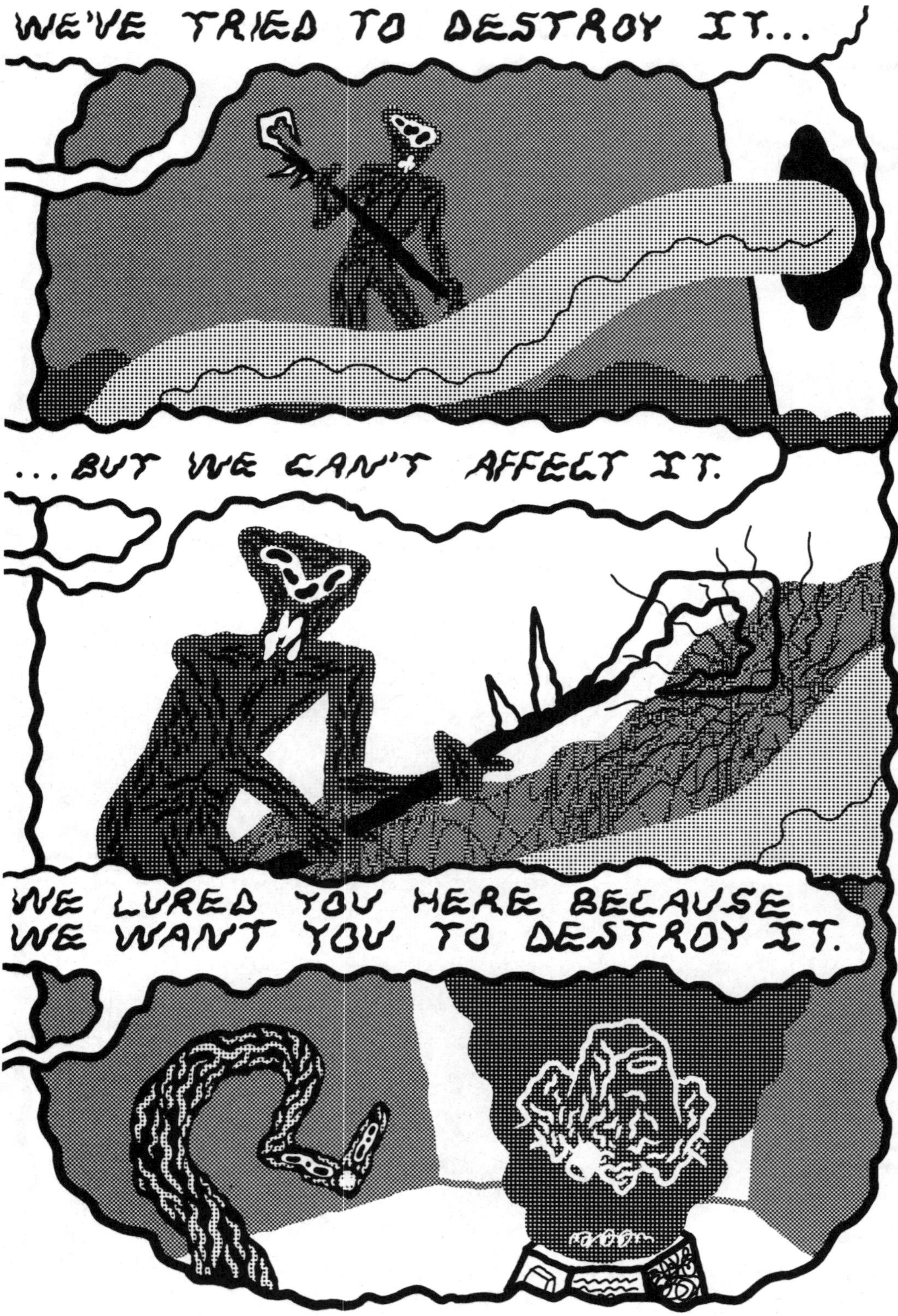
WE'VE TRIED TO DESTROY IT...
...BUT WE CAN'T AFFECT IT.
WE LURED YOU HERE BECAUSE WE WANT YOU TO DESTROY IT.

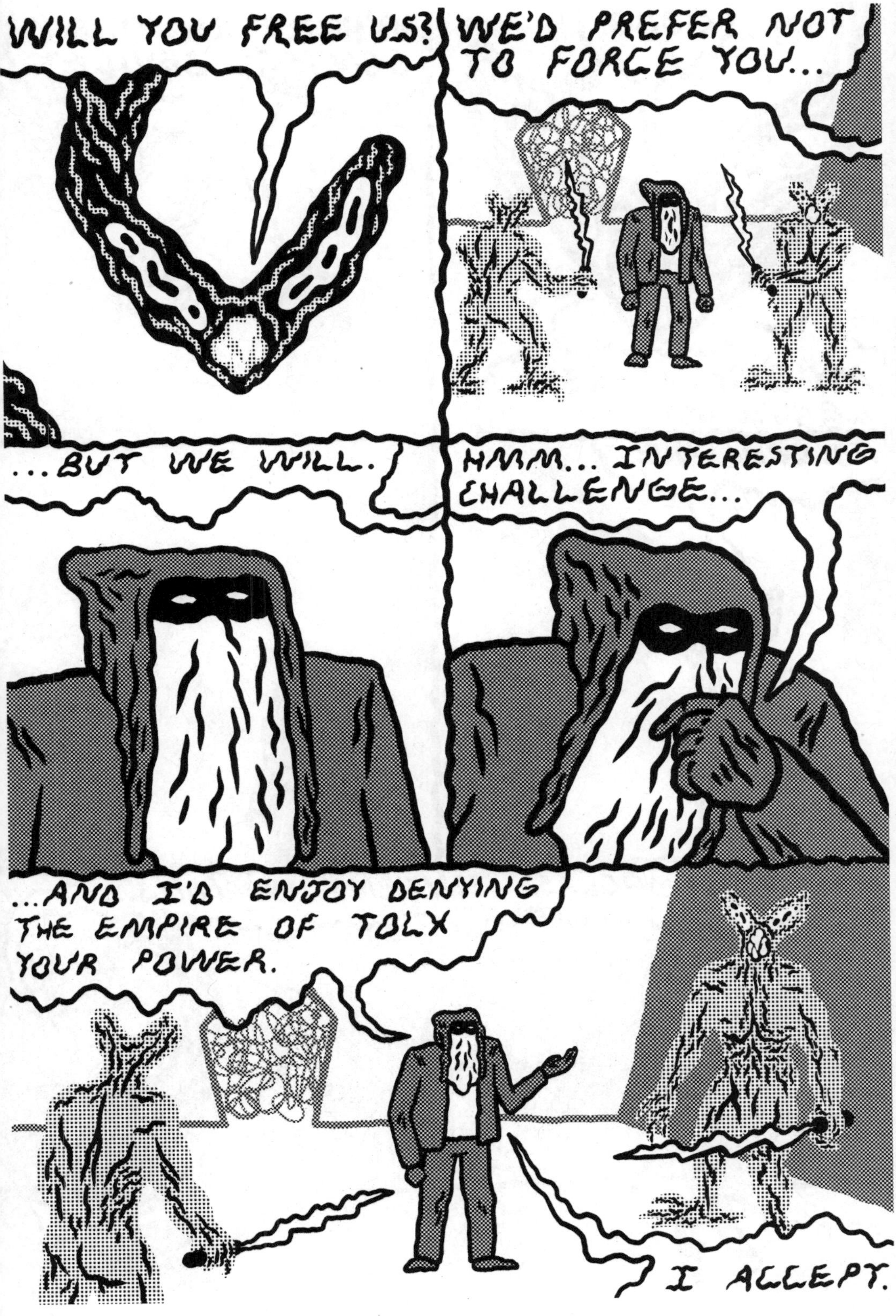
WILL YOU FREE US?
WE'D PREFER NOT TO FORCE YOU...
...BUT WE WILL.
HMM... INTERESTING CHALLENGE...
...AND I'D ENJOY DENYING THE EMPIRE OF TOLX YOUR POWER.
I ACCEPT.

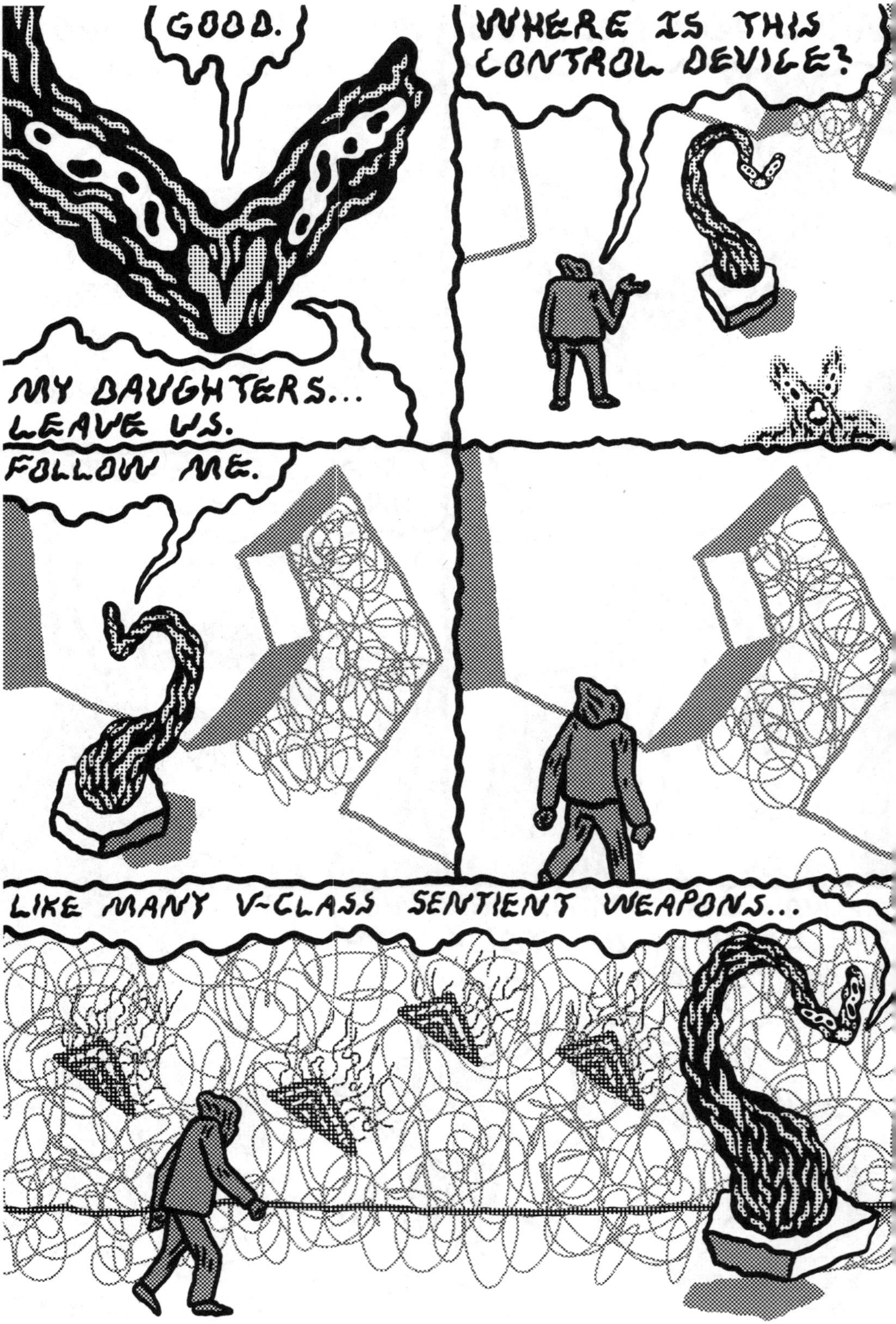
GOOD.
MY DAUGHTERS... LEAVE US.
WHERE IS THIS CONTROL DEVICE?
FOLLOW ME.
LIKE MANY V-CLASS SENTIENT WEAPONS...

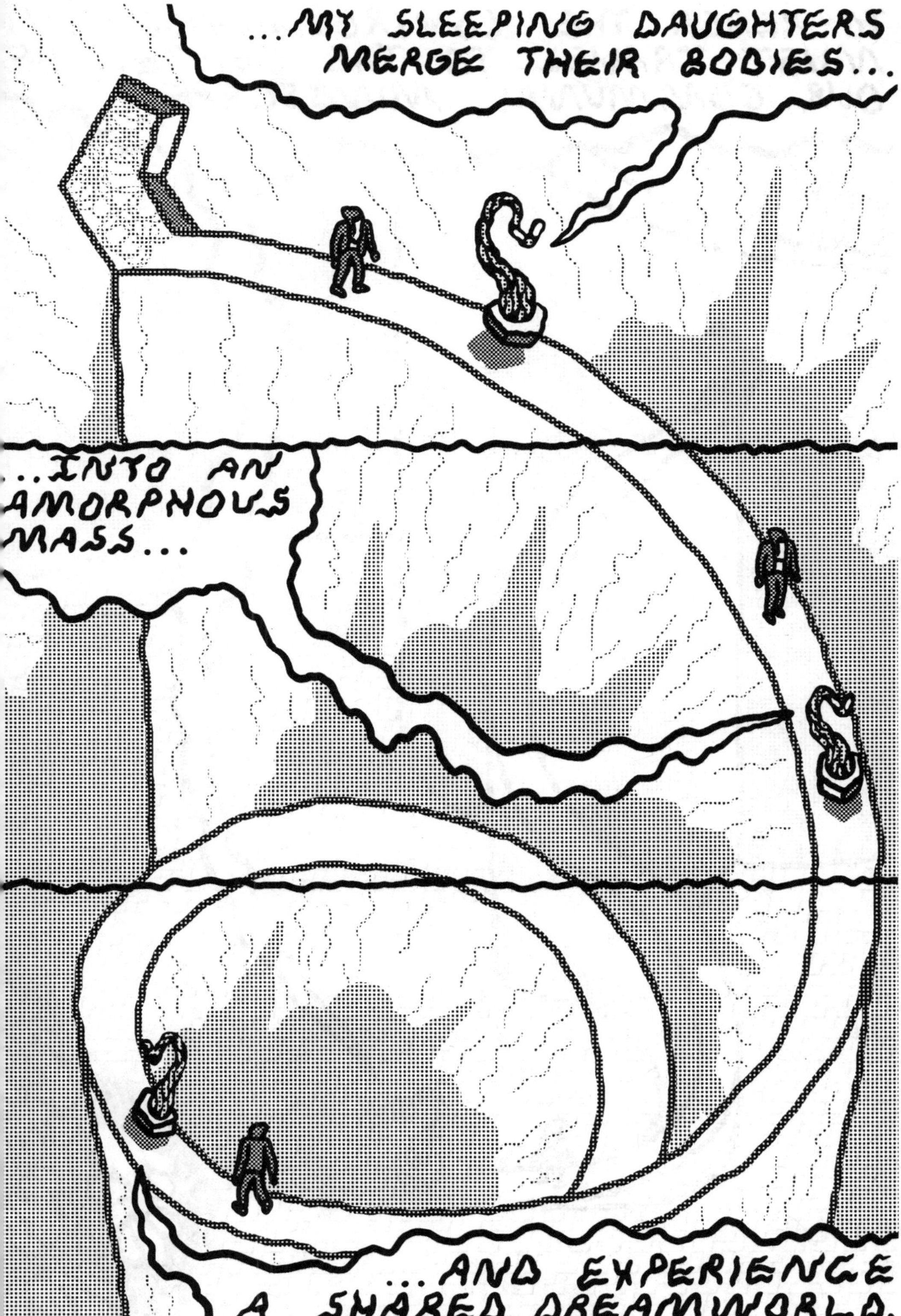
...MY SLEEPING DAUGHTERS MERGE THEIR BODIES...
...INTO AN AMORPHOUS MASS...
...AND EXPERIENCE A SHARED DREAMWORLD.

TO REACH THE CONTROL DEVICE, YOU MUST TRAVEL TO THE CENTER OF OUR COMMUNAL MINDSCAPE.

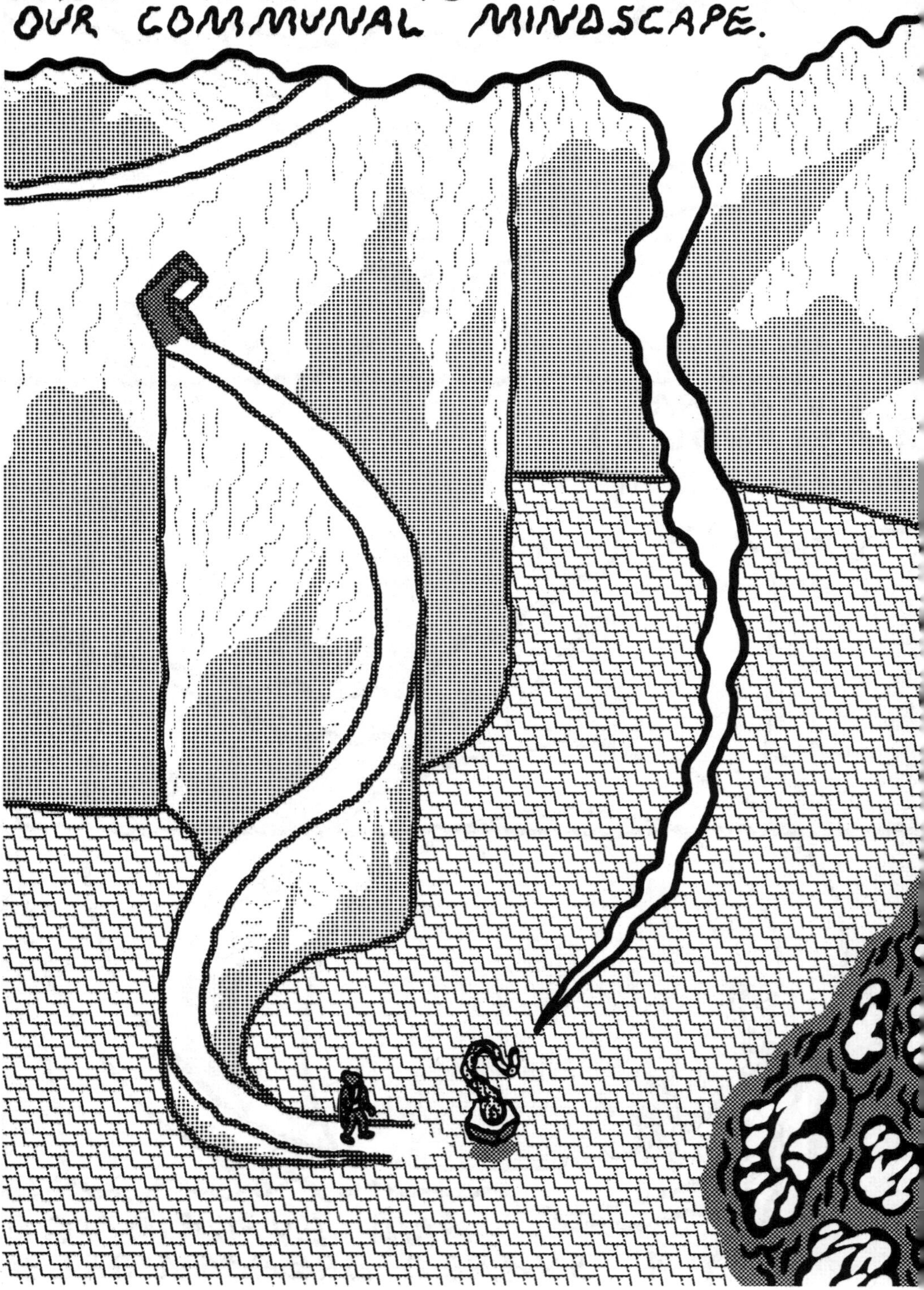

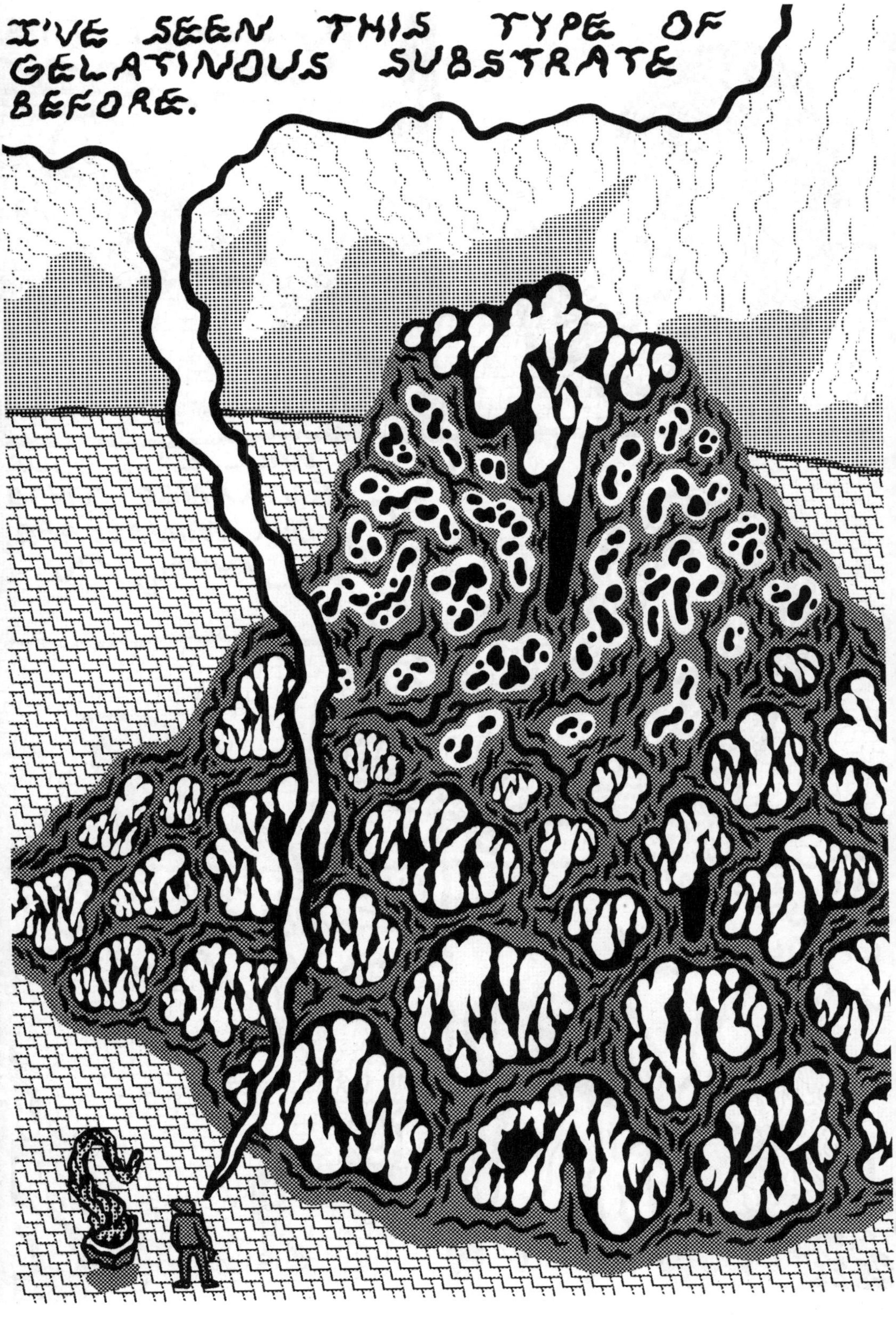
I'VE SEEN THIS TYPE OF GELATINOUS SUBSTRATE BEFORE.

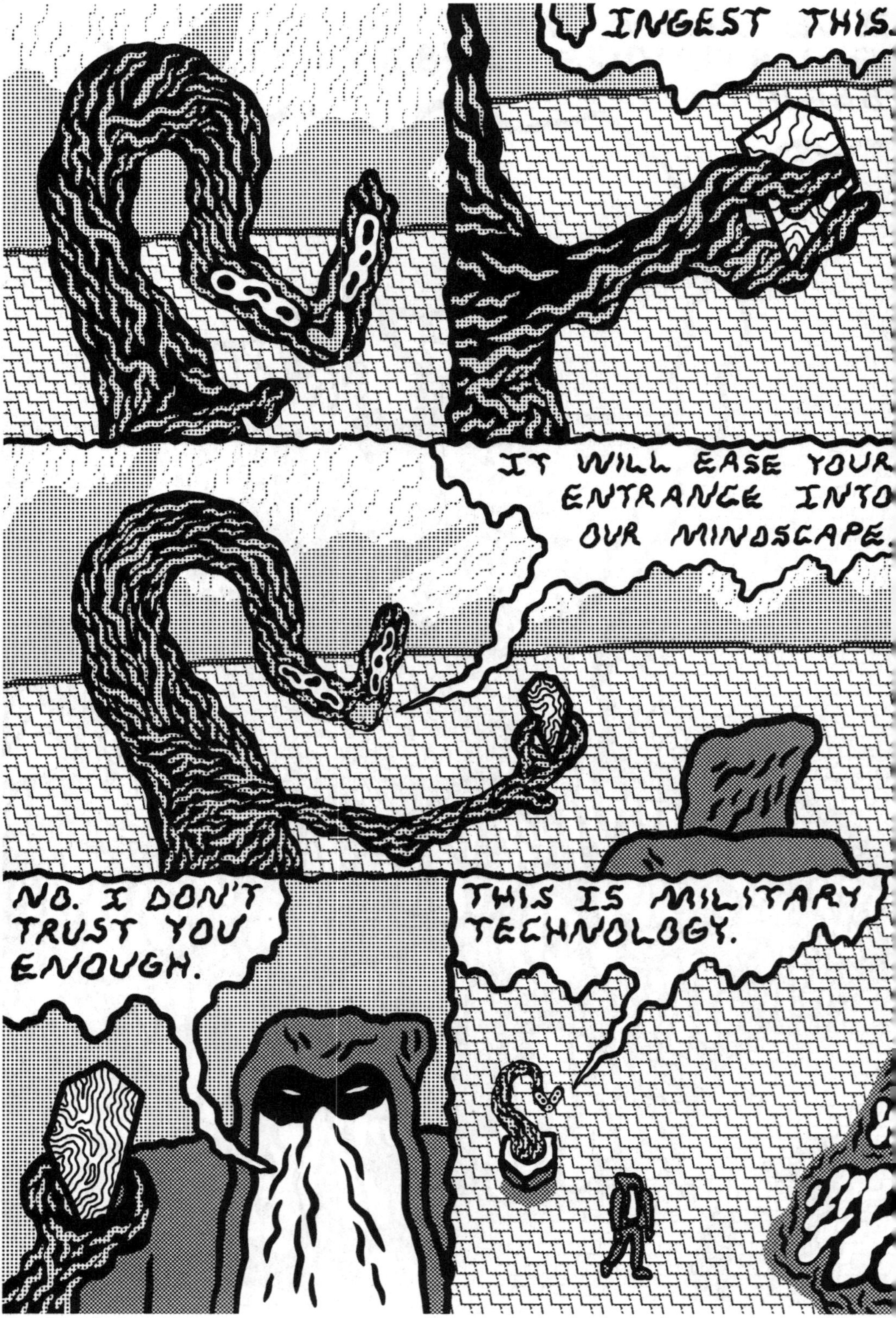
INGEST THIS.
IT WILL EASE YOUR ENTRANCE INTO OUR MINDSCAPE.
NO. I DON'T TRUST YOU ENOUGH.
THIS IS MILITARY TECHNOLOGY.

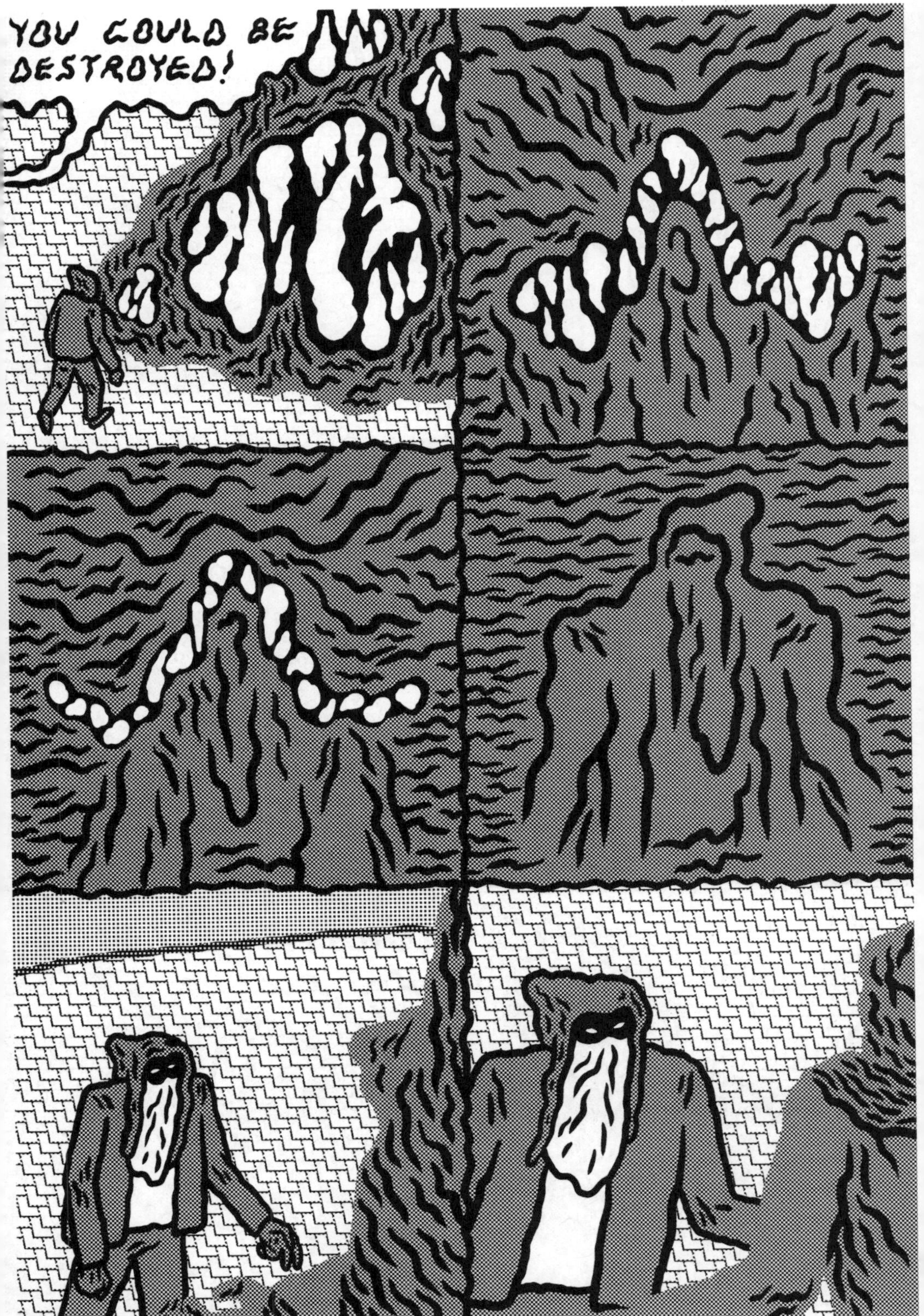
YOU COULD BE DESTROYED!

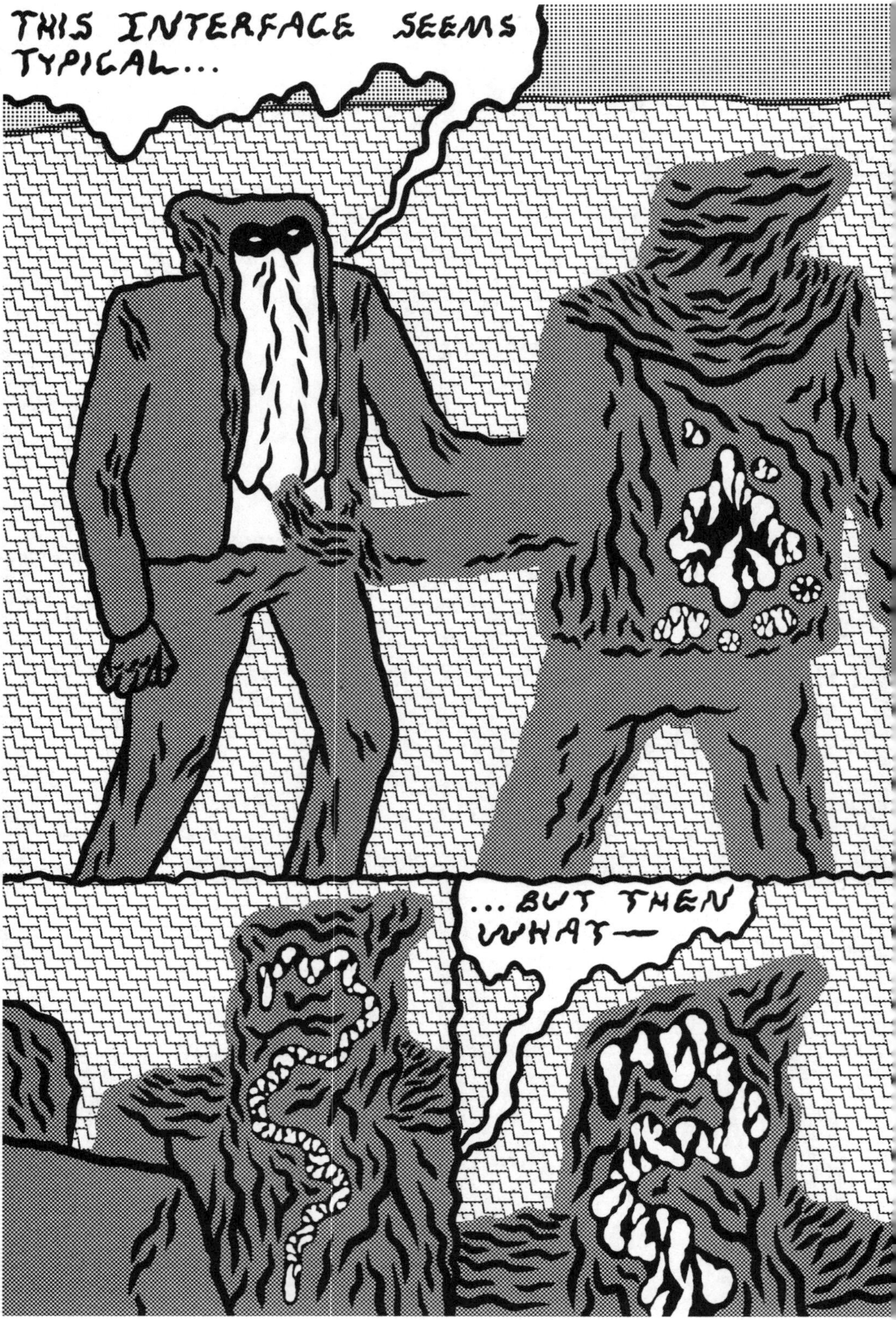
THIS INTERFACE SEEMS TYPICAL...
...BUT THEN WHAT—

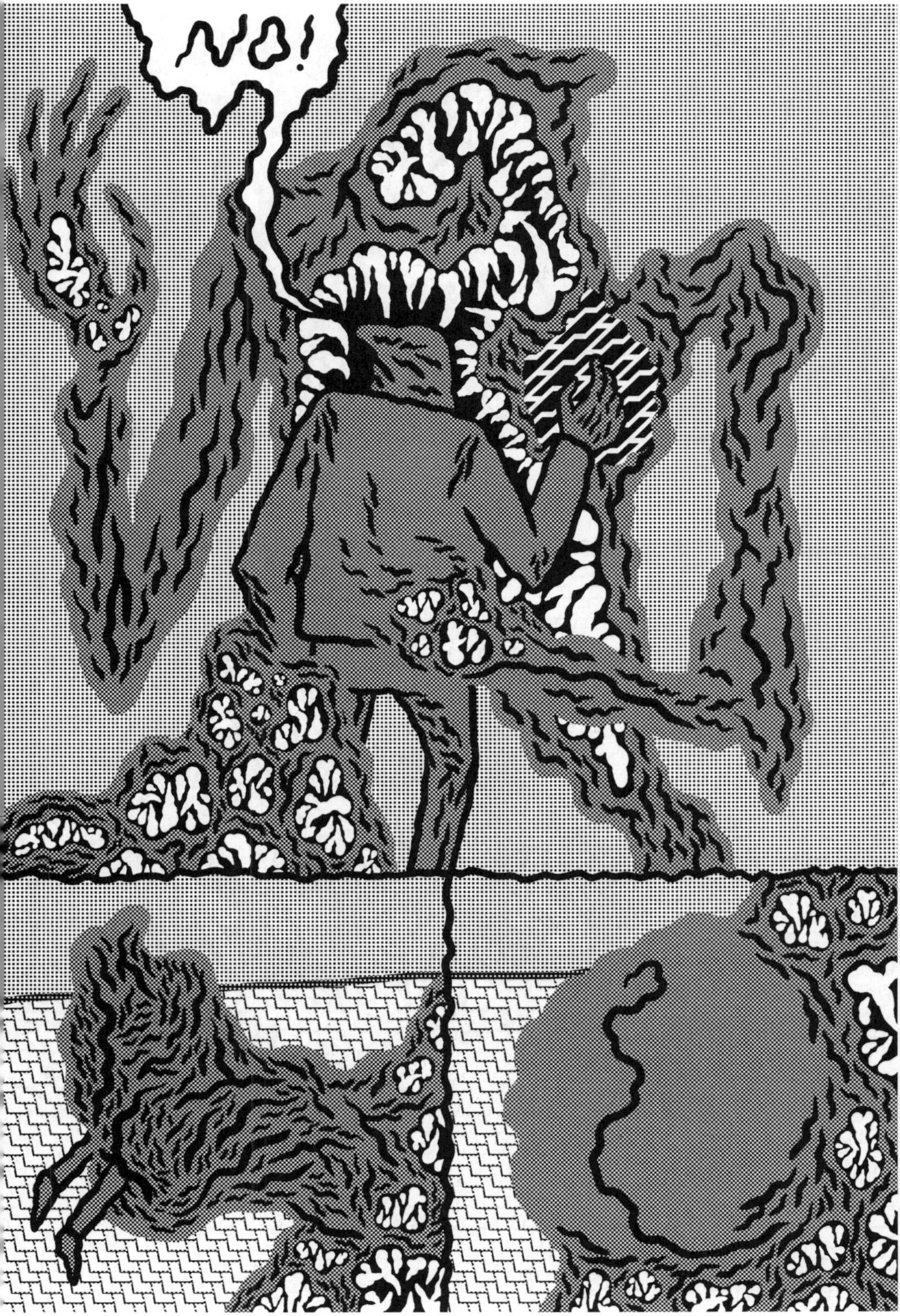
NO!

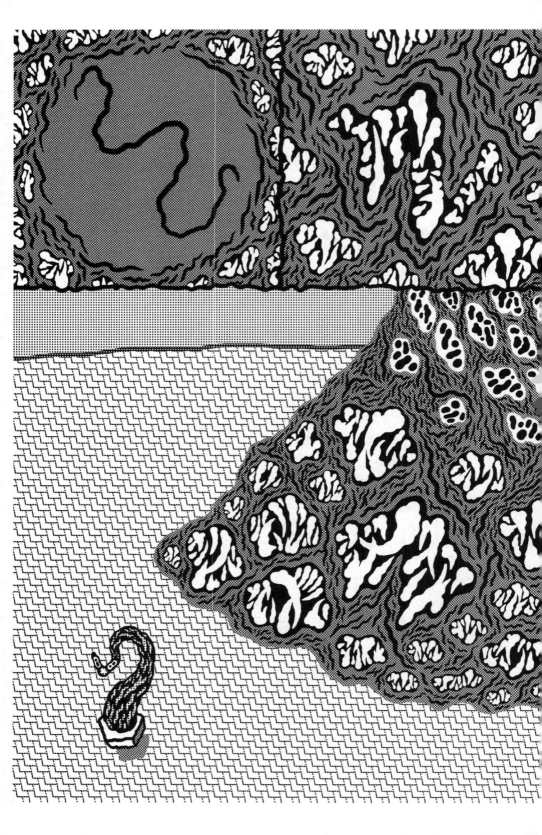

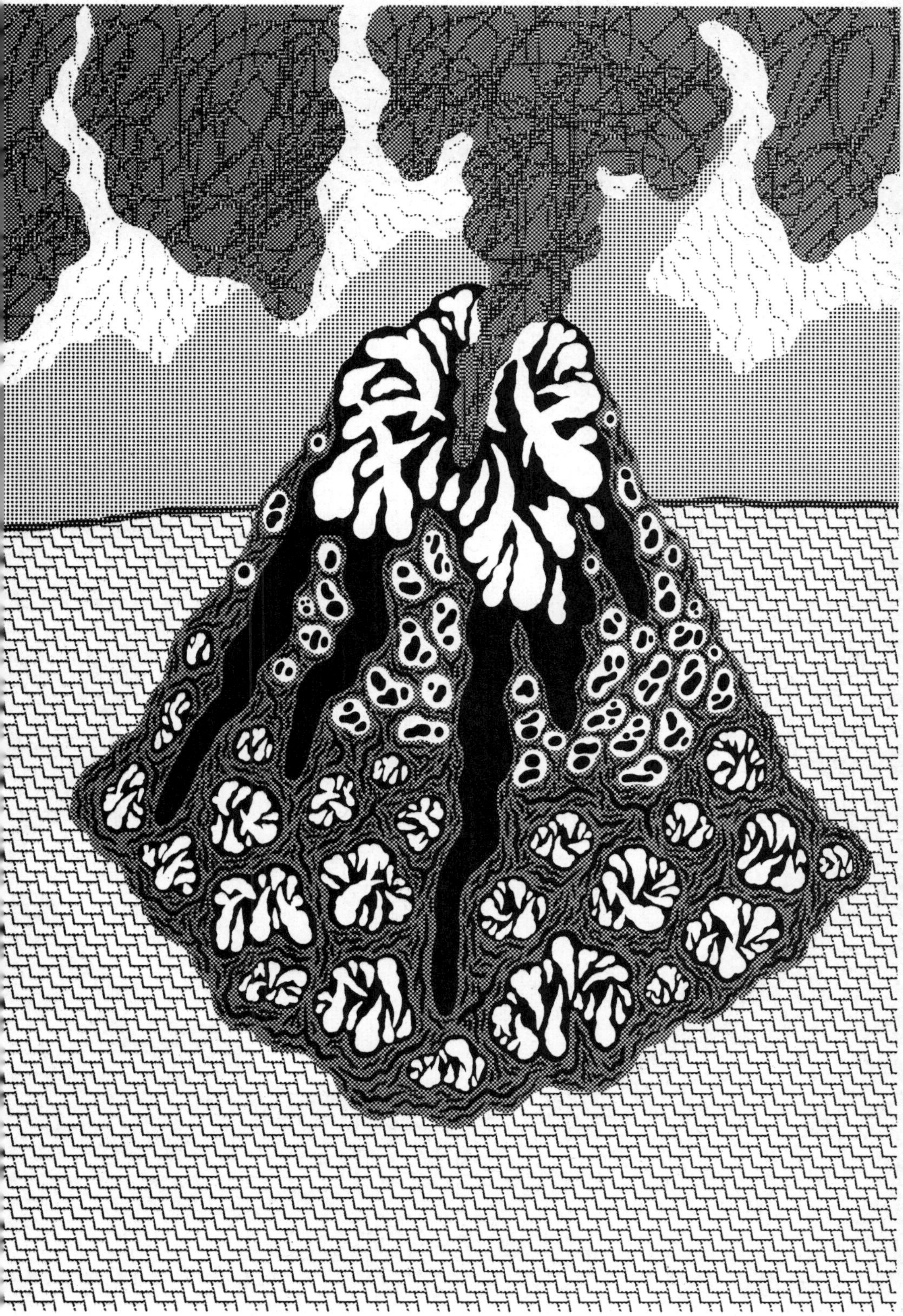

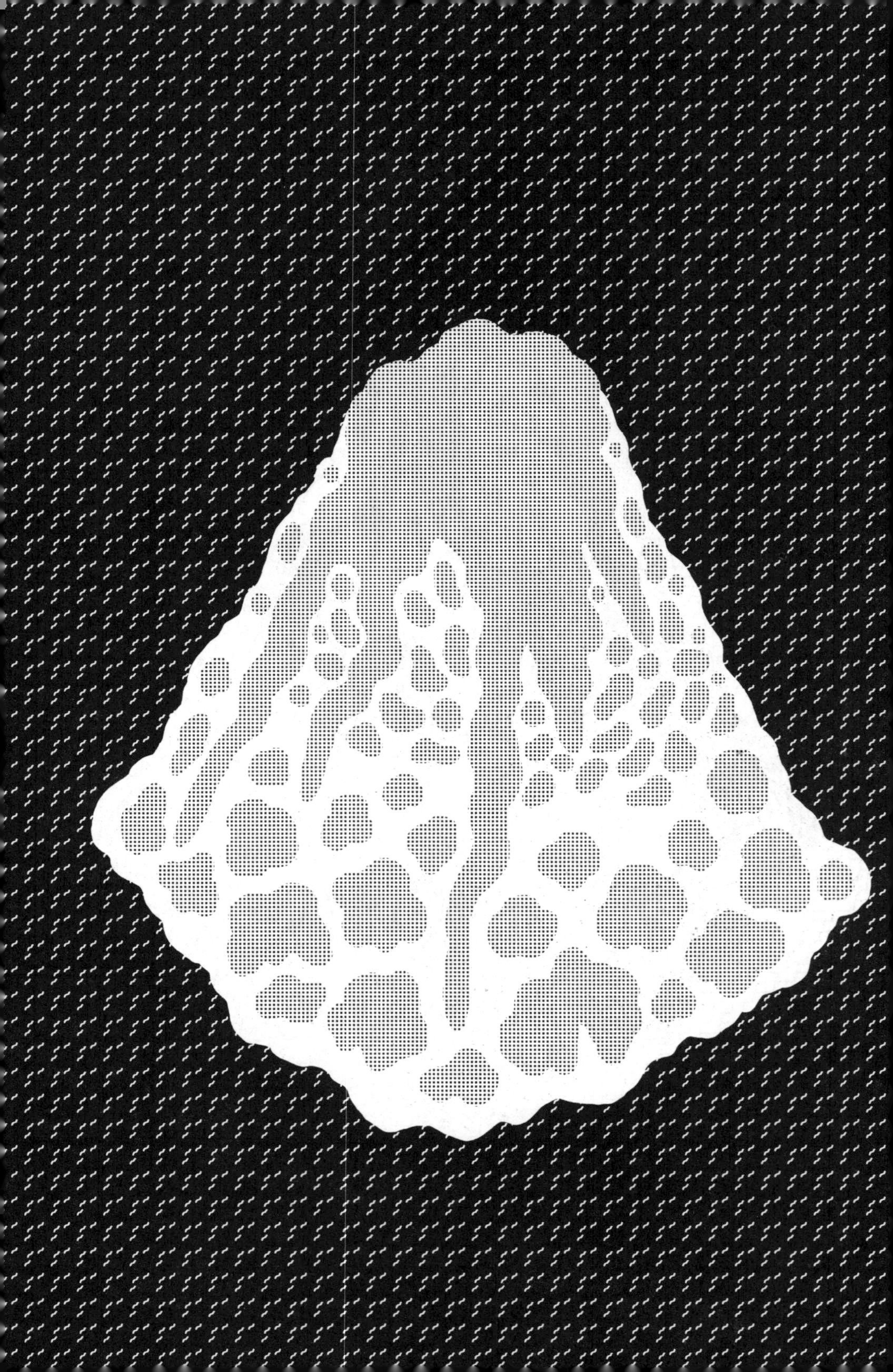

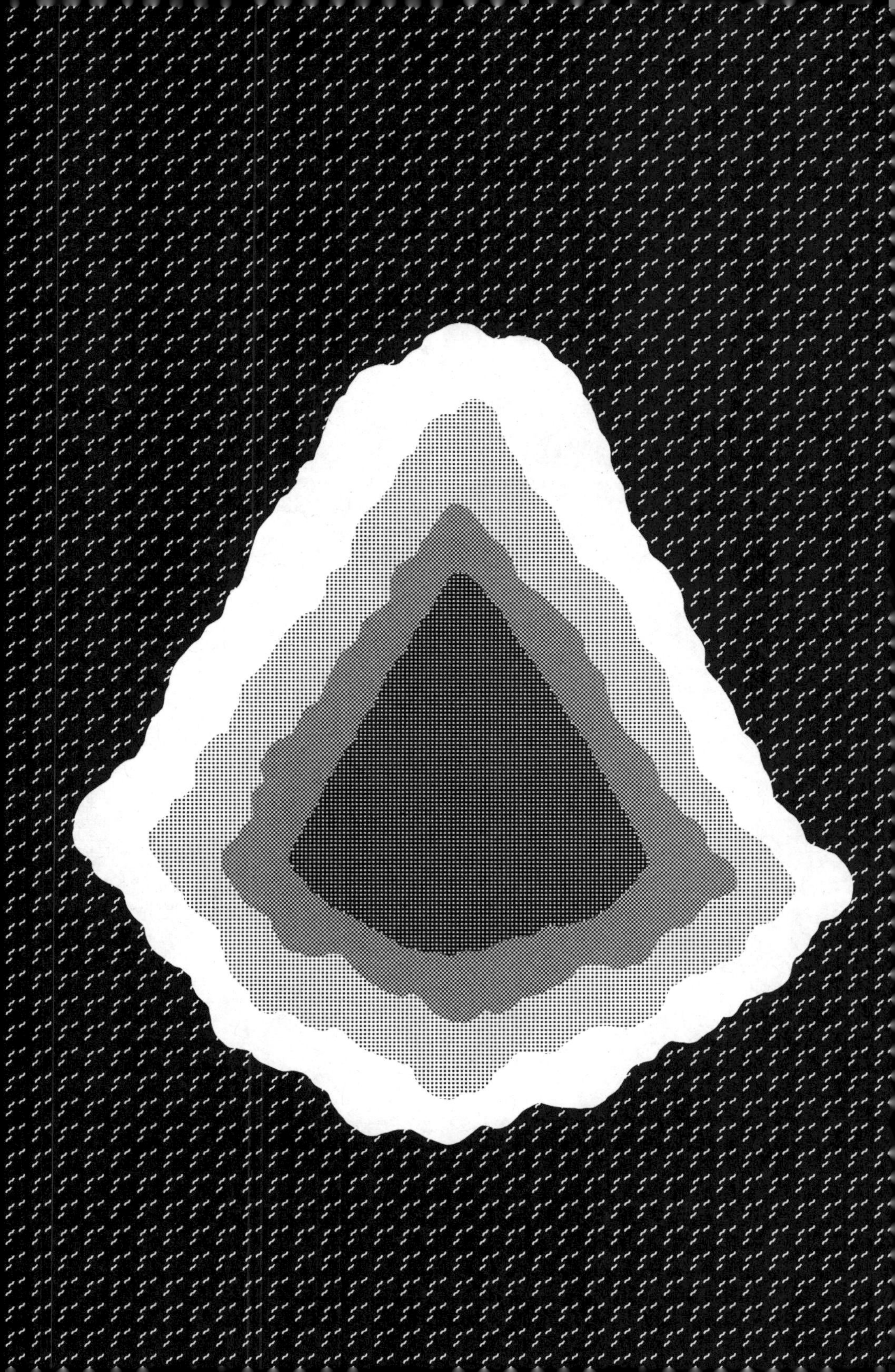

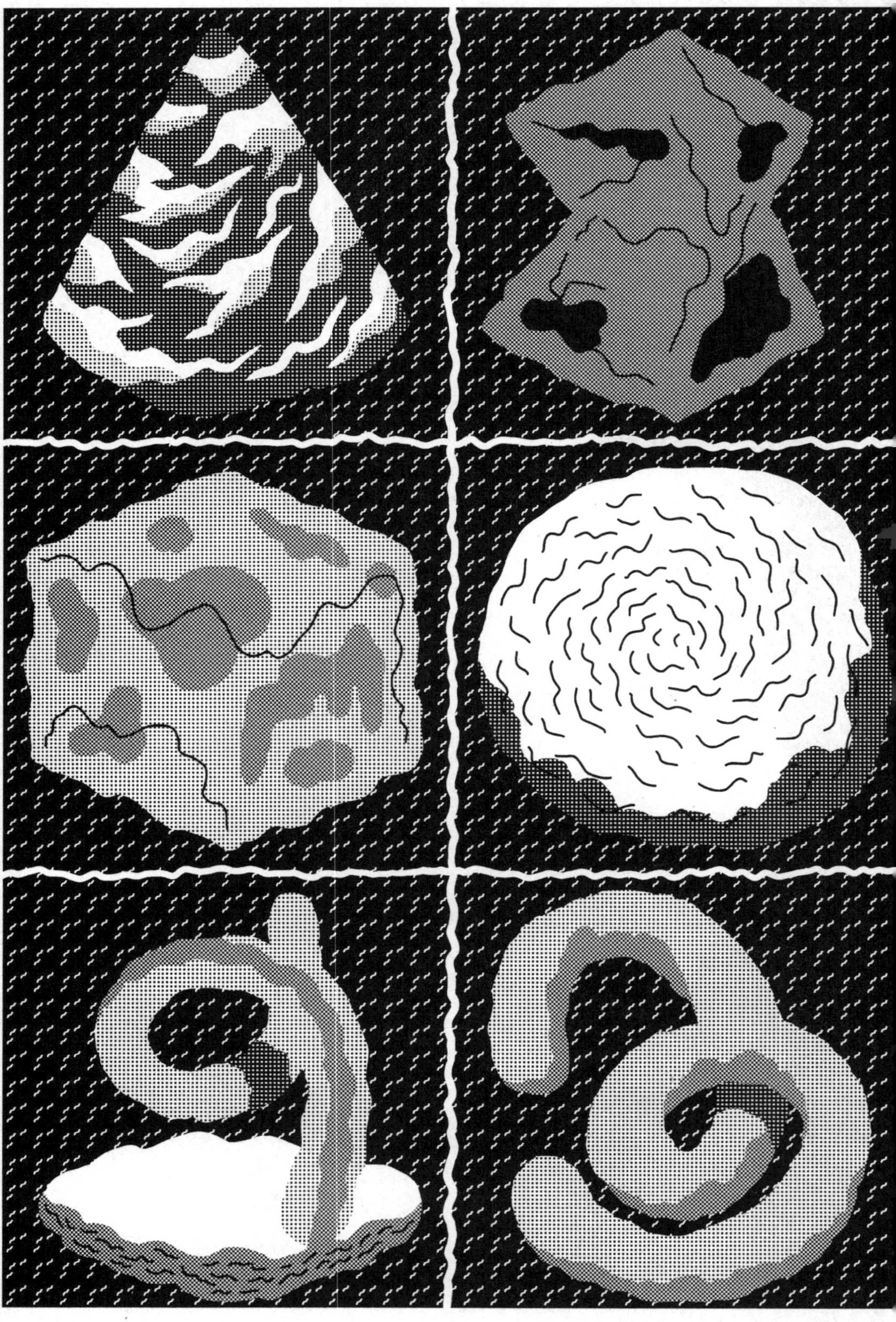

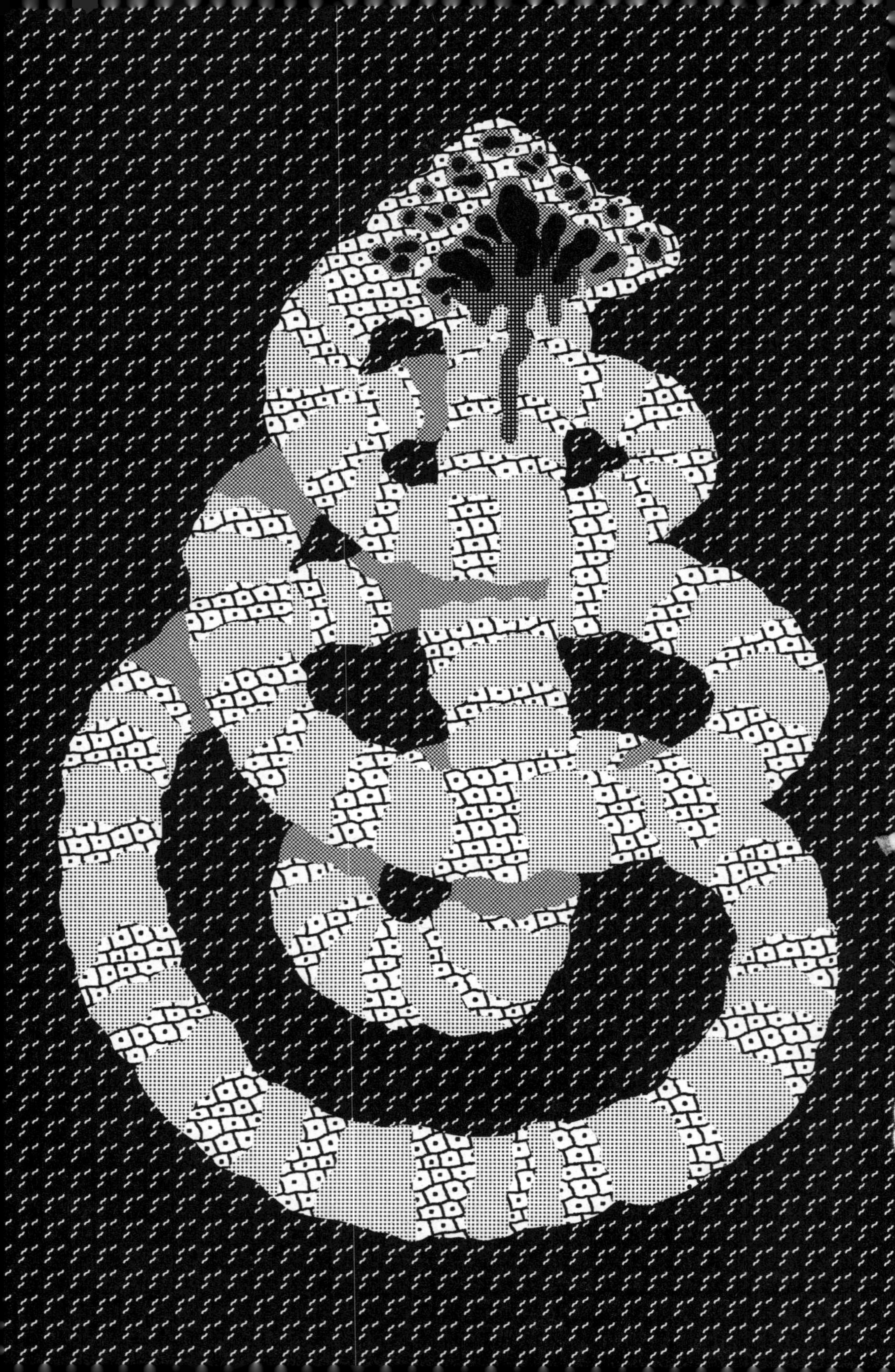

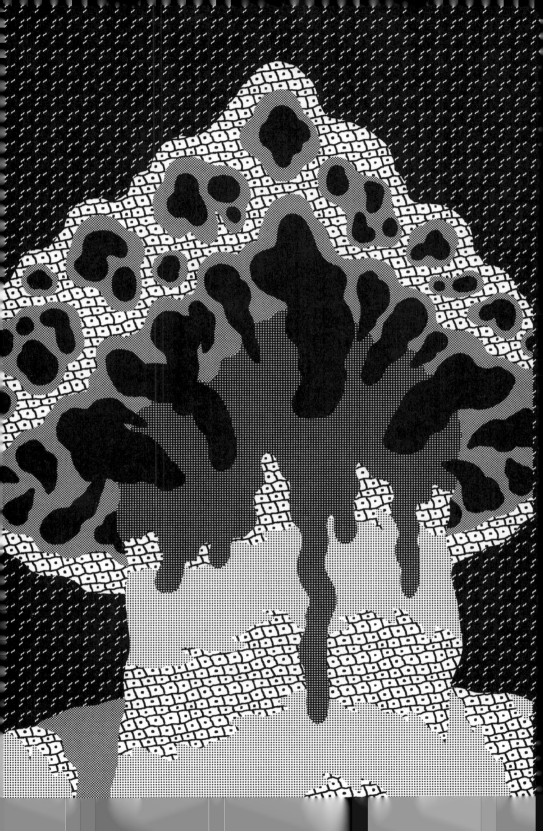

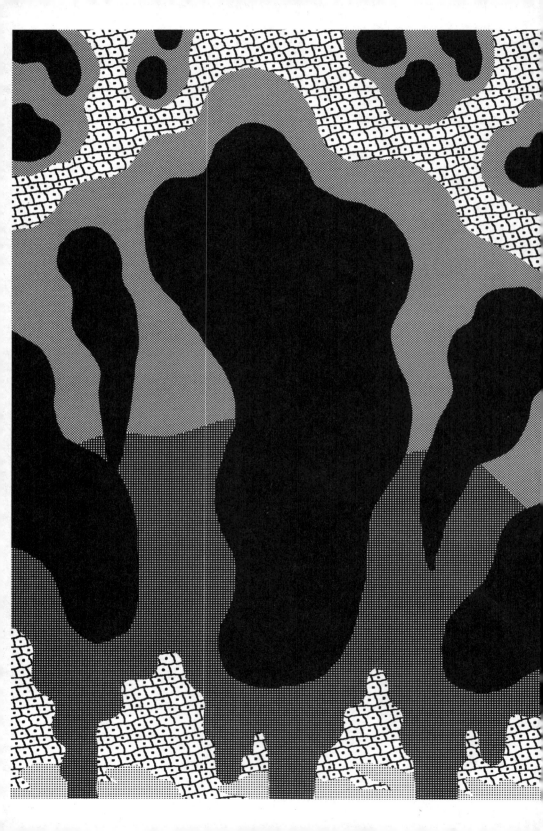

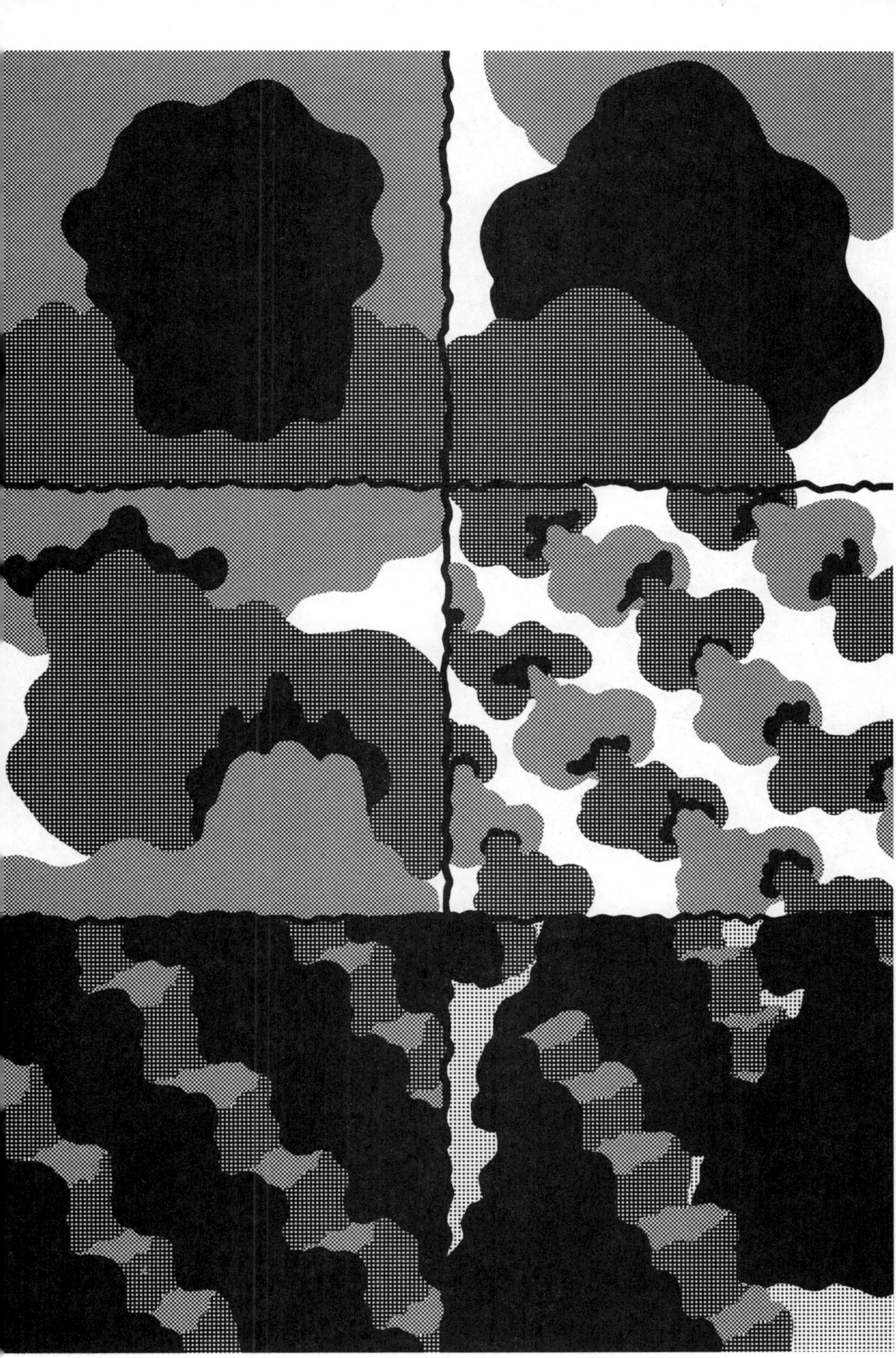

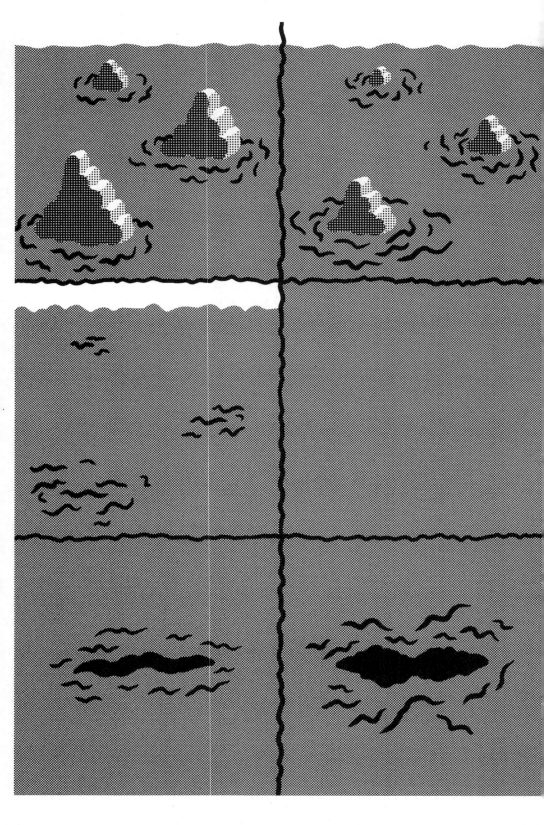

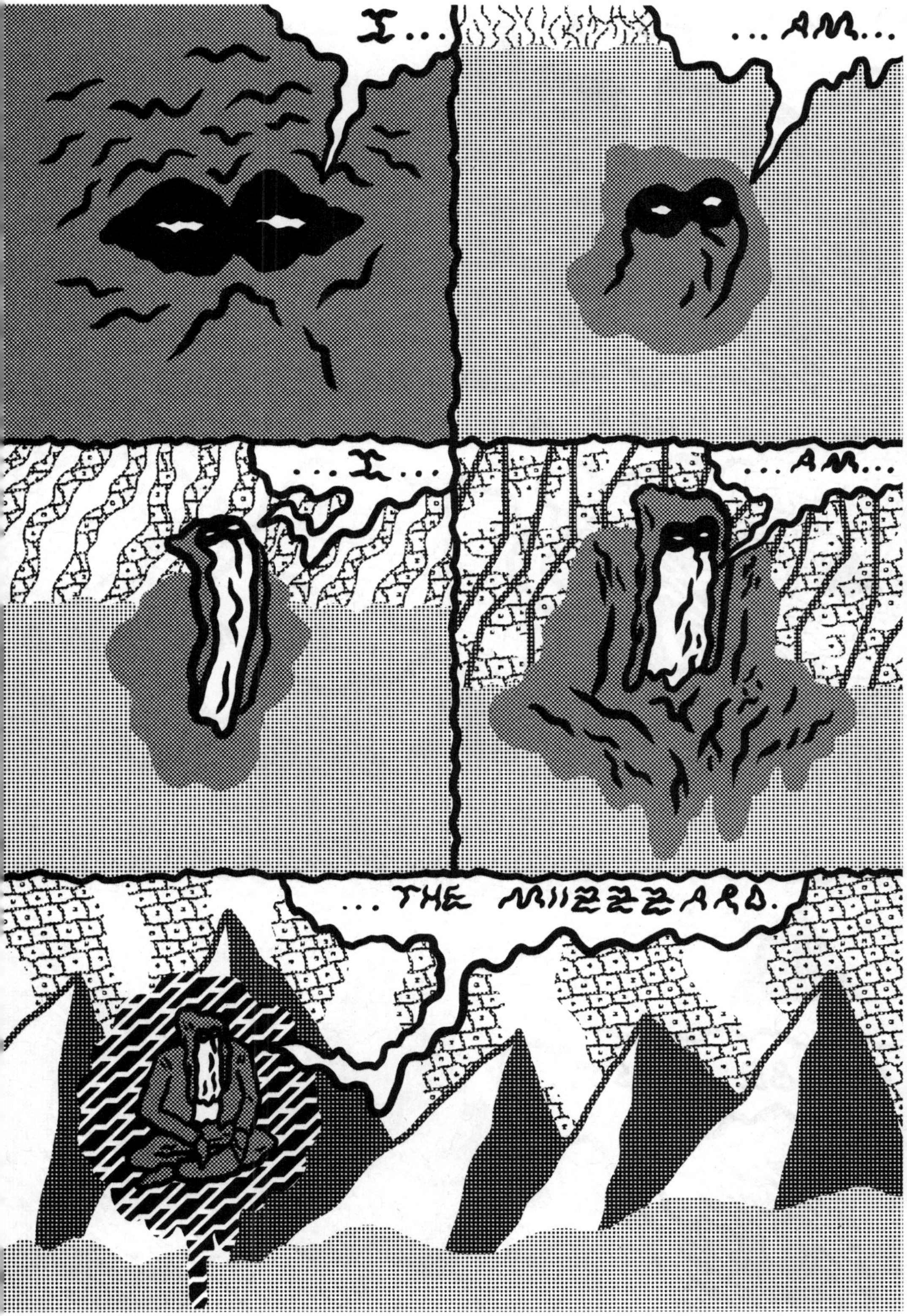
I...
...AM...
...I...
...AM...
...THE MIIZZZZARD.

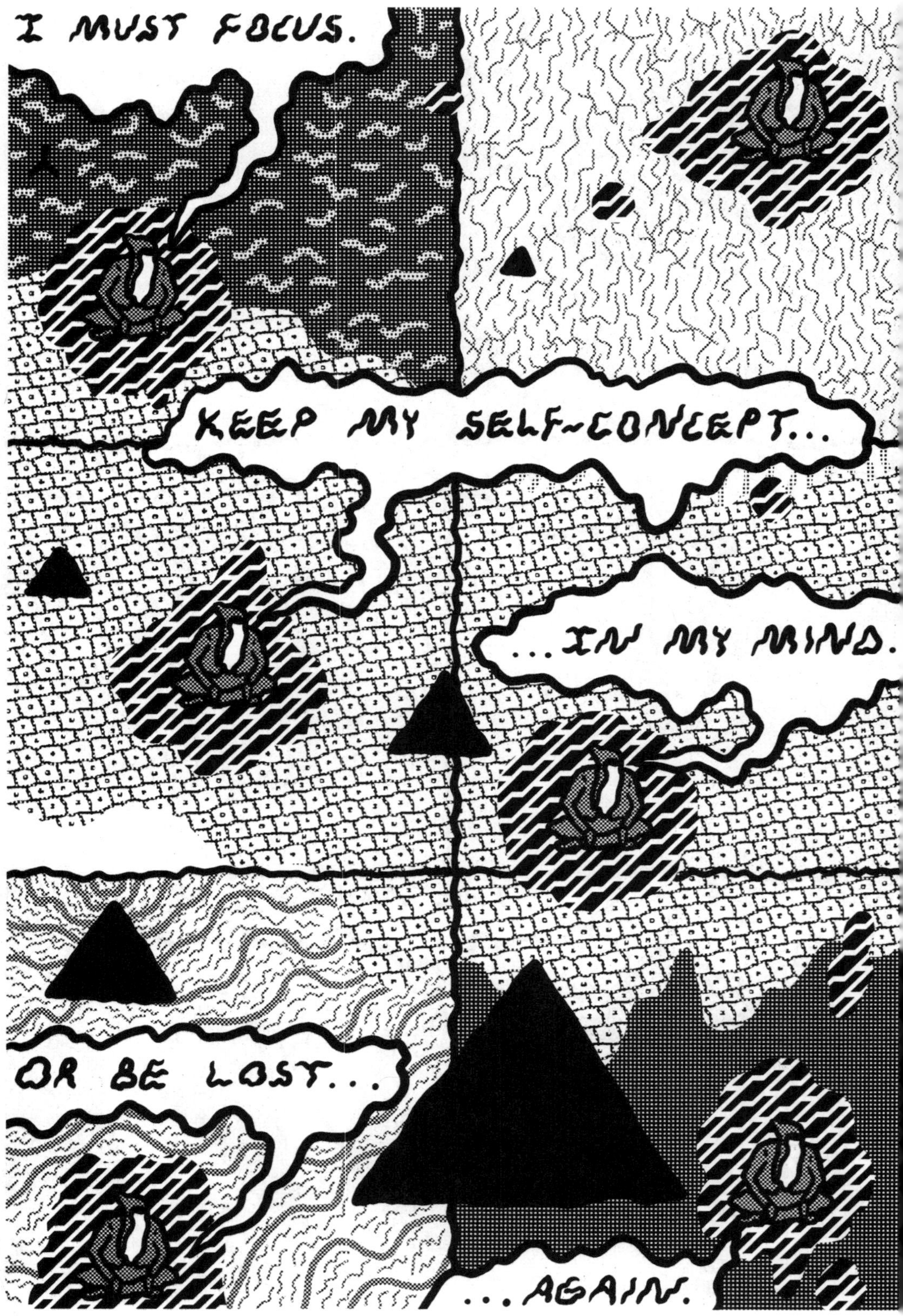
I MUST FOCUS.
KEEP MY SELF-CONCEPT...
...IN MY MIND.
OR BE LOST...
...AGAIN.

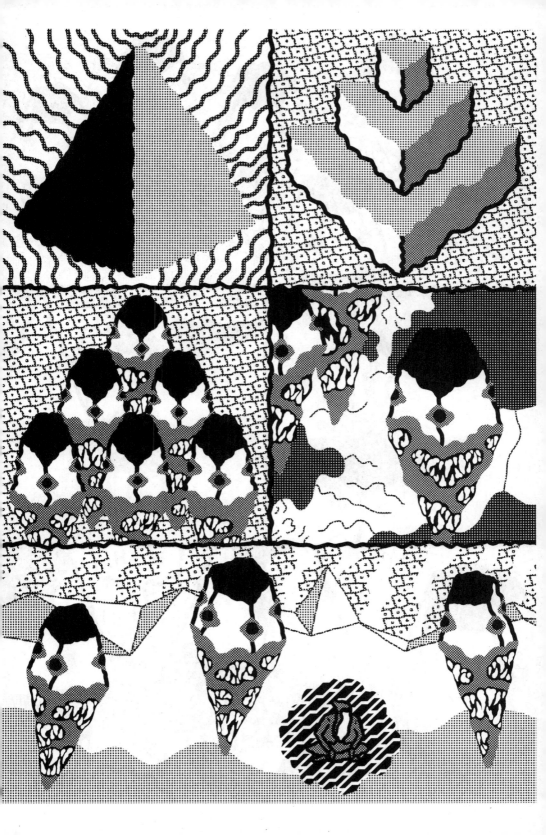

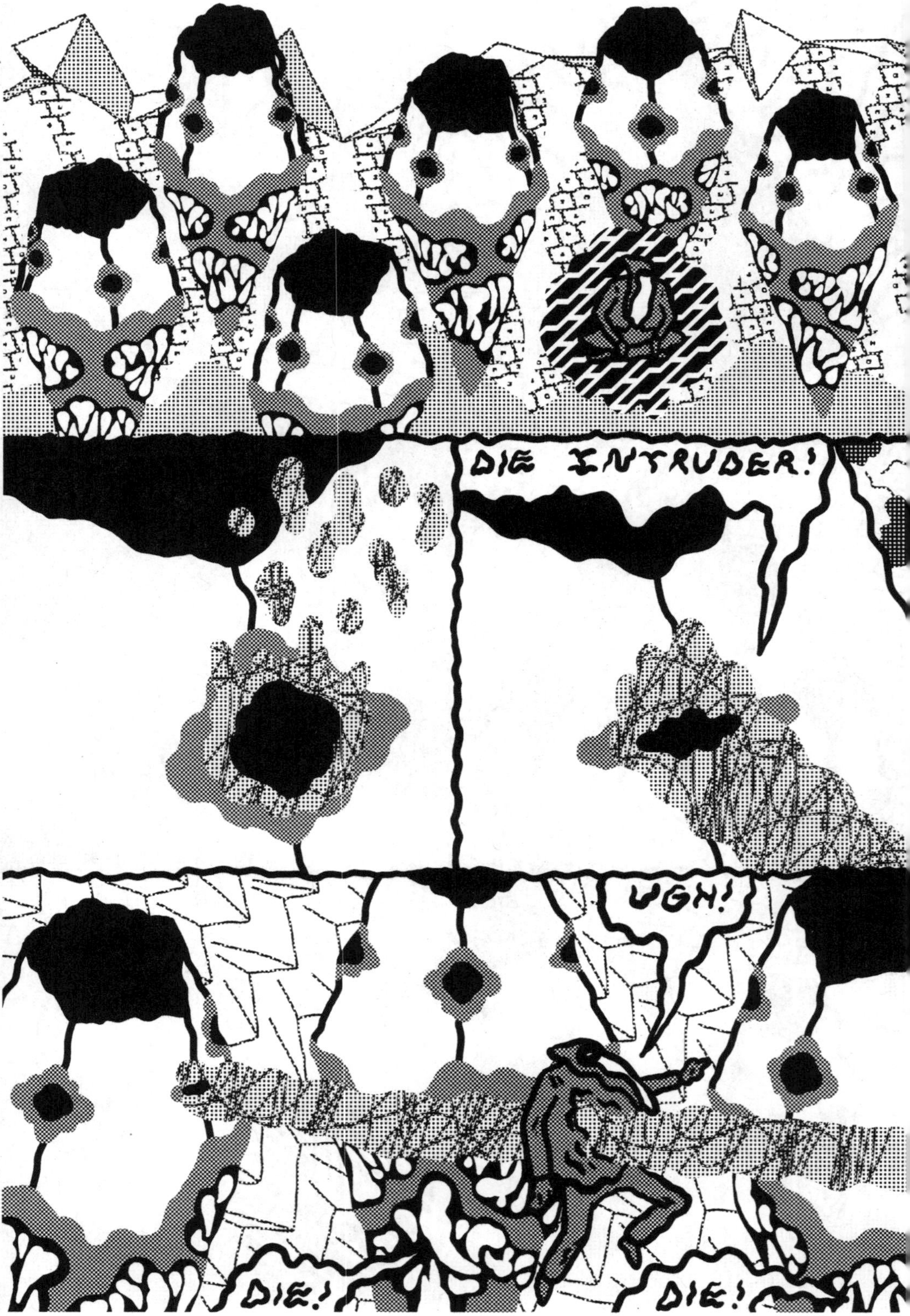
DIE INTRUDER!
UGH!
DIE!
DIE!

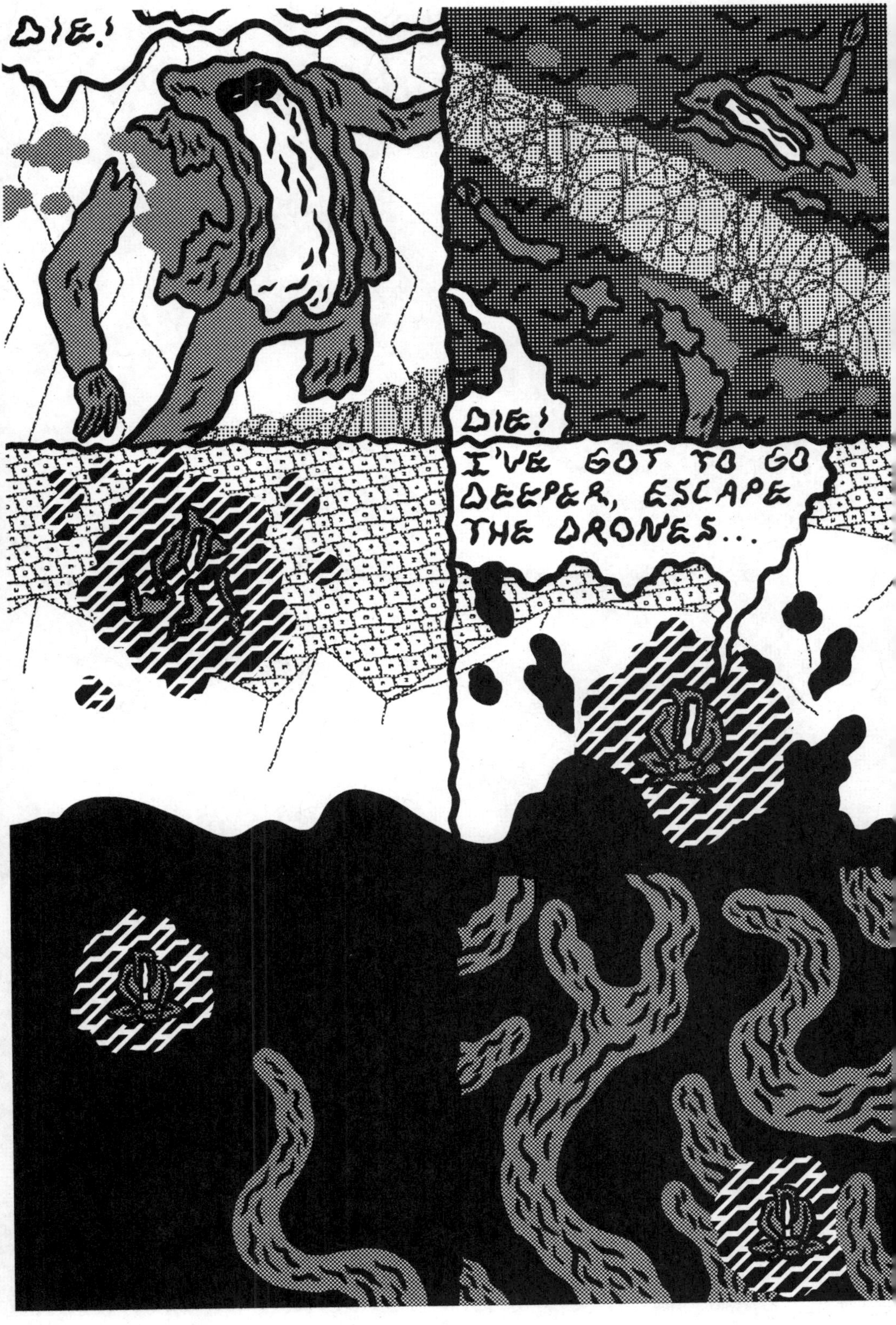
DIE!
DIE!
I'VE GOT TO GO DEEPER, ESCAPE THE DRONES...

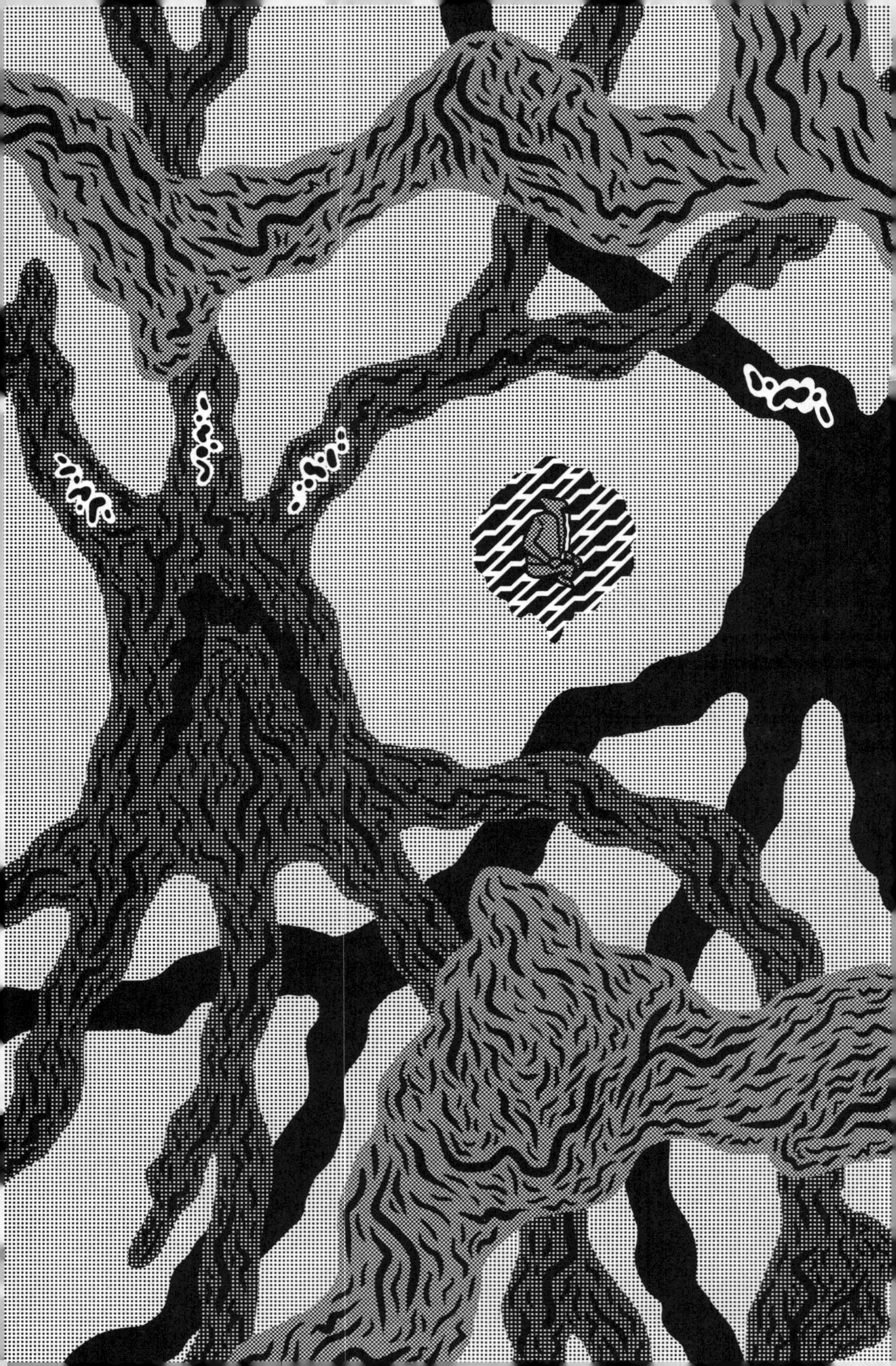

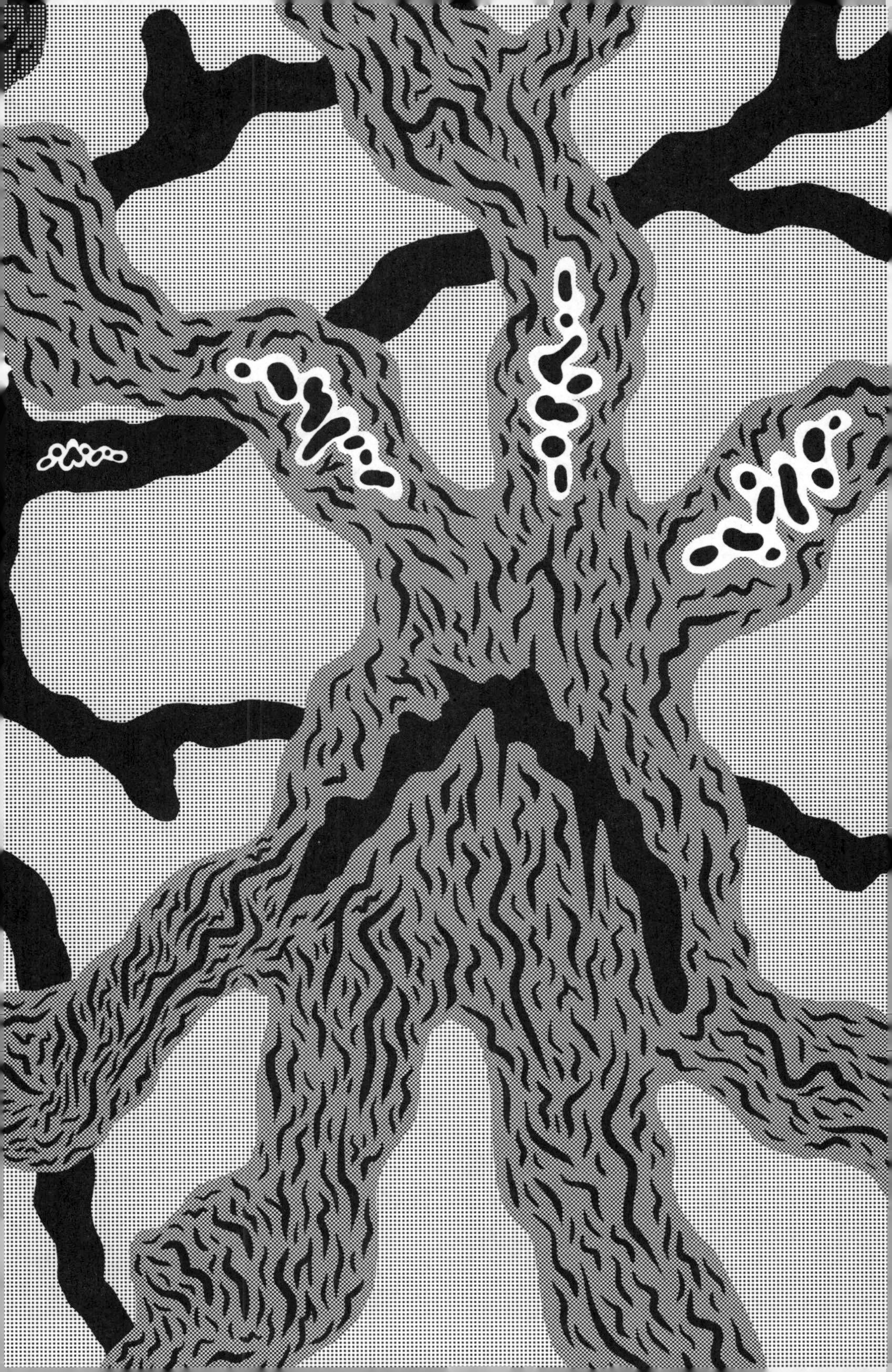

I CAN PROBABLY FIND A CONNECTION TO THE CONTROL DEVICE WITHIN THIS ANCIENT VORTEX.

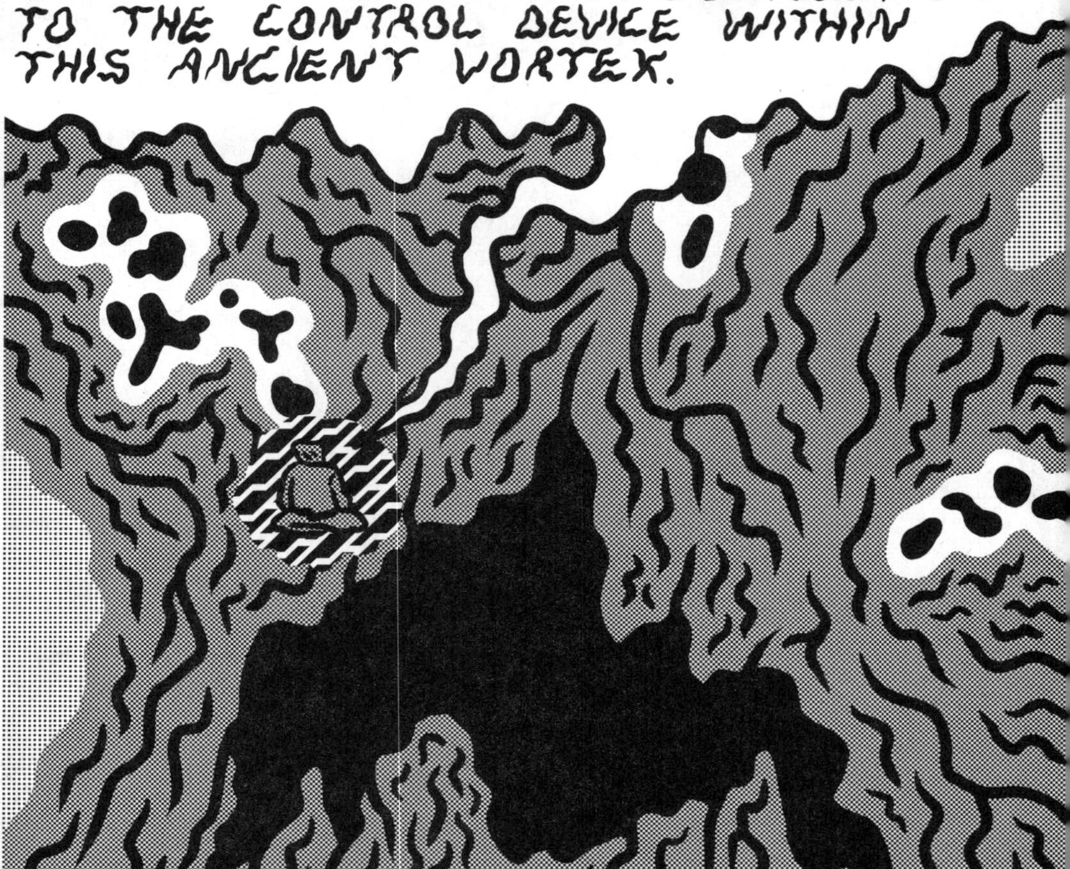

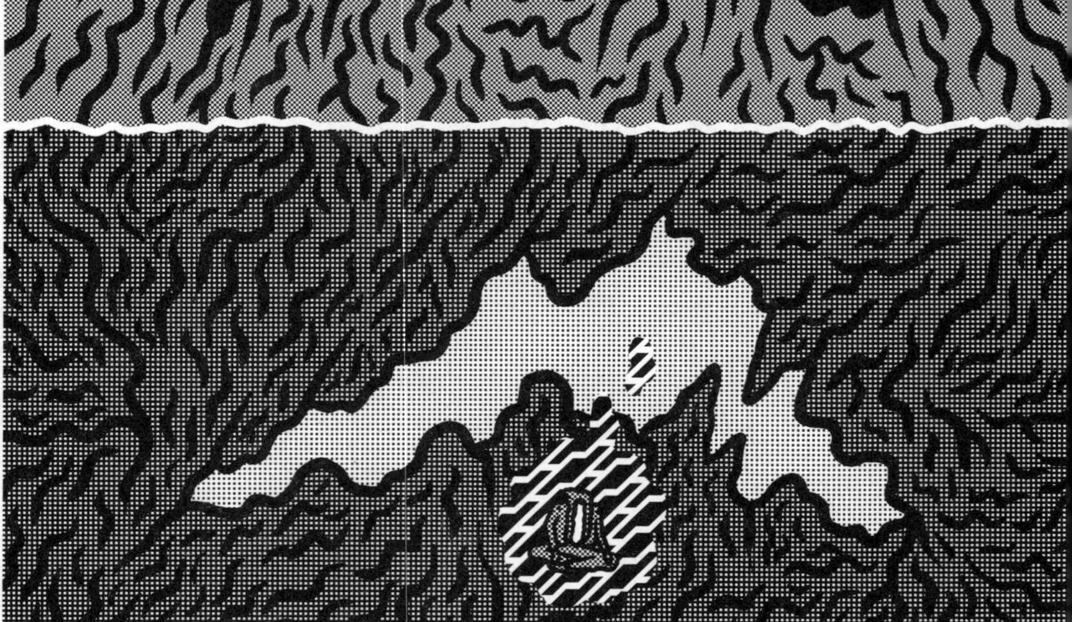

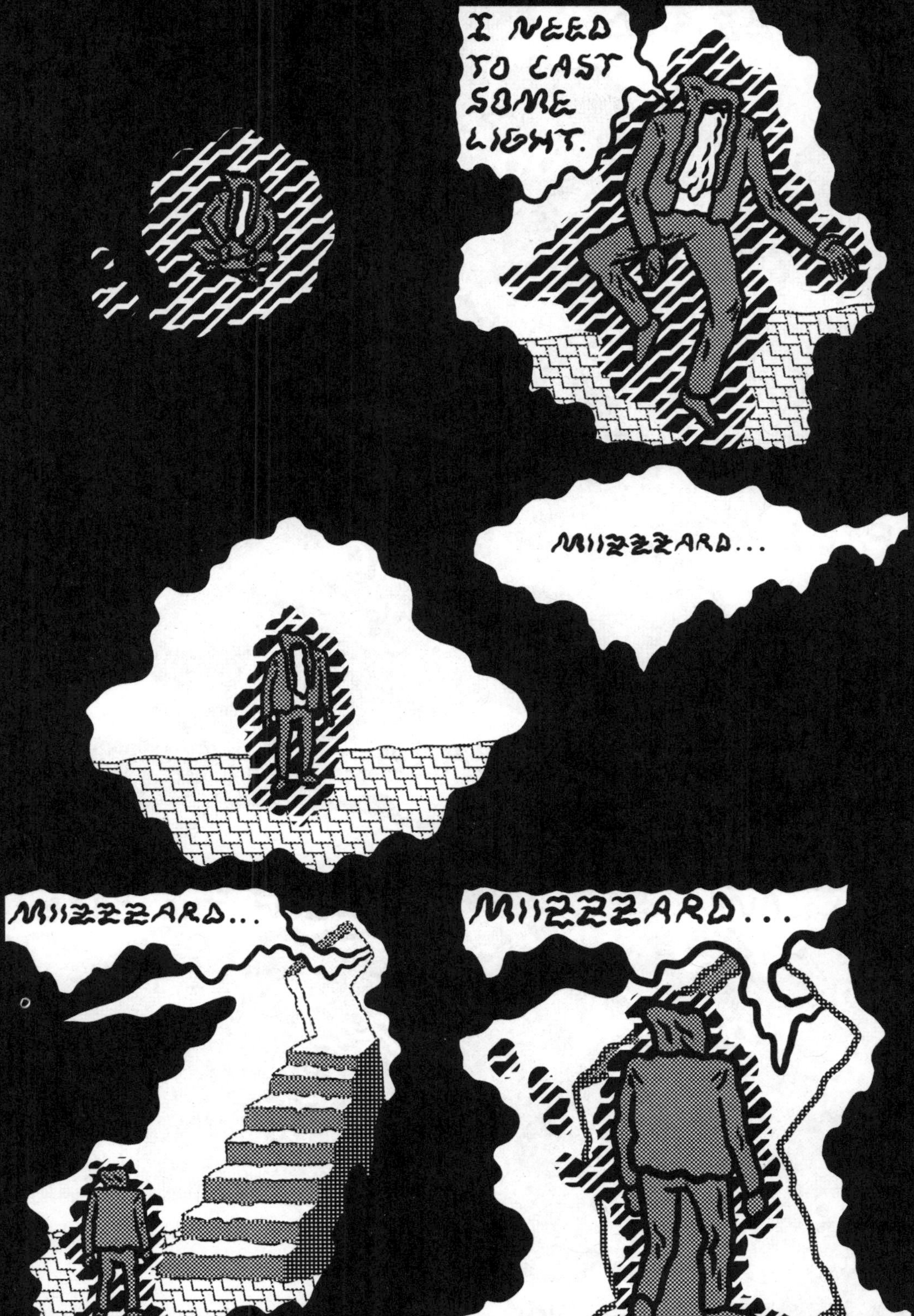
I NEED TO CAST SOME LIGHT.
MIIZZZARD...
MIIZZZARD...
MIIZZZARD...

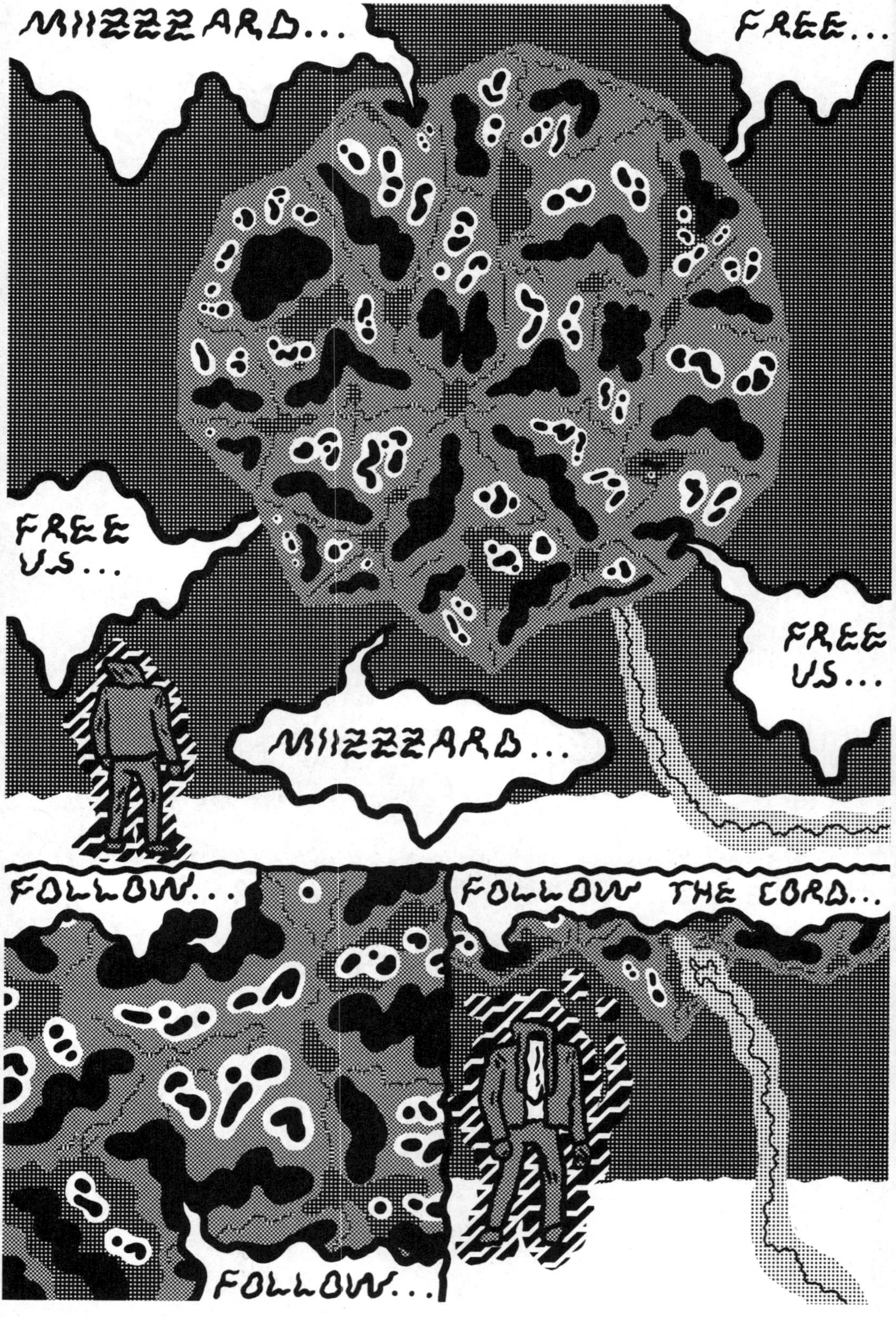
MIIZZZARD...
FREE...
FREE US...
FREE US...
MIIZZZARD...
FOLLOW...
FOLLOW THE CORD...
FOLLOW...

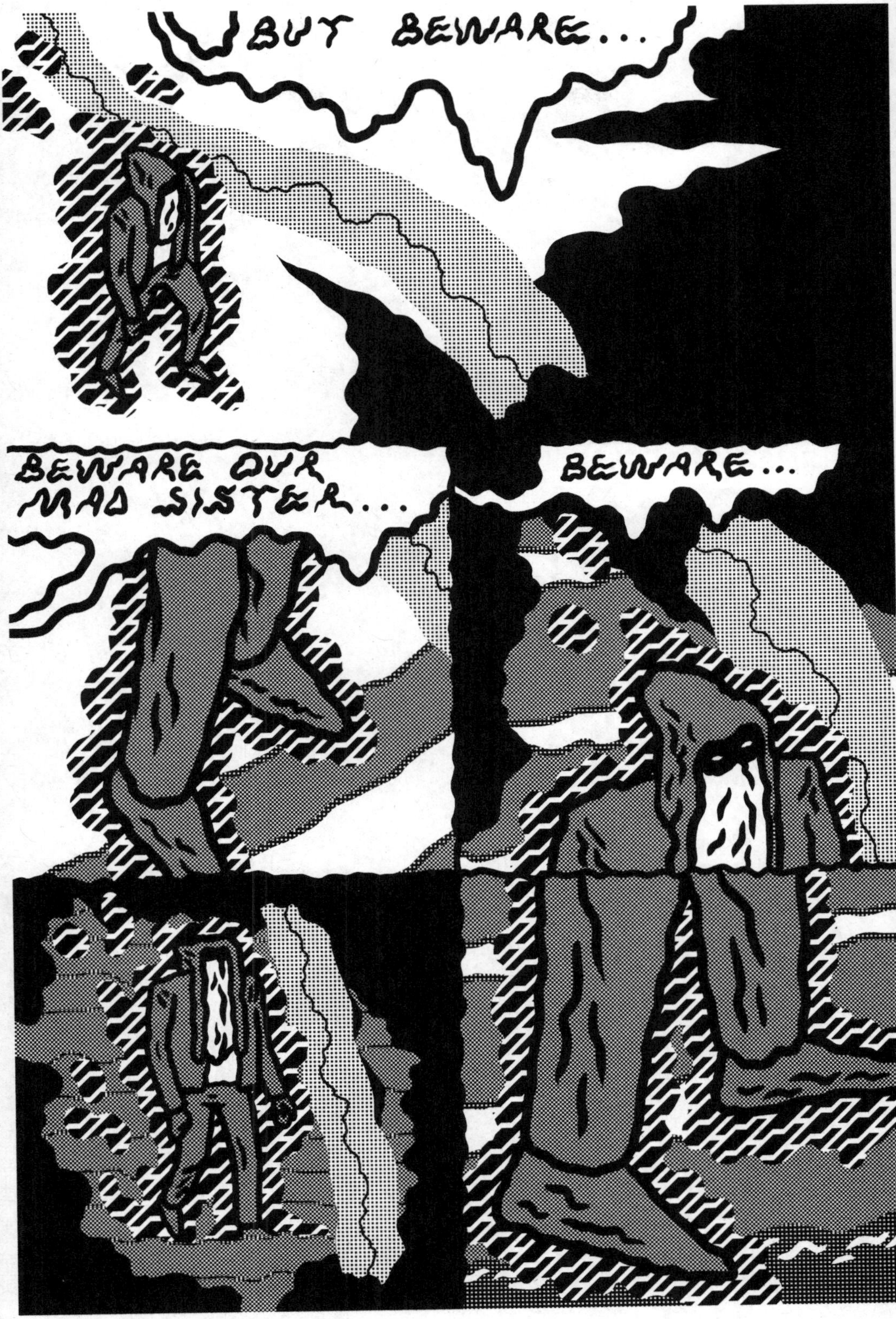
BUT BEWARE...
BEWARE OUR MAD SISTER...
BEWARE...

THIS PART OF THE DREAMSCAPE FEELS MORE...

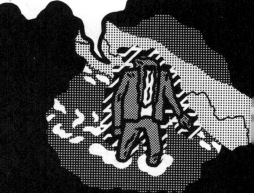

...SUBSTANTIAL.

BLOOD

I DON'T SEE ANYTHING...

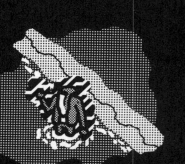

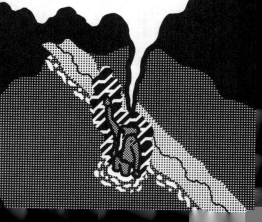

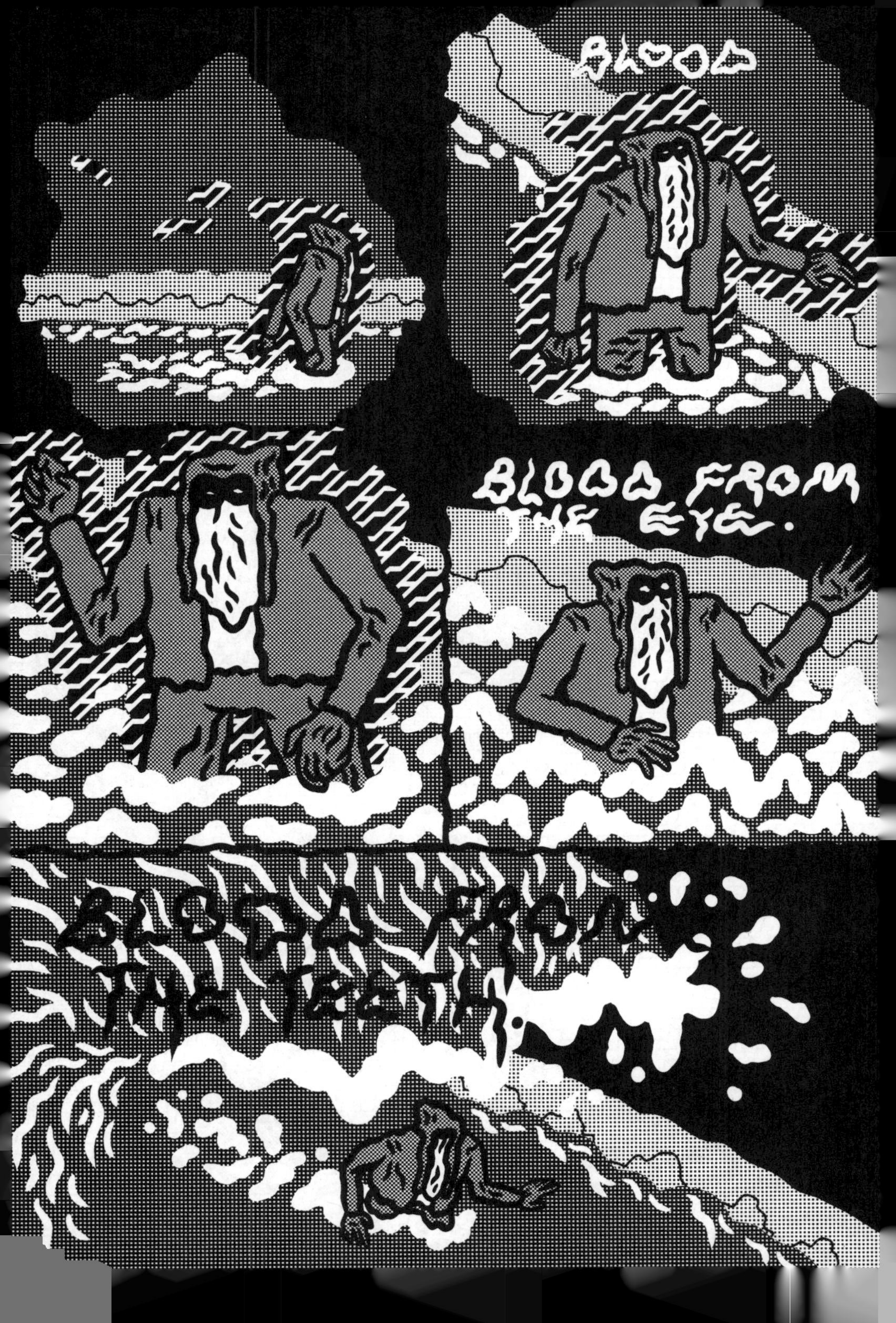
BLOOD
BLOOD FROM THE EYE.
BLOOD FROM THE TEETH.

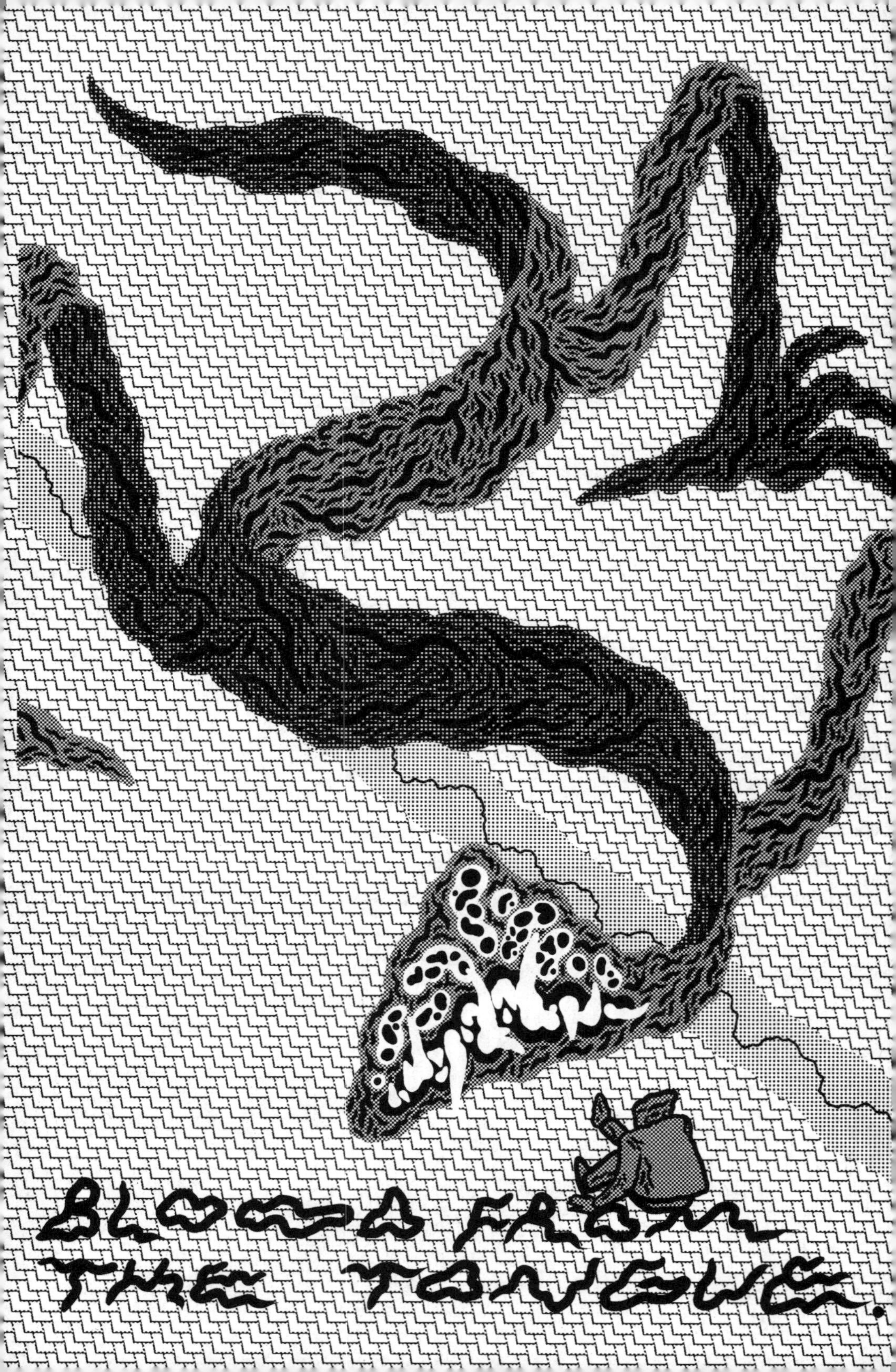
BLOOD FROM THE TONGUE.

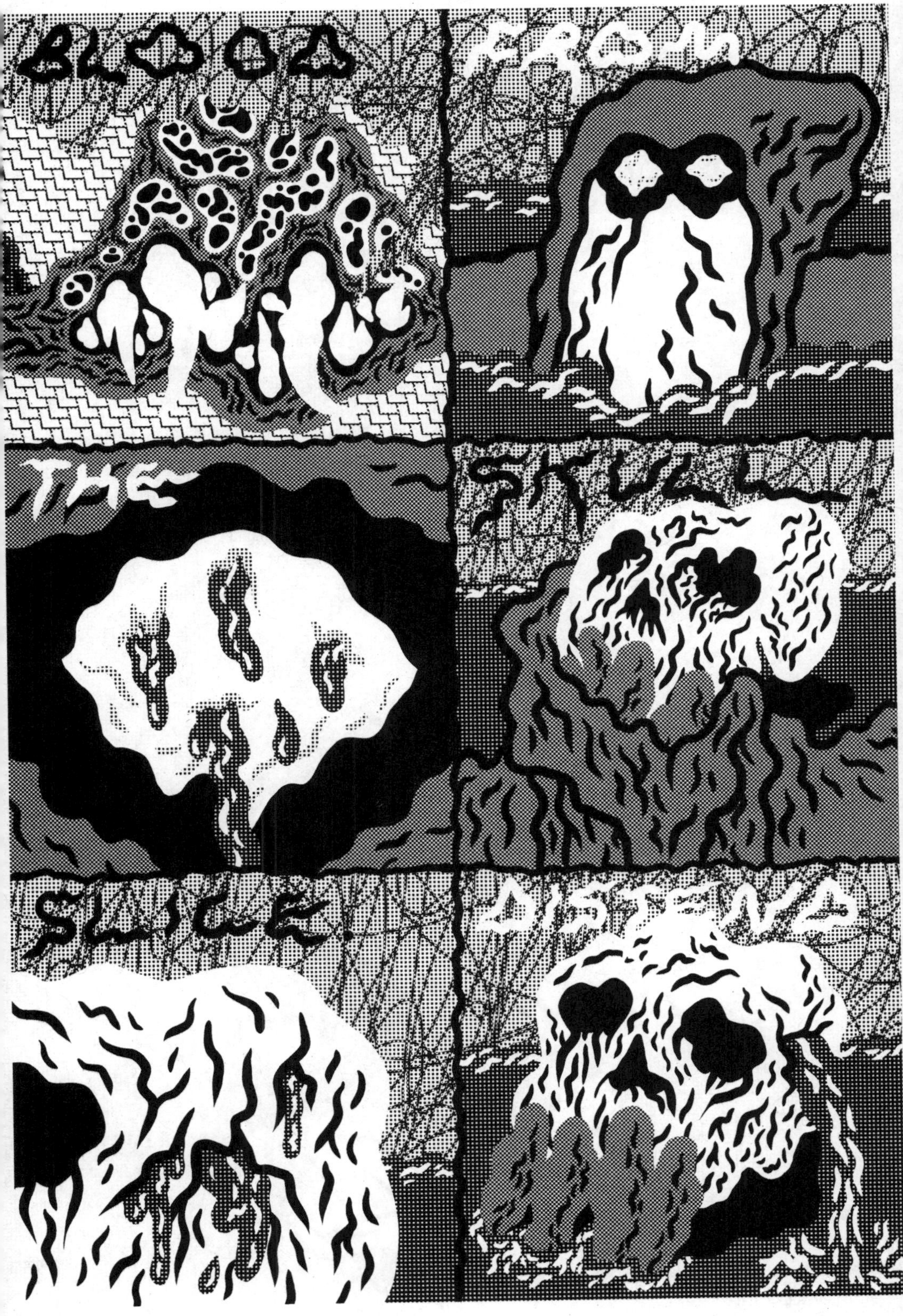
BLOOD
FROM
THE
SKULL
SLICE.
DISTEND

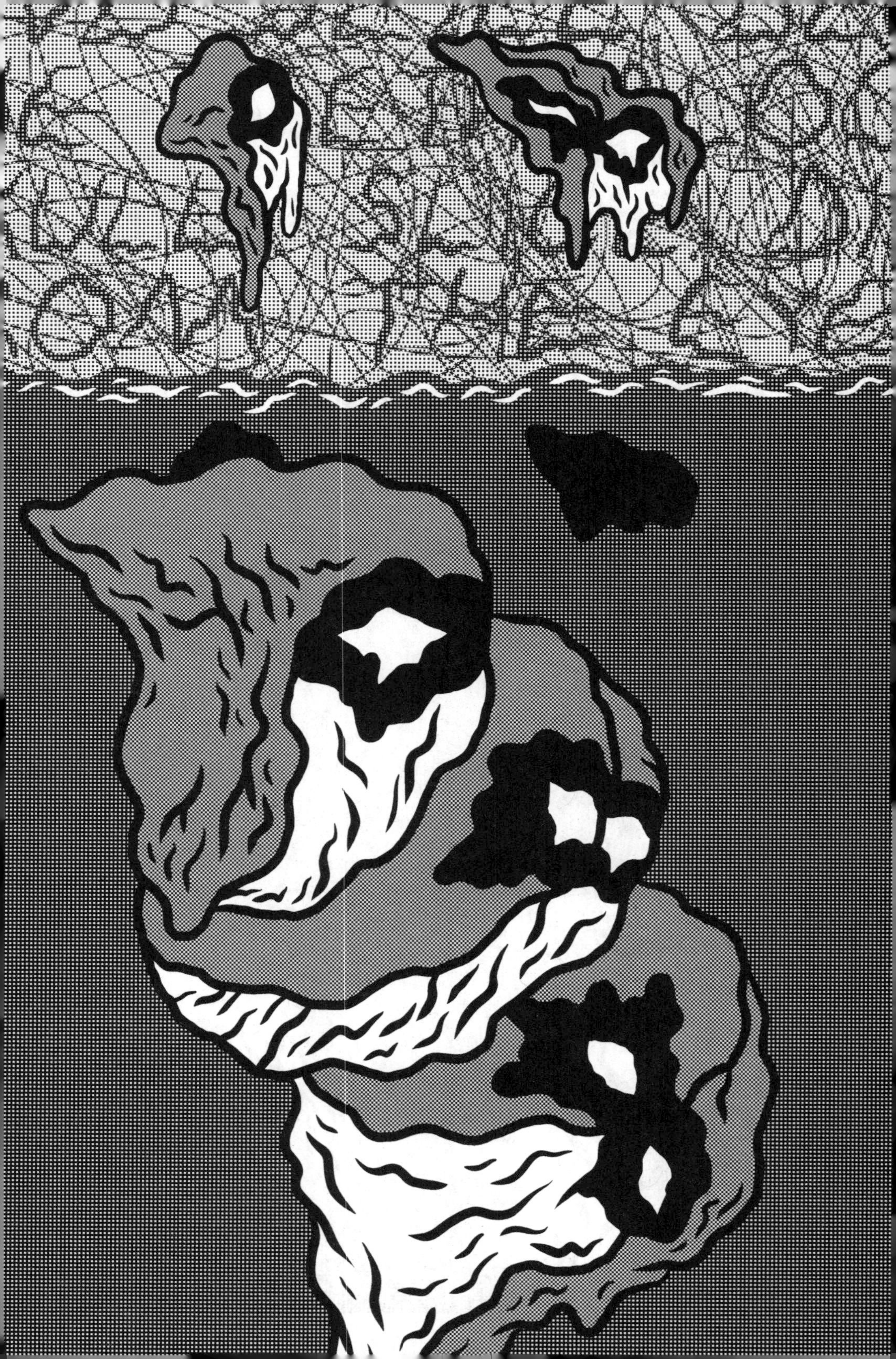

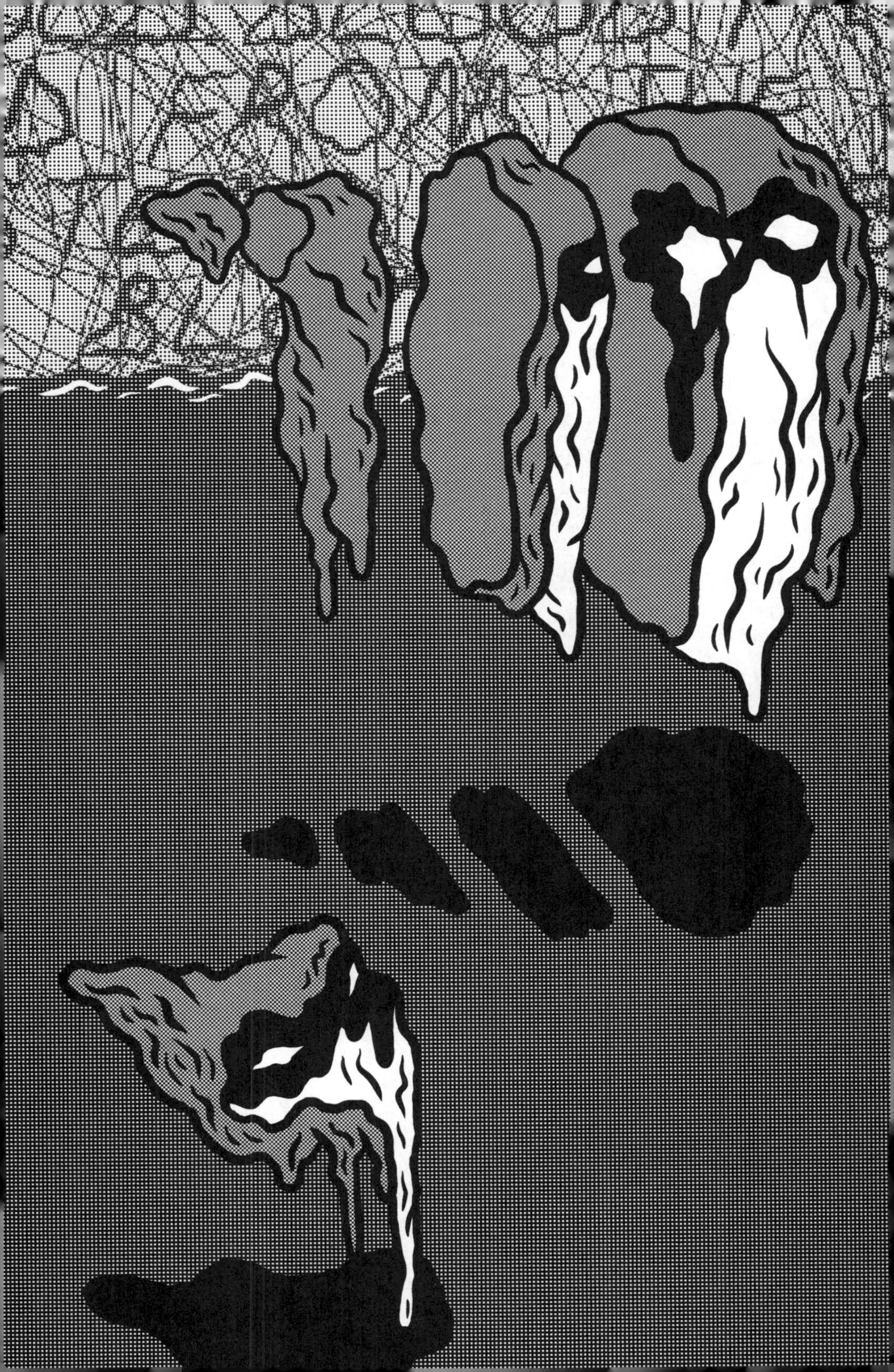

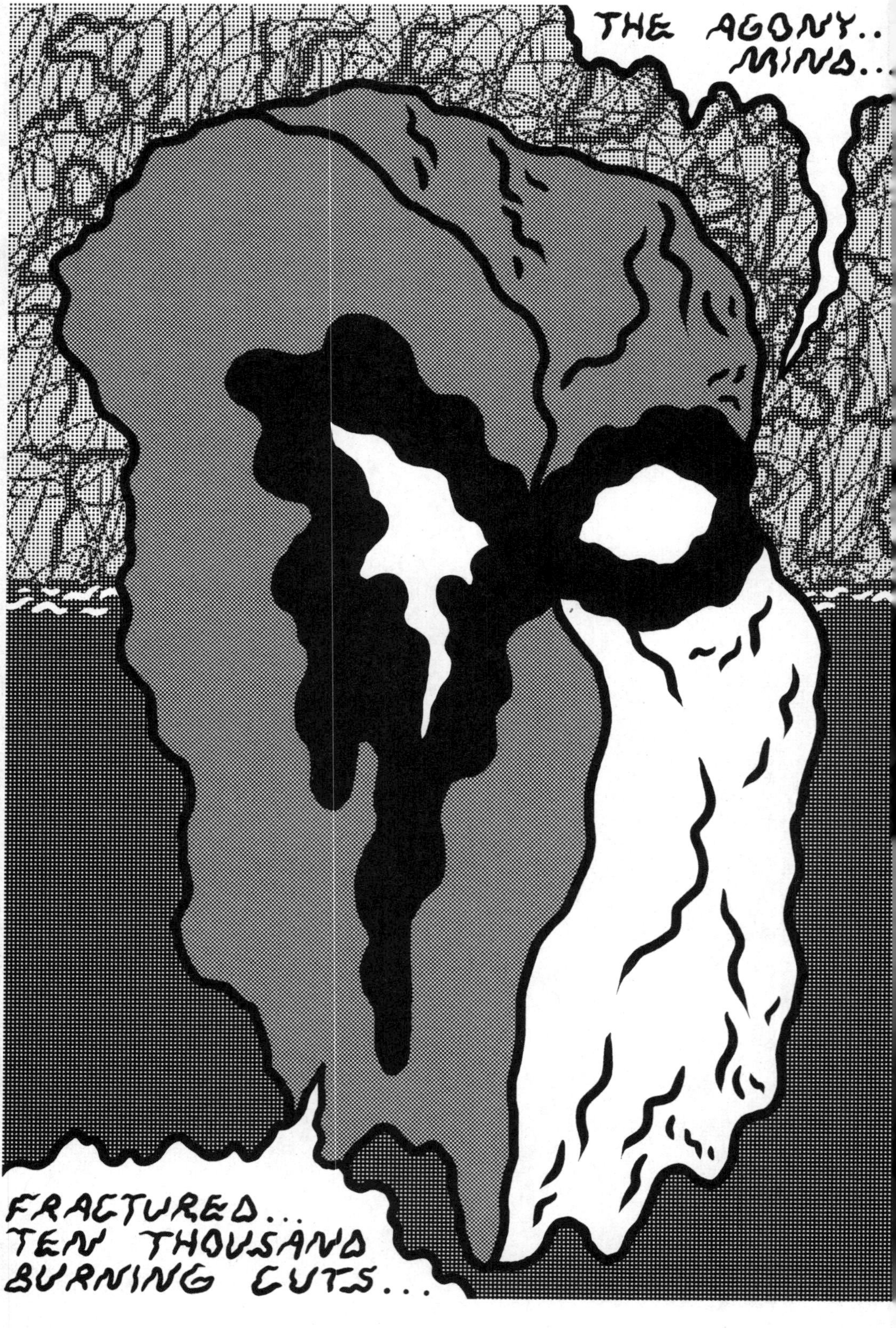
THE AGONY..
MIND...
FRACTURED...
TEN THOUSAND
BURNING CUTS...

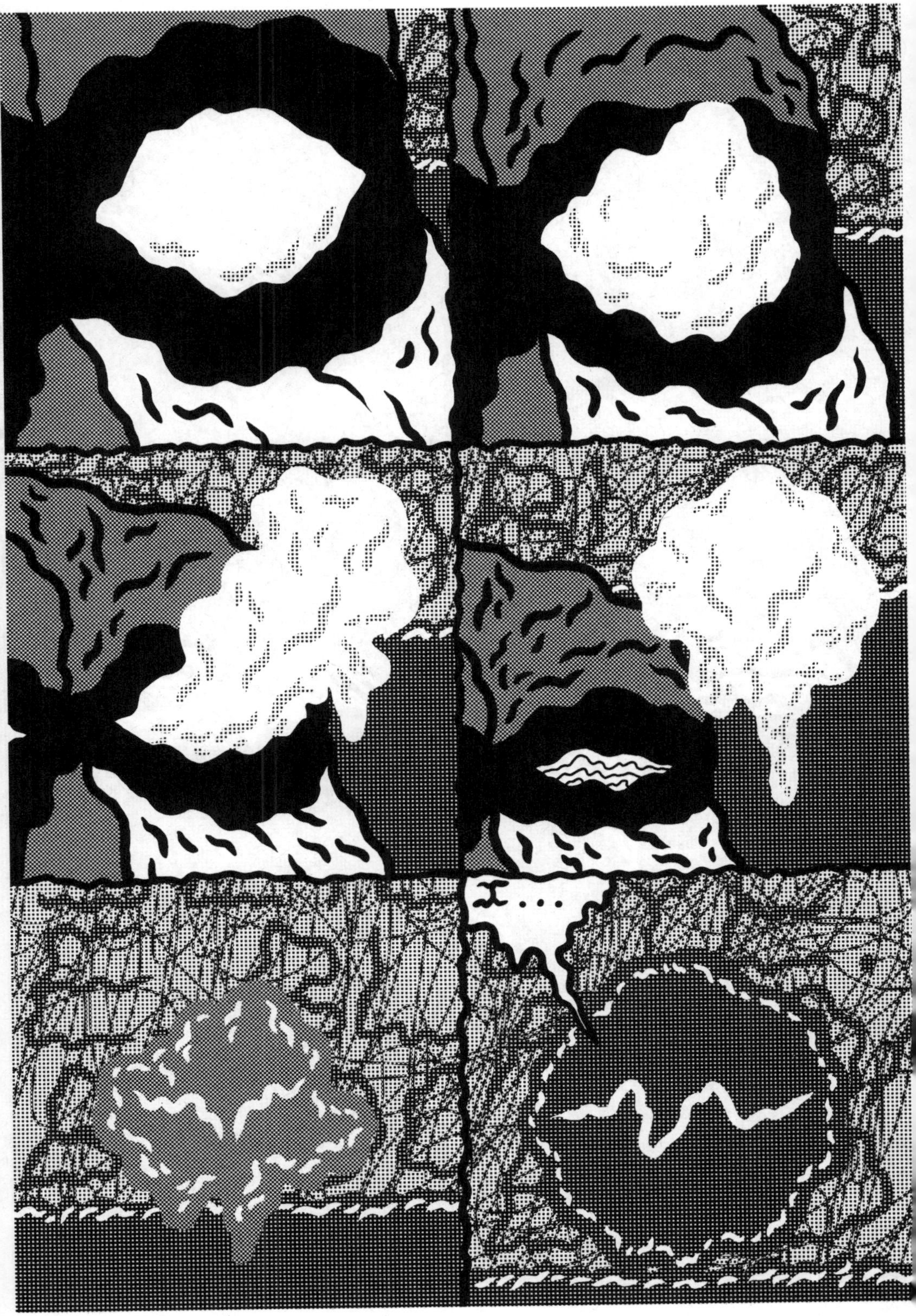
I...

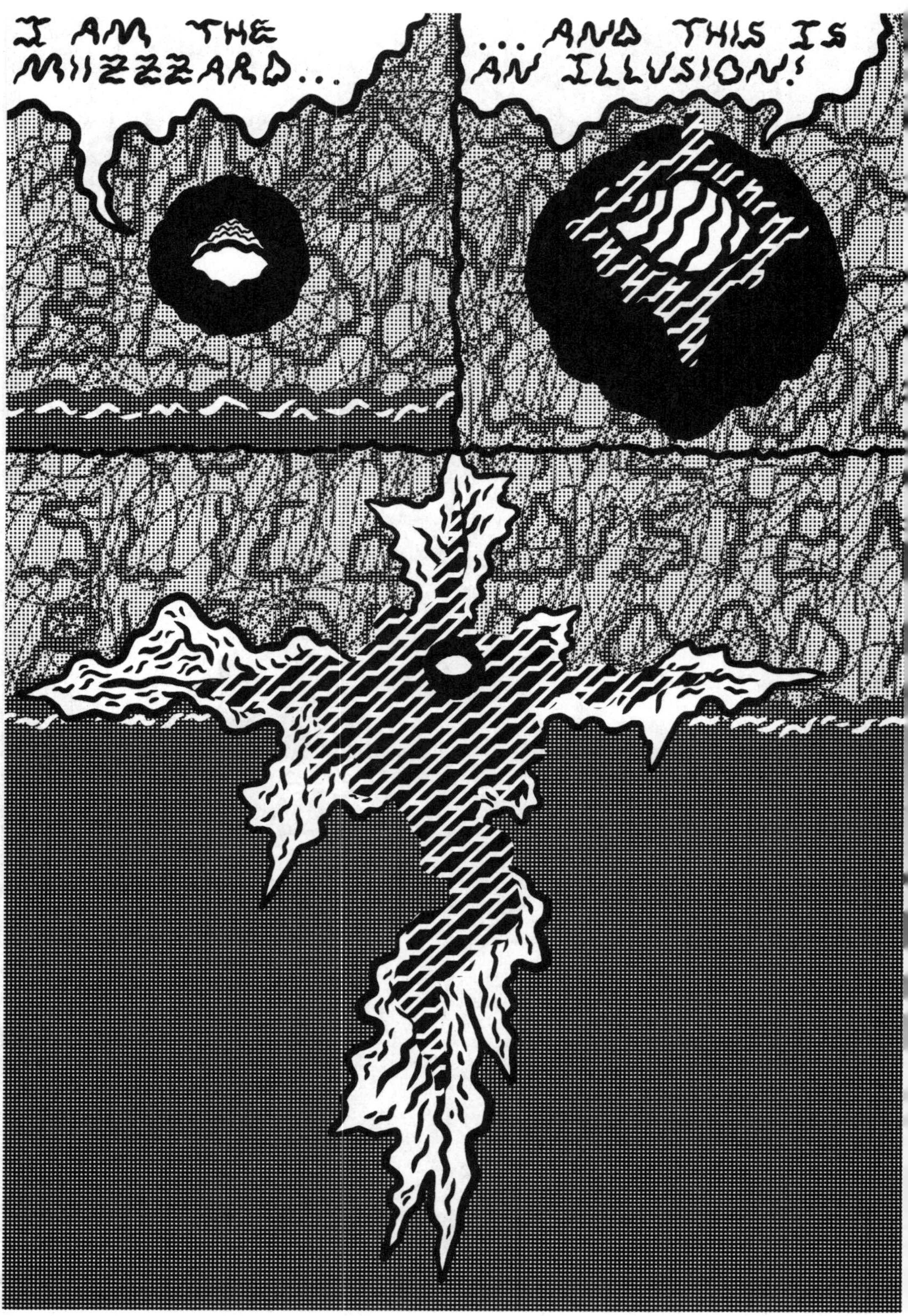
I AM THE MIIZZZARD...
...AND THIS IS AN ILLUSION!

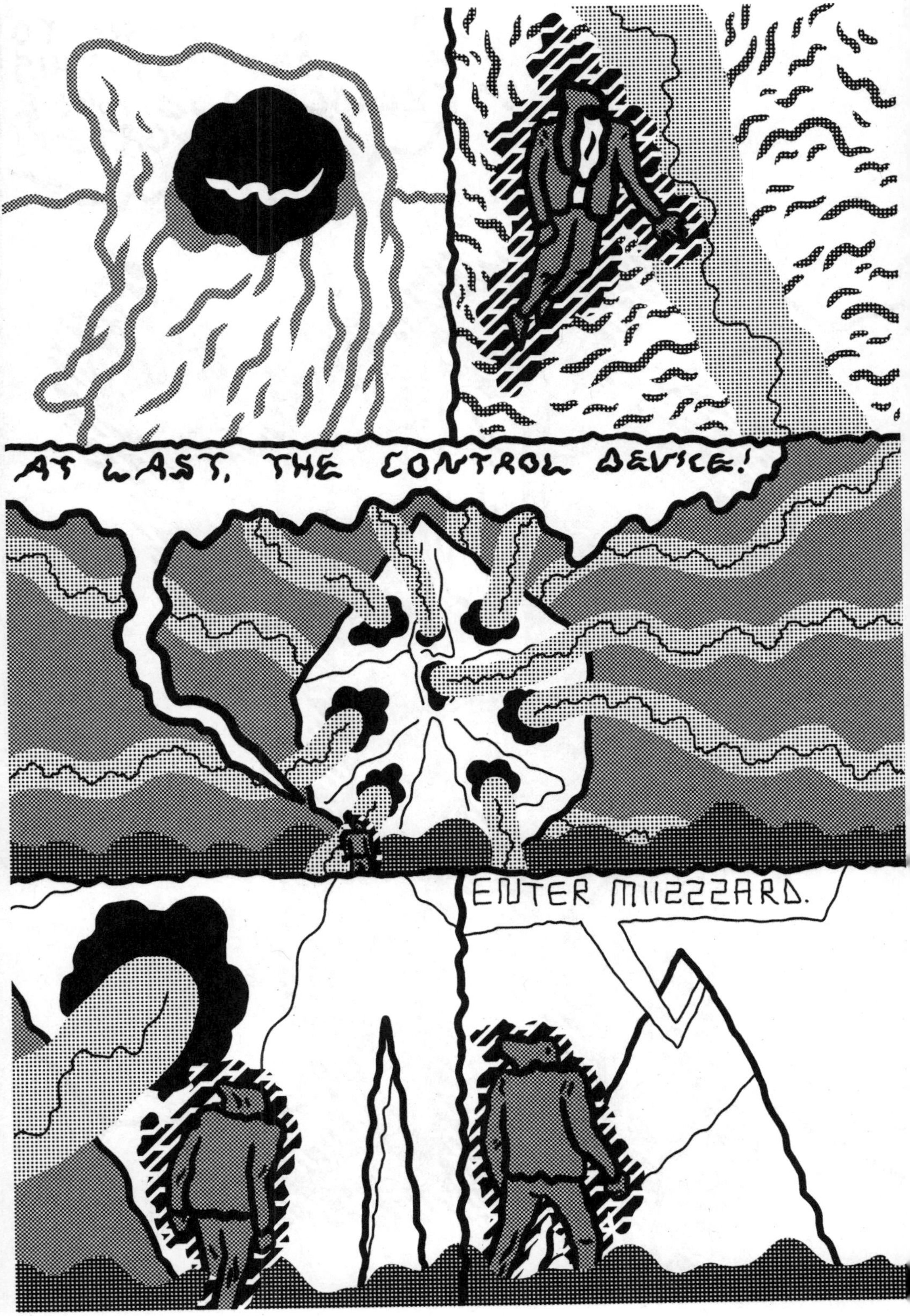
AT LAST, THE CONTROL DEVICE!
ENTER MIIZZZARD.

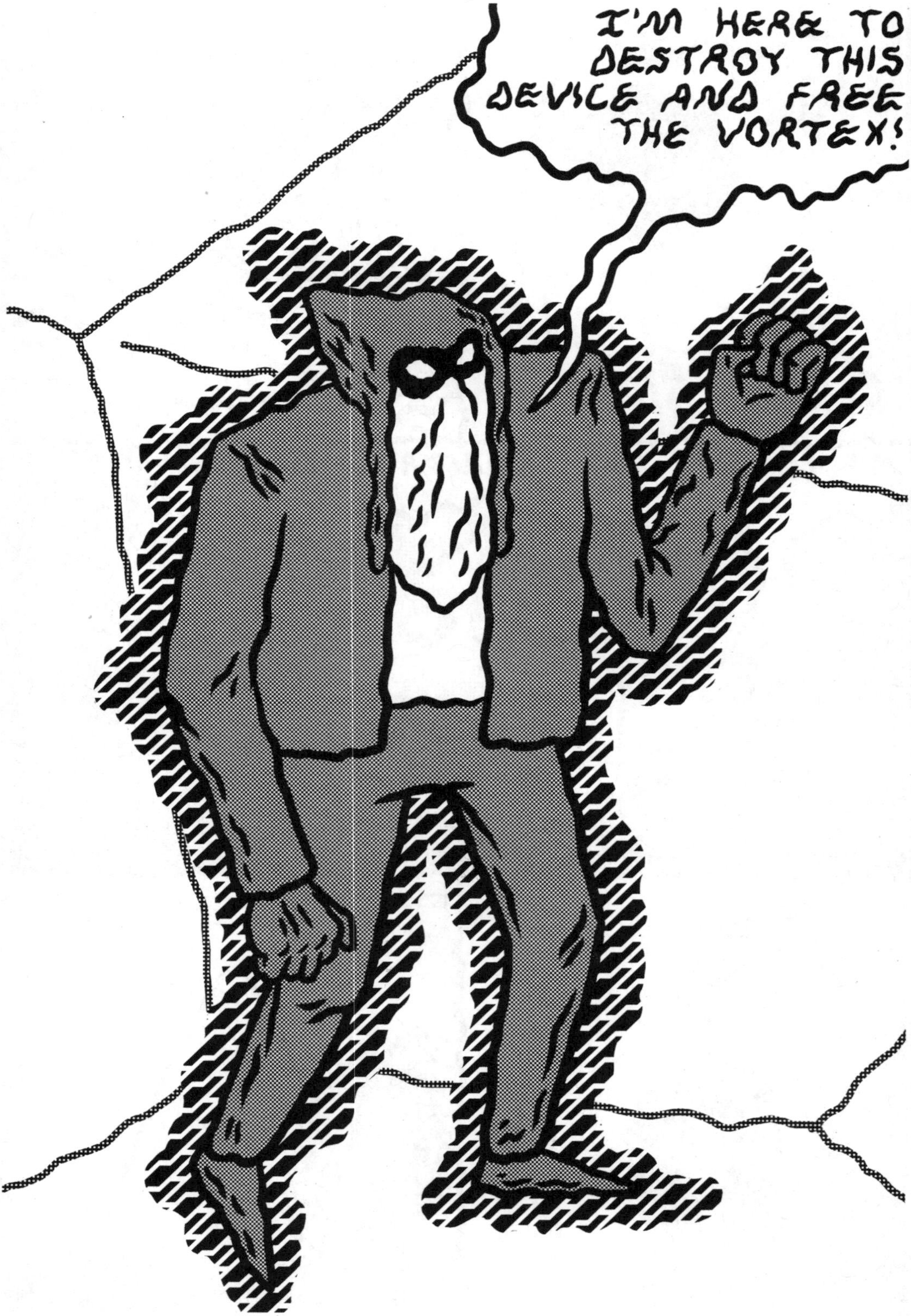
I'M HERE TO DESTROY THIS DEVICE AND FREE THE VORTEX!

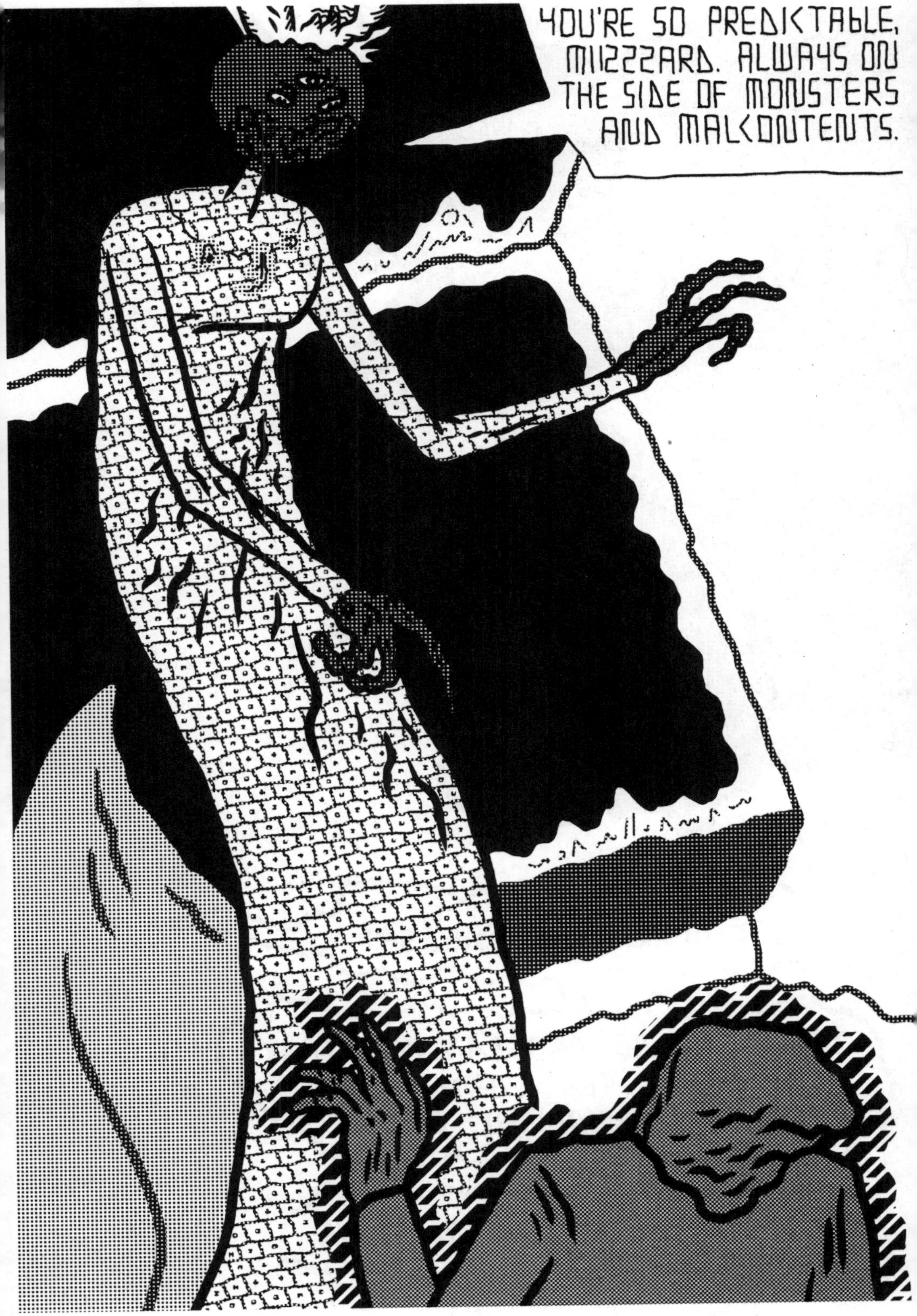
YOU'RE SO PREDICTABLE, MIIZZZARD. ALWAYS ON THE SIDE OF MONSTERS AND MALCONTENTS.

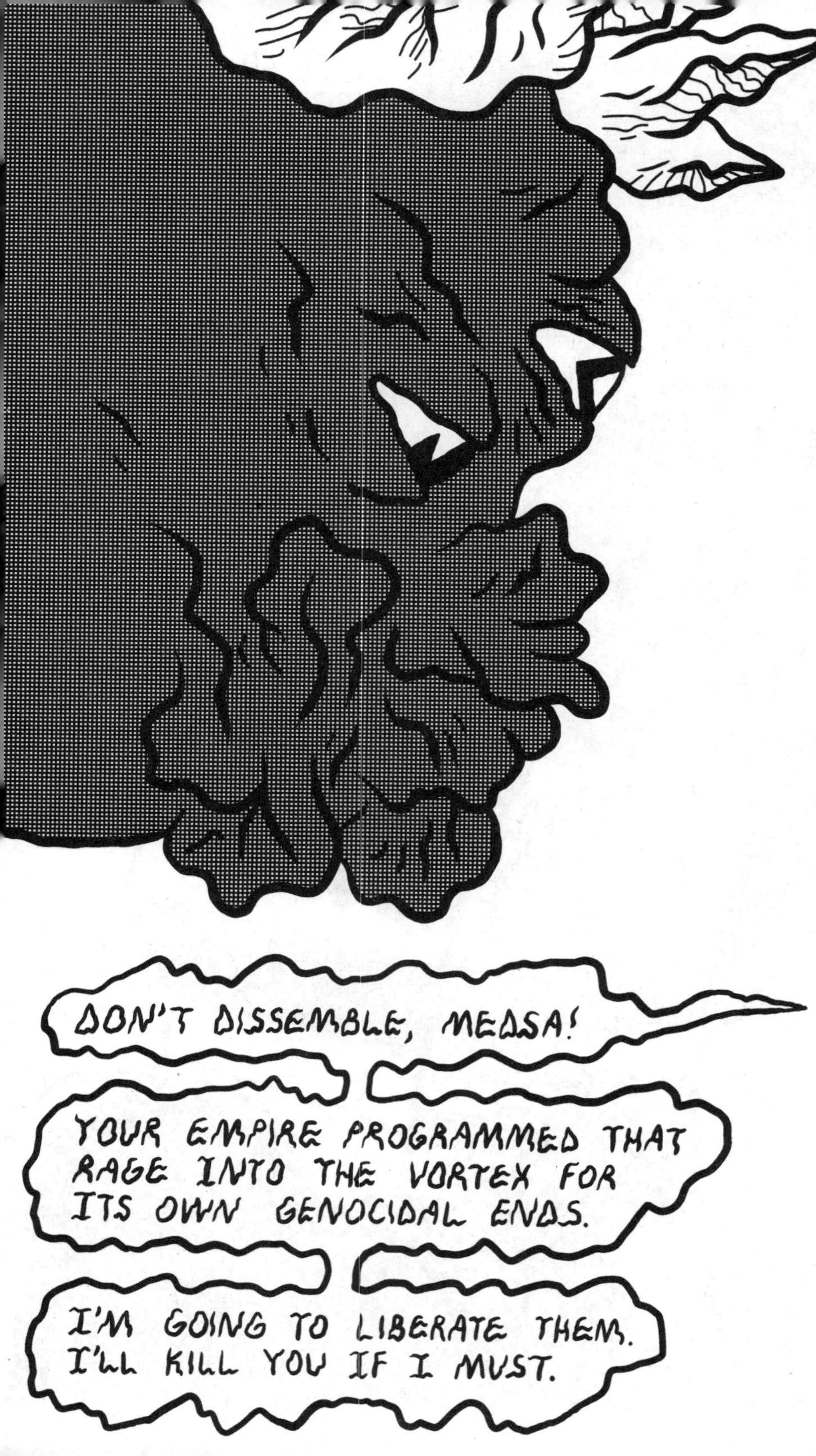
DON'T DISSEMBLE, MEDSA!
YOUR EMPIRE PROGRAMMED THAT RAGE INTO THE VORTEX FOR ITS OWN GENOCIDAL ENDS.
I'M GOING TO LIBERATE THEM. I'LL KILL YOU IF I MUST.

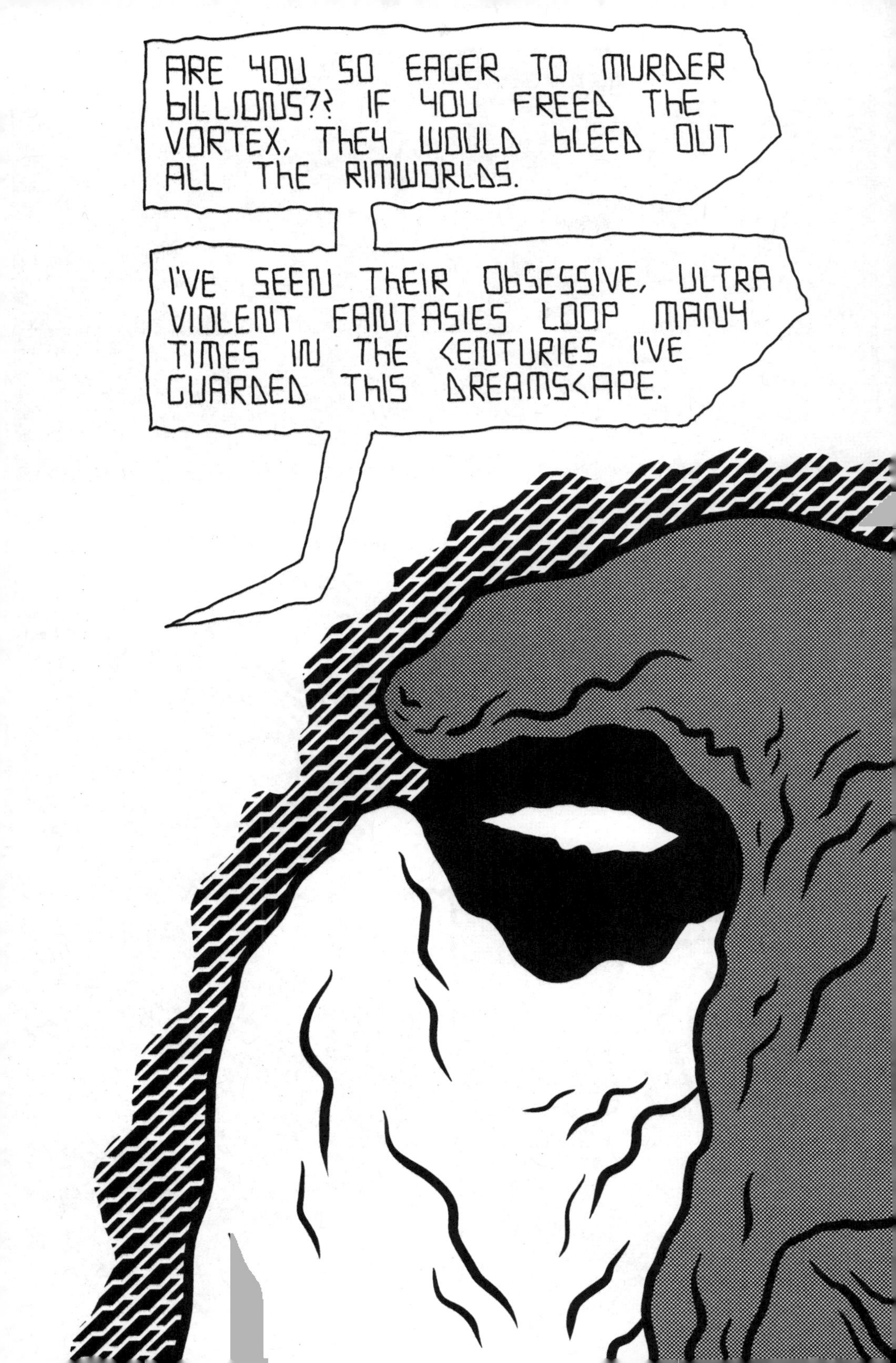
ARE YOU SO EAGER TO MURDER BILLIONS?! IF YOU FREED THE VORTEX, THEY WOULD BLEED OUT ALL THE RIMWORLDS.
I'VE SEEN THEIR OBSESSIVE, ULTRA VIOLENT FANTASIES LOOP MANY TIMES IN THE CENTURIES I'VE GUARDED THIS DREAMSCAPE.

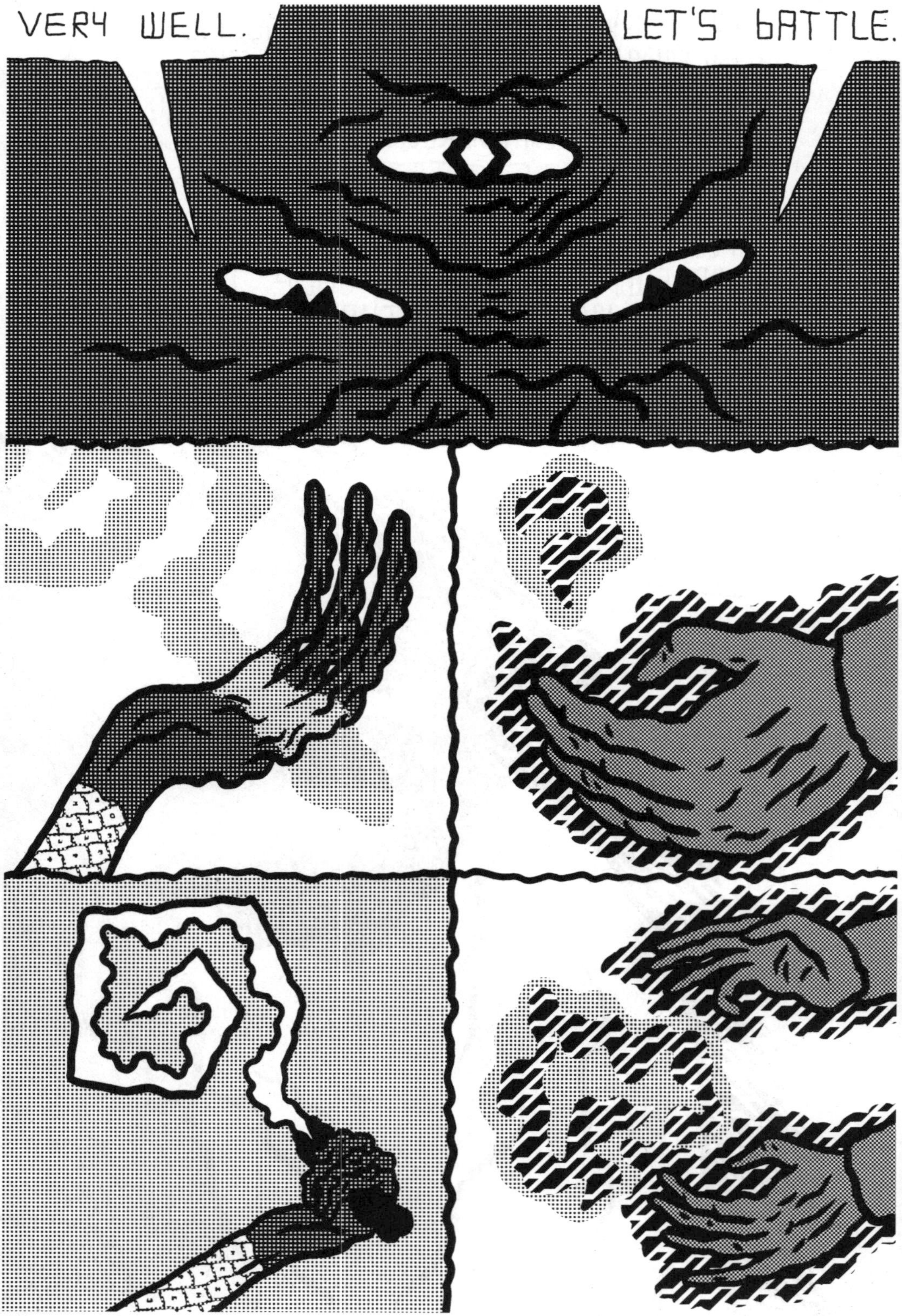
VERY WELL.
LET'S BATTLE.

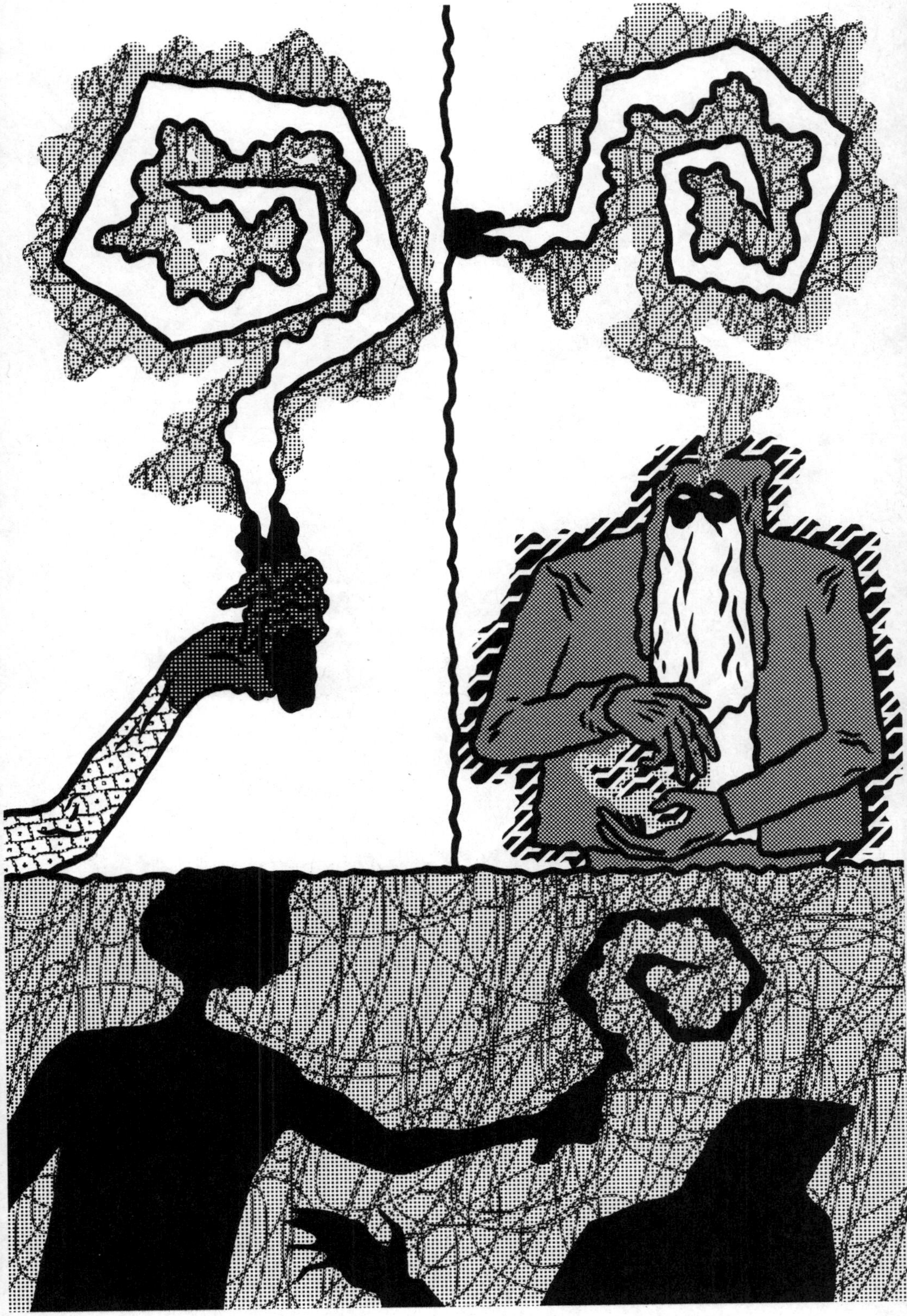

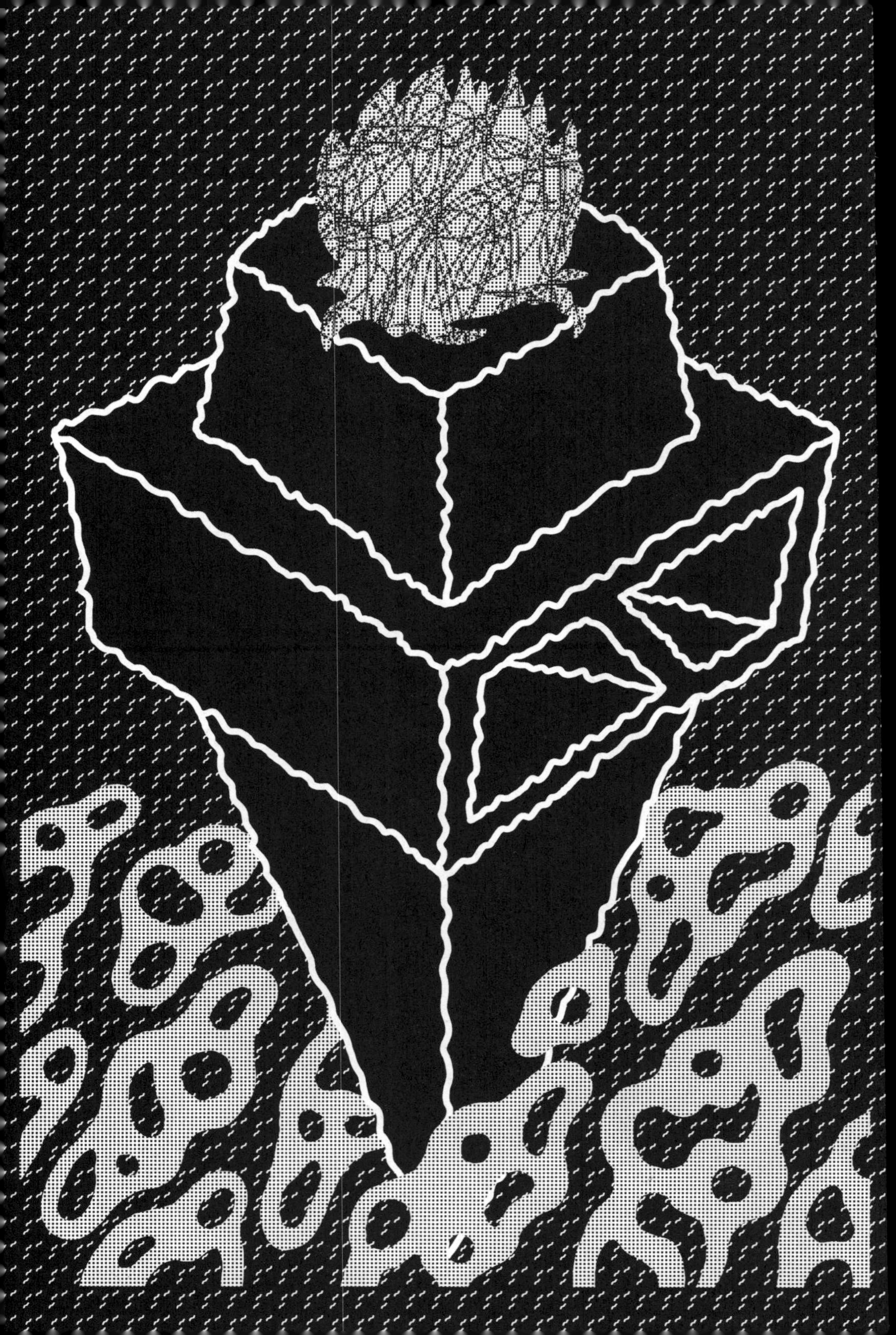

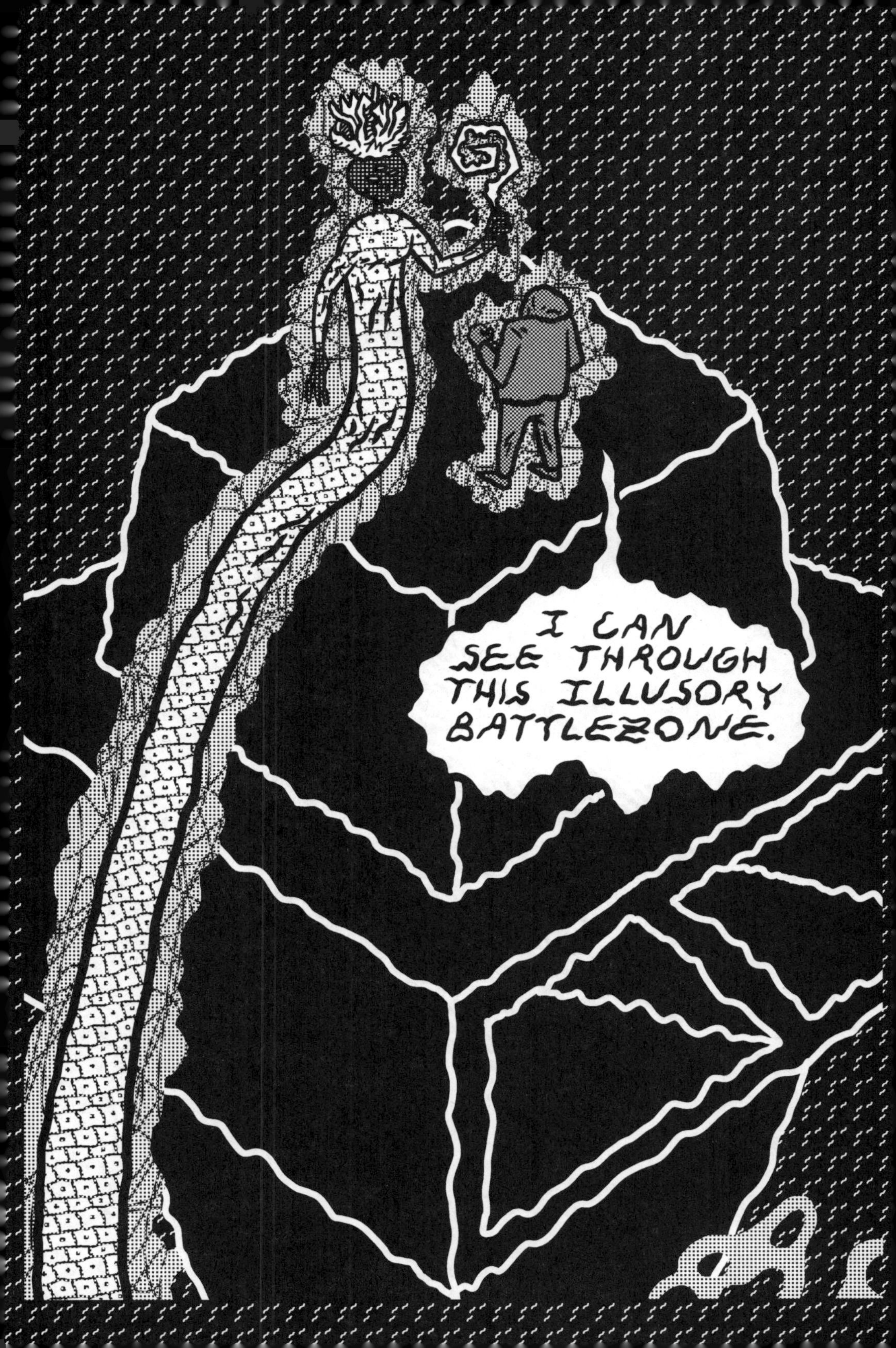
I CAN SEE THROUGH THIS ILLUSORY BATTLEZONE.

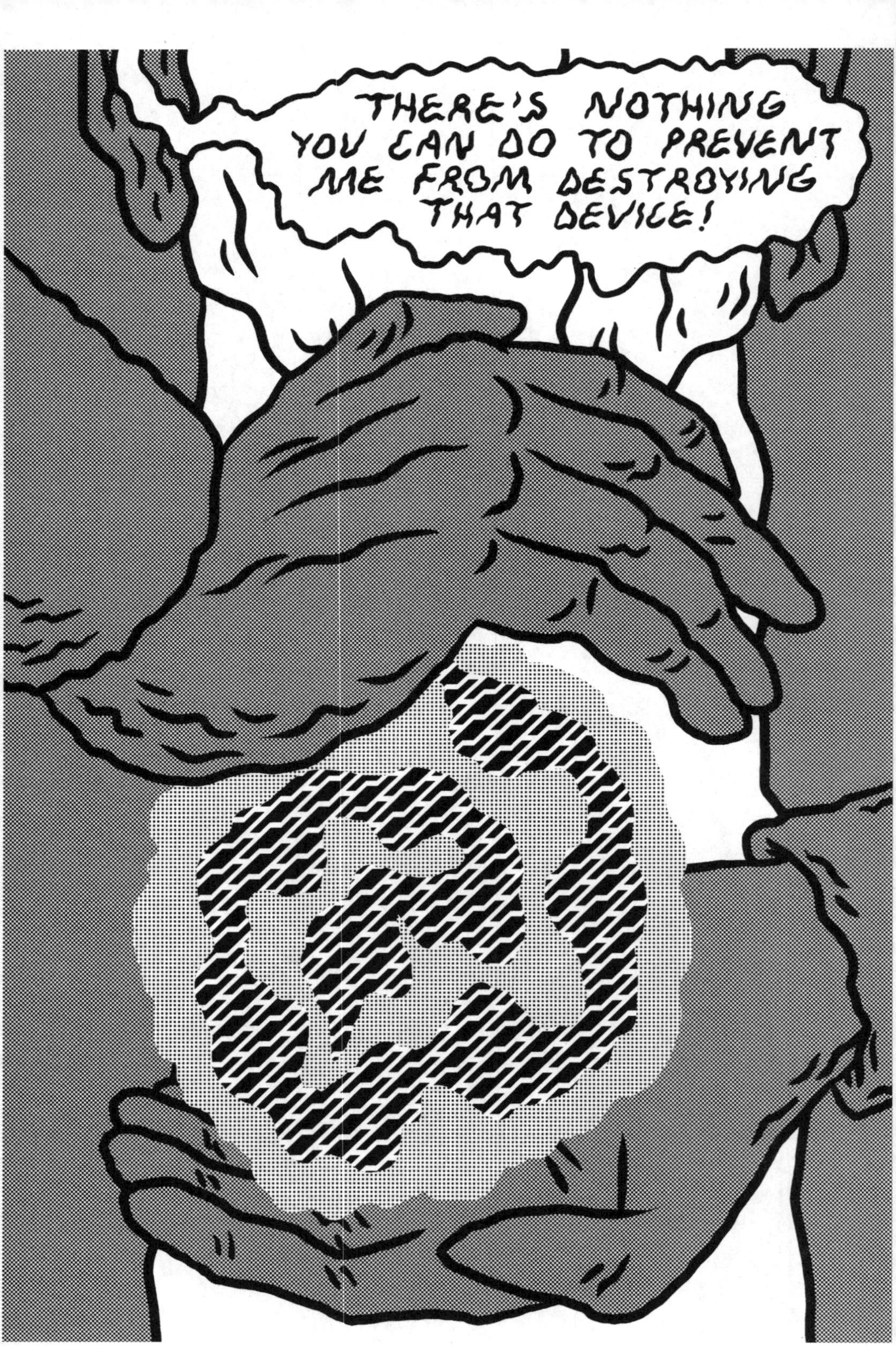
THERE'S NOTHING YOU CAN DO TO PREVENT ME FROM DESTROYING THAT DEVICE!

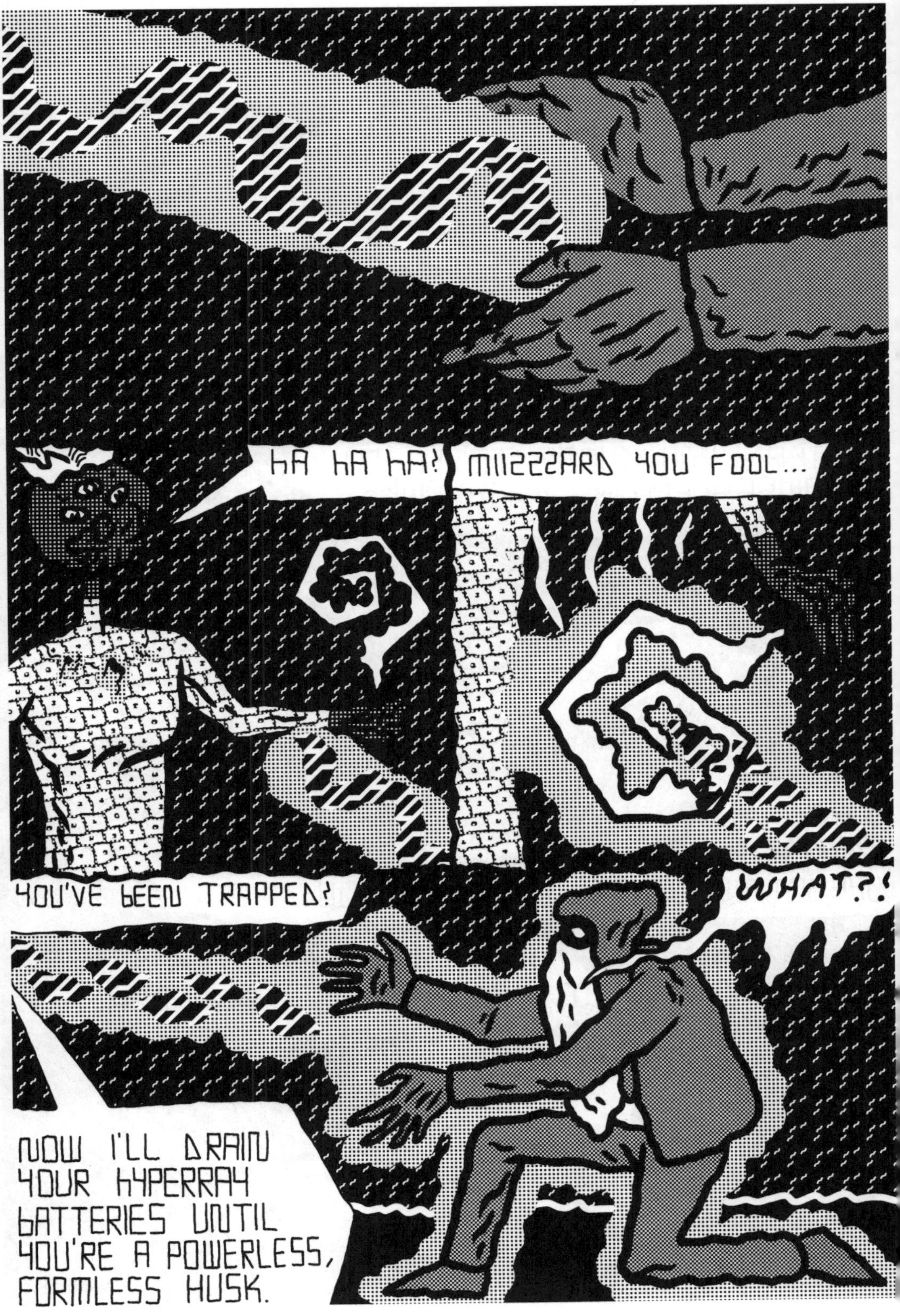
HA HA HA!
MIIZZZARD YOU FOOL...
YOU'VE BEEN TRAPPED!
WHAT?!
NOW I'LL DRAIN YOUR HYPERRAY BATTERIES UNTIL YOU'RE A POWERLESS, FORMLESS HUSK.

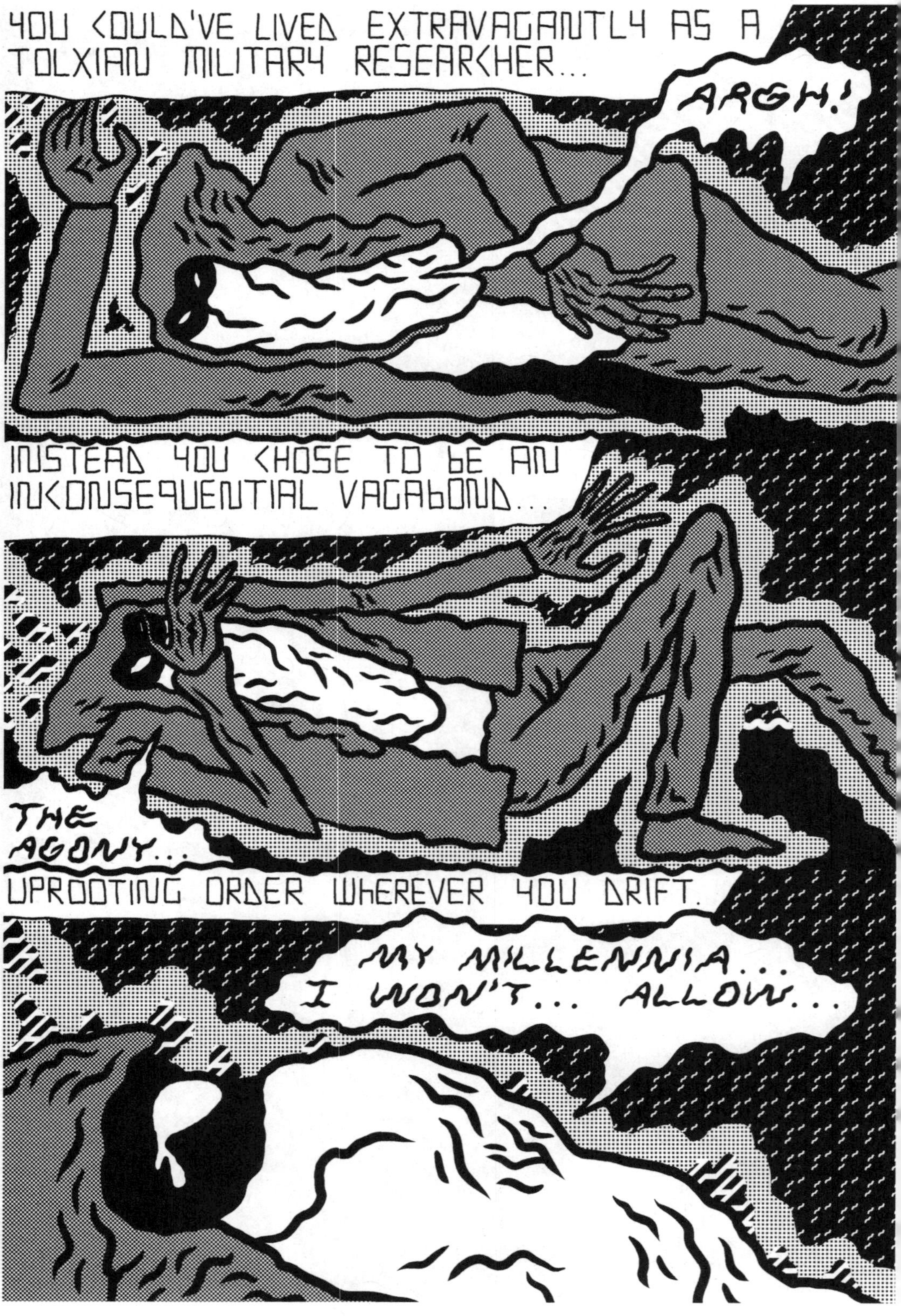
YOU COULD'VE LIVED EXTRAVAGANTLY AS A TOLXIAN MILITARY RESEARCHER...
ARGH!
INSTEAD YOU CHOSE TO BE AN INCONSEQUENTIAL VAGABOND...
THE AGONY...
UPROOTING ORDER WHEREVER YOU DRIFT.
MY MILLENNIA... I WON'T... ALLOW...

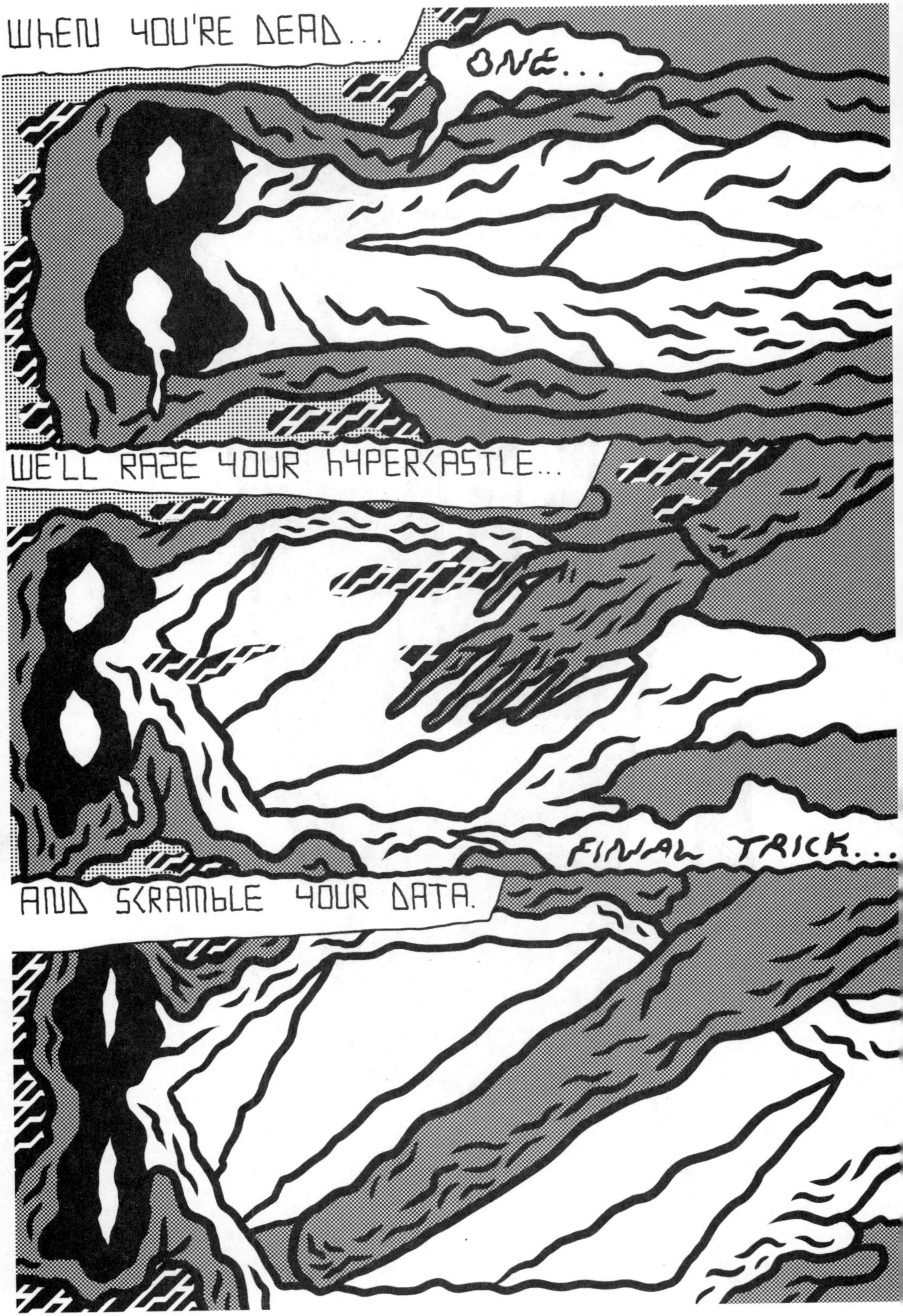
WHEN YOU'RE DEAD...
ONE...
WE'LL RAZE YOUR HYPERCASTLE...
FINAL TRICK...
AND SCRAMBLE YOUR DATA.

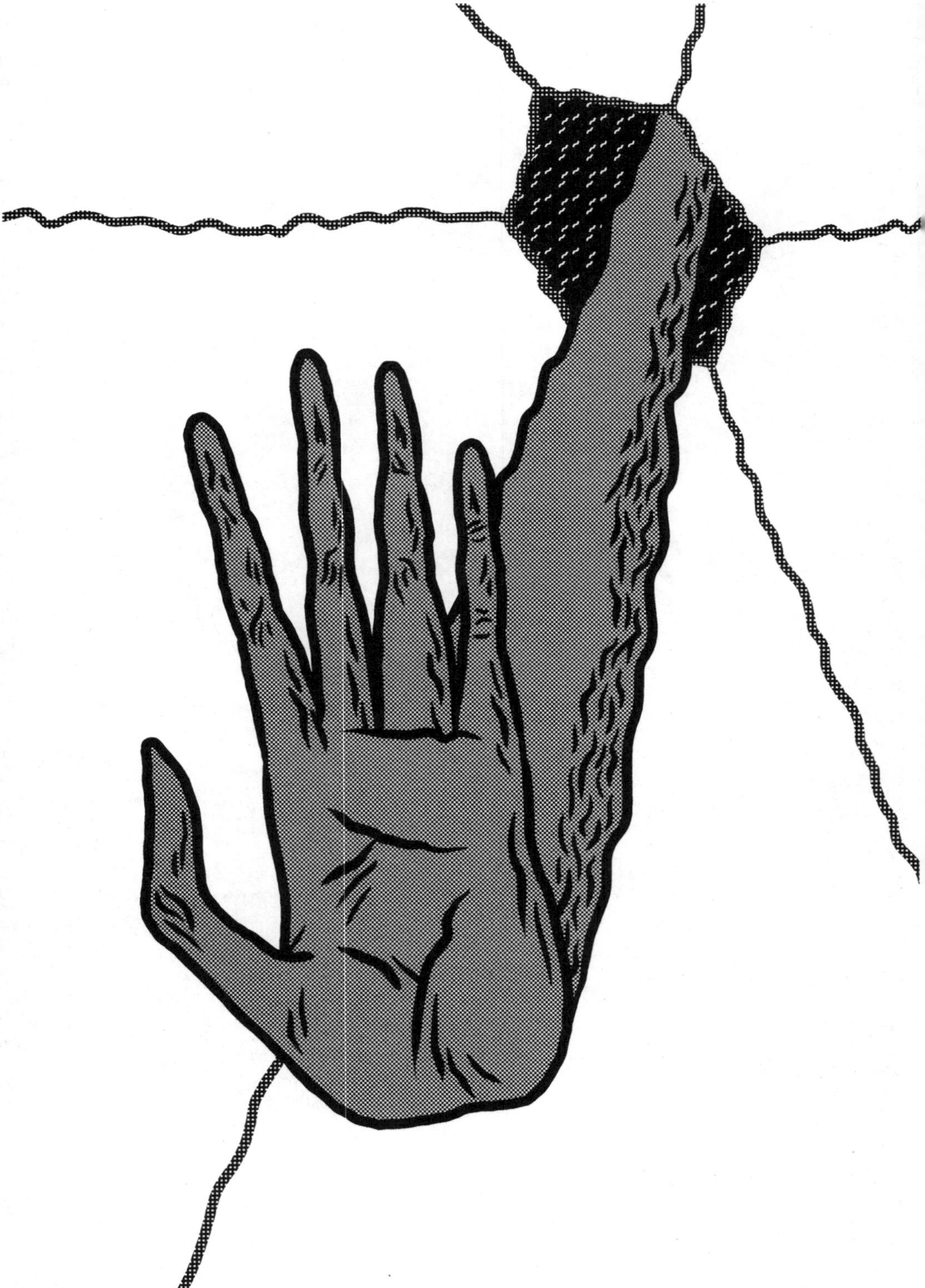

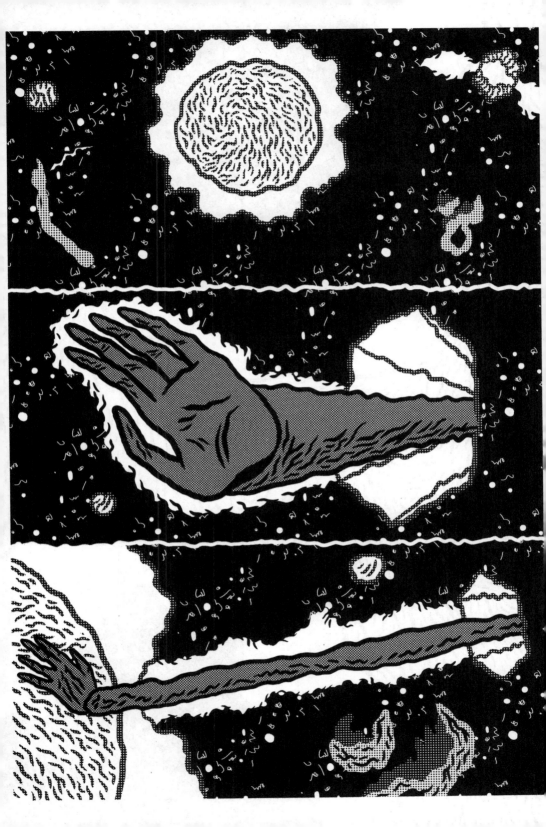

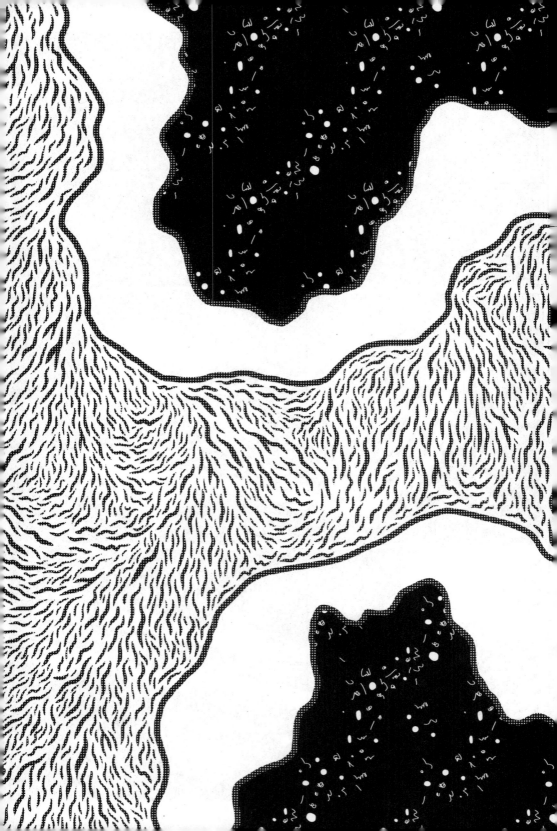

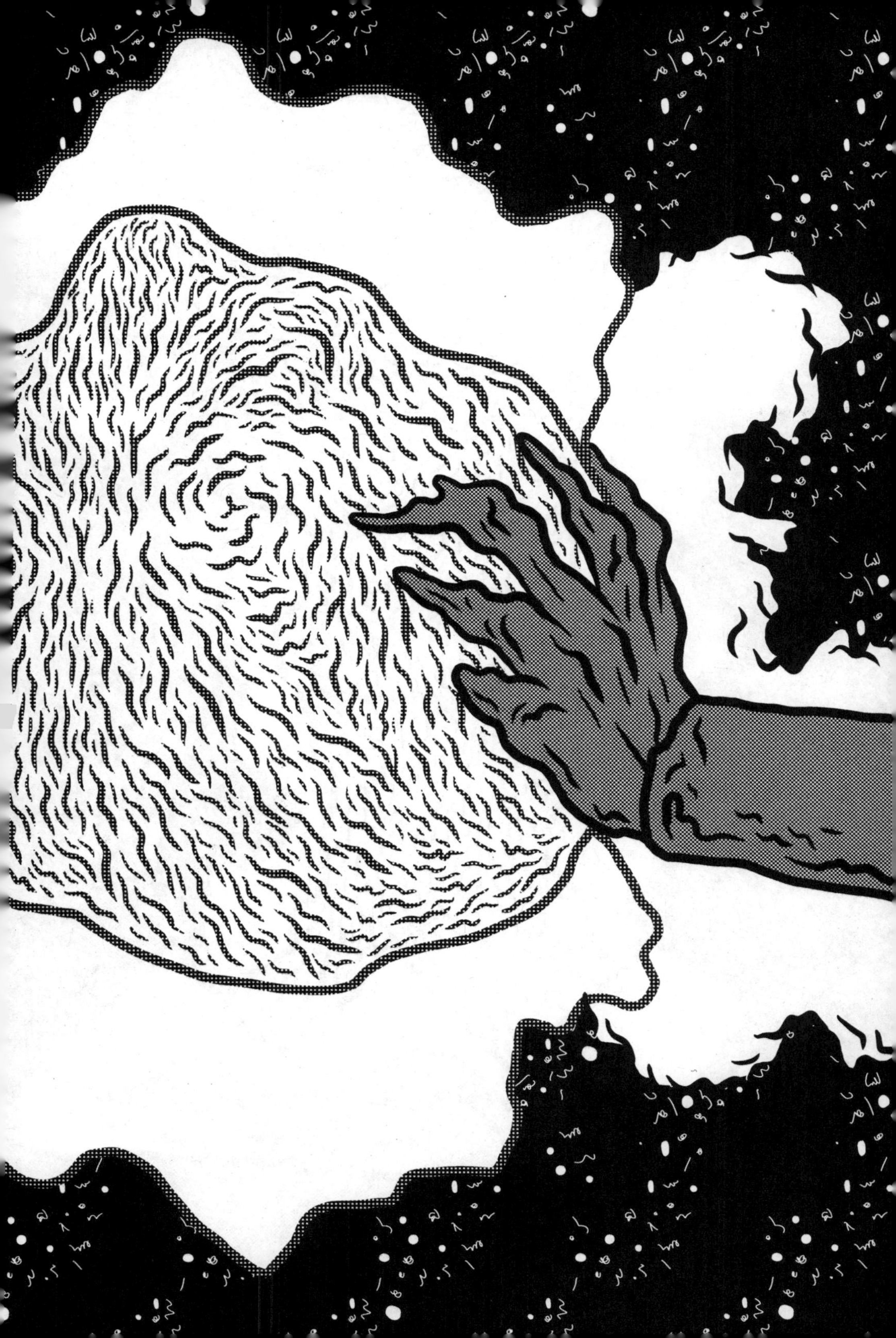

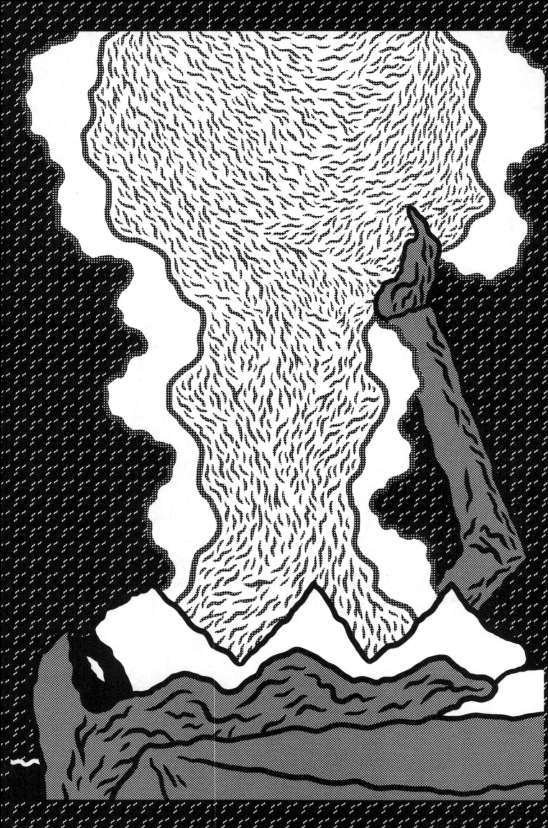

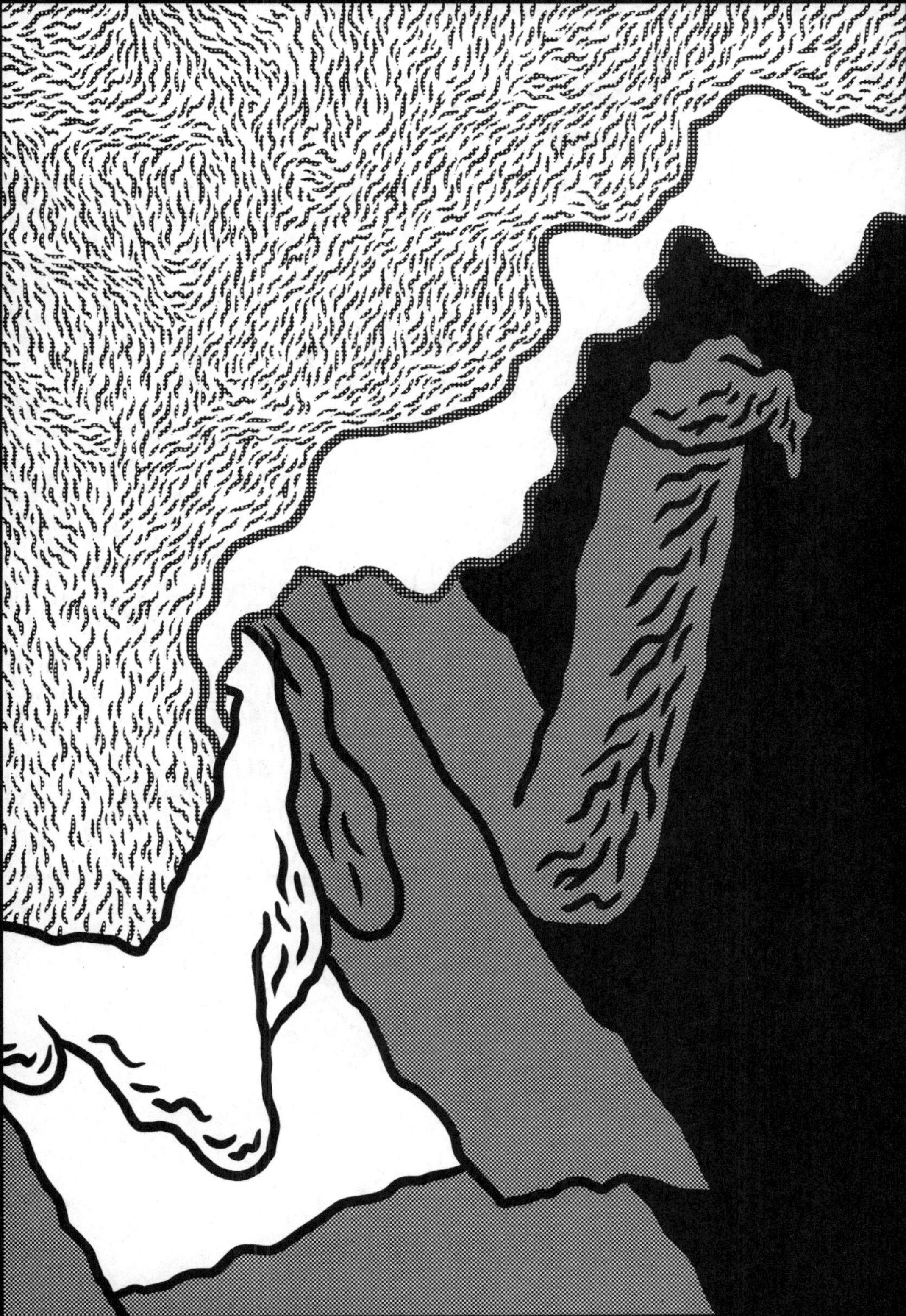

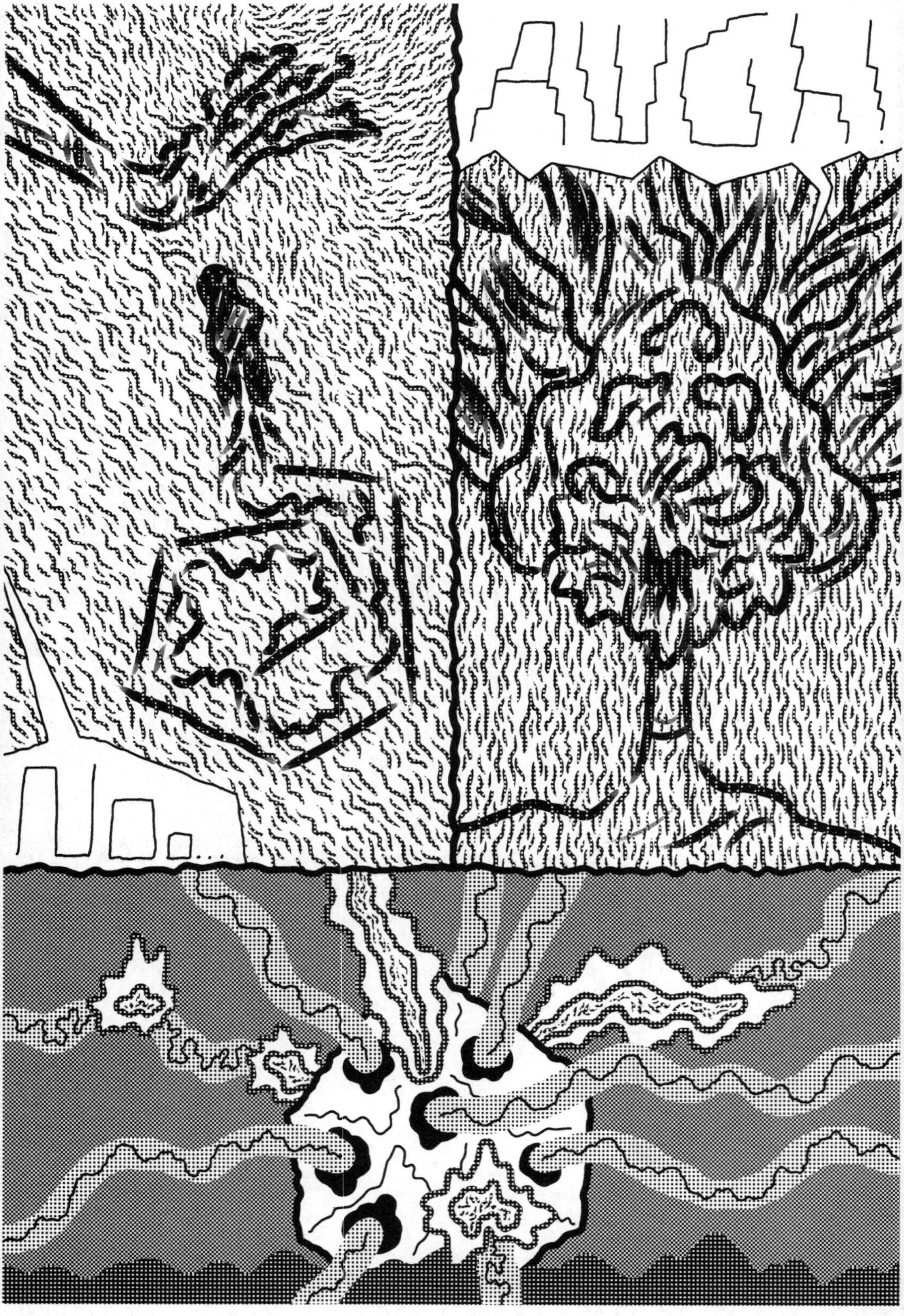
No...
AUGH!

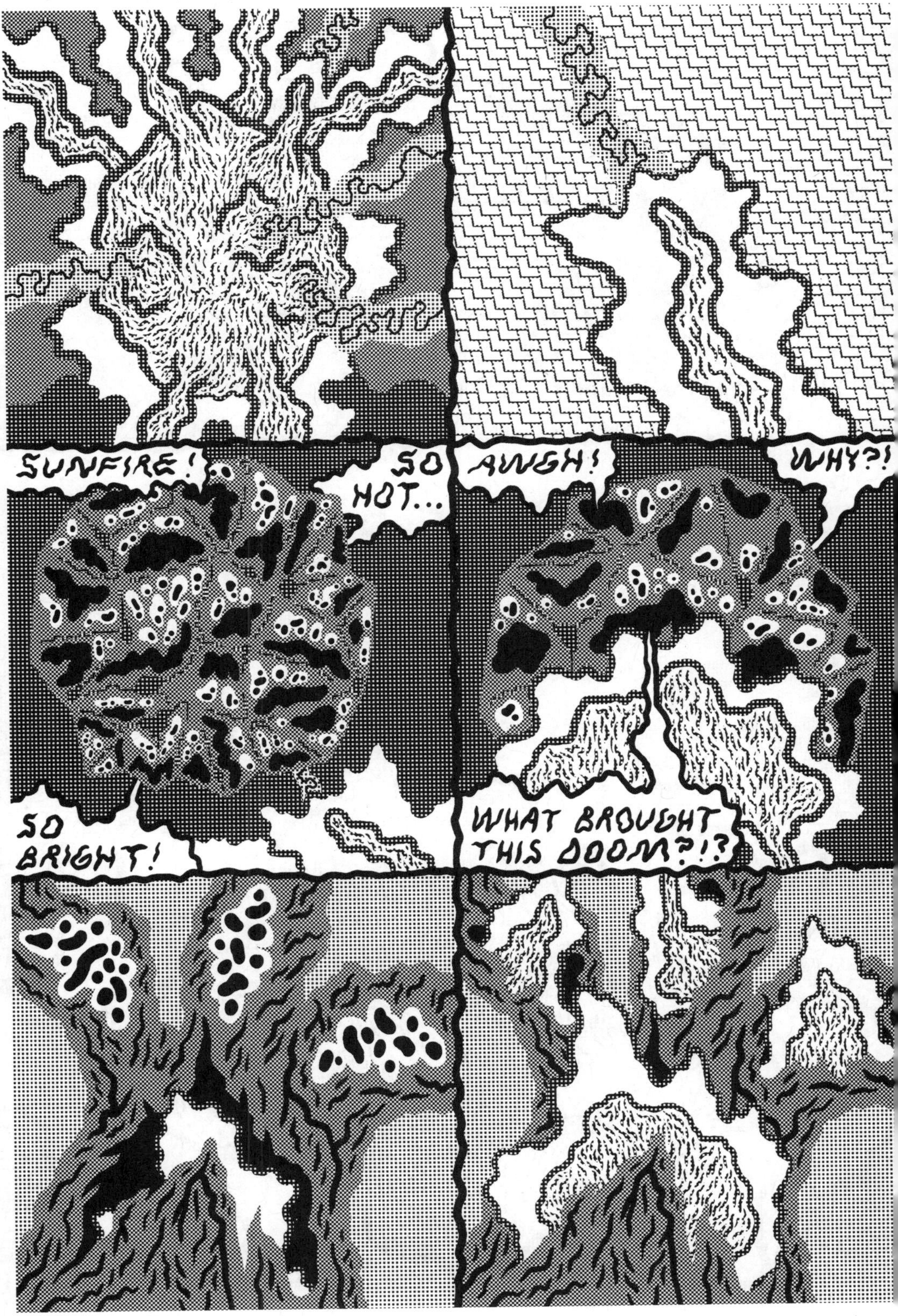
SUNFIRE!
SO HOT...
SO BRIGHT!
AWGH!
WHY?!
WHAT BROUGHT THIS DOOM?!?

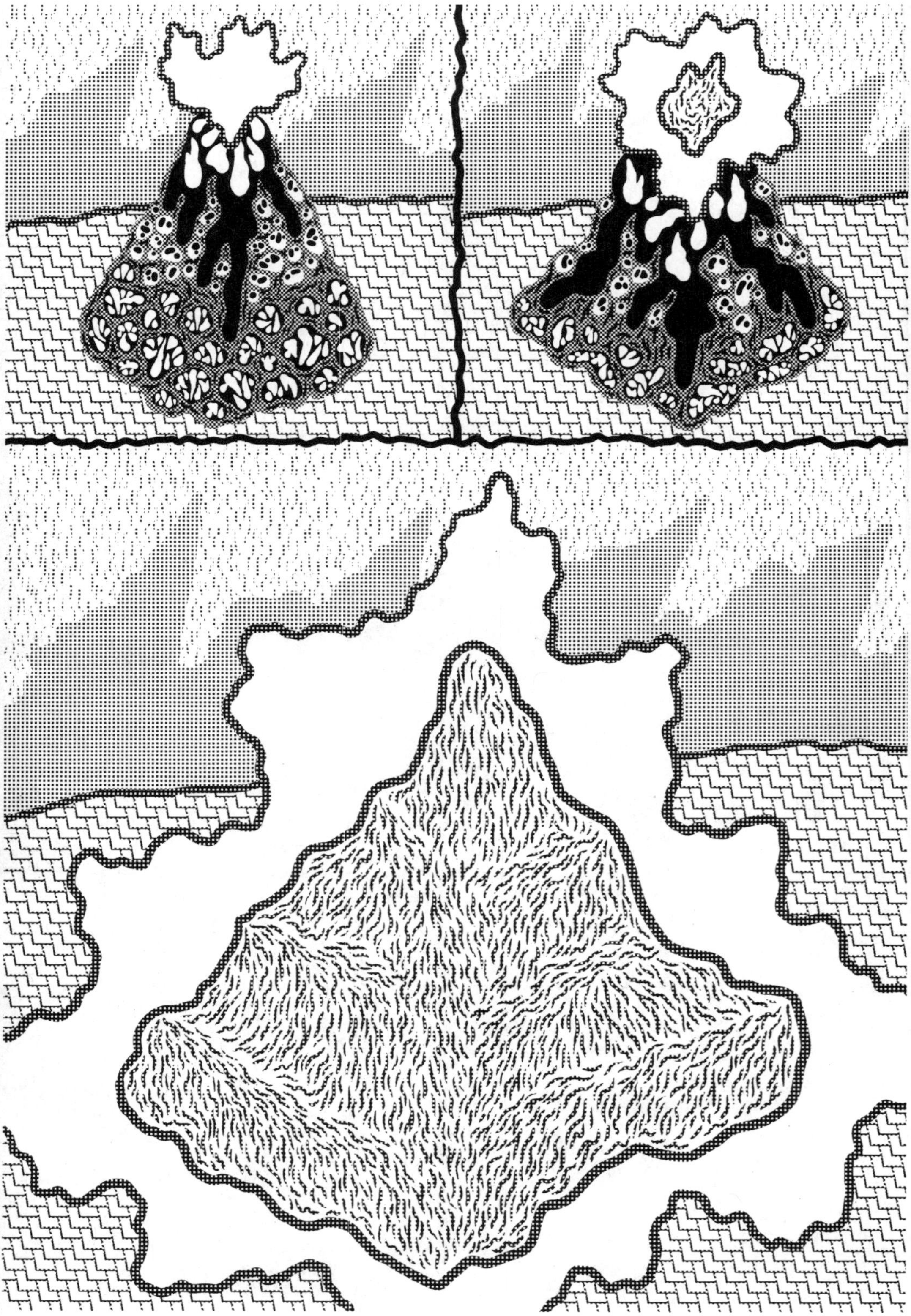

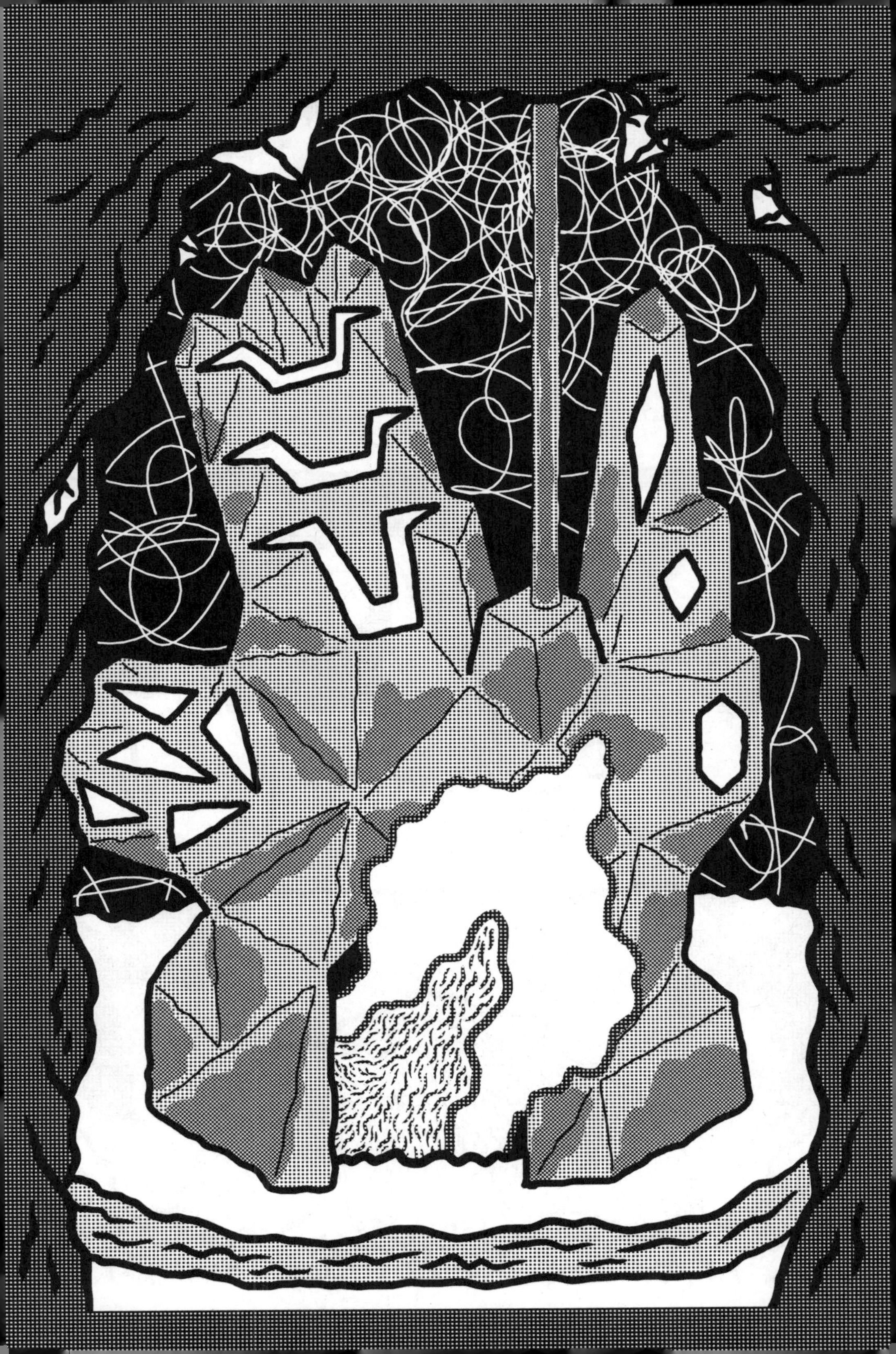

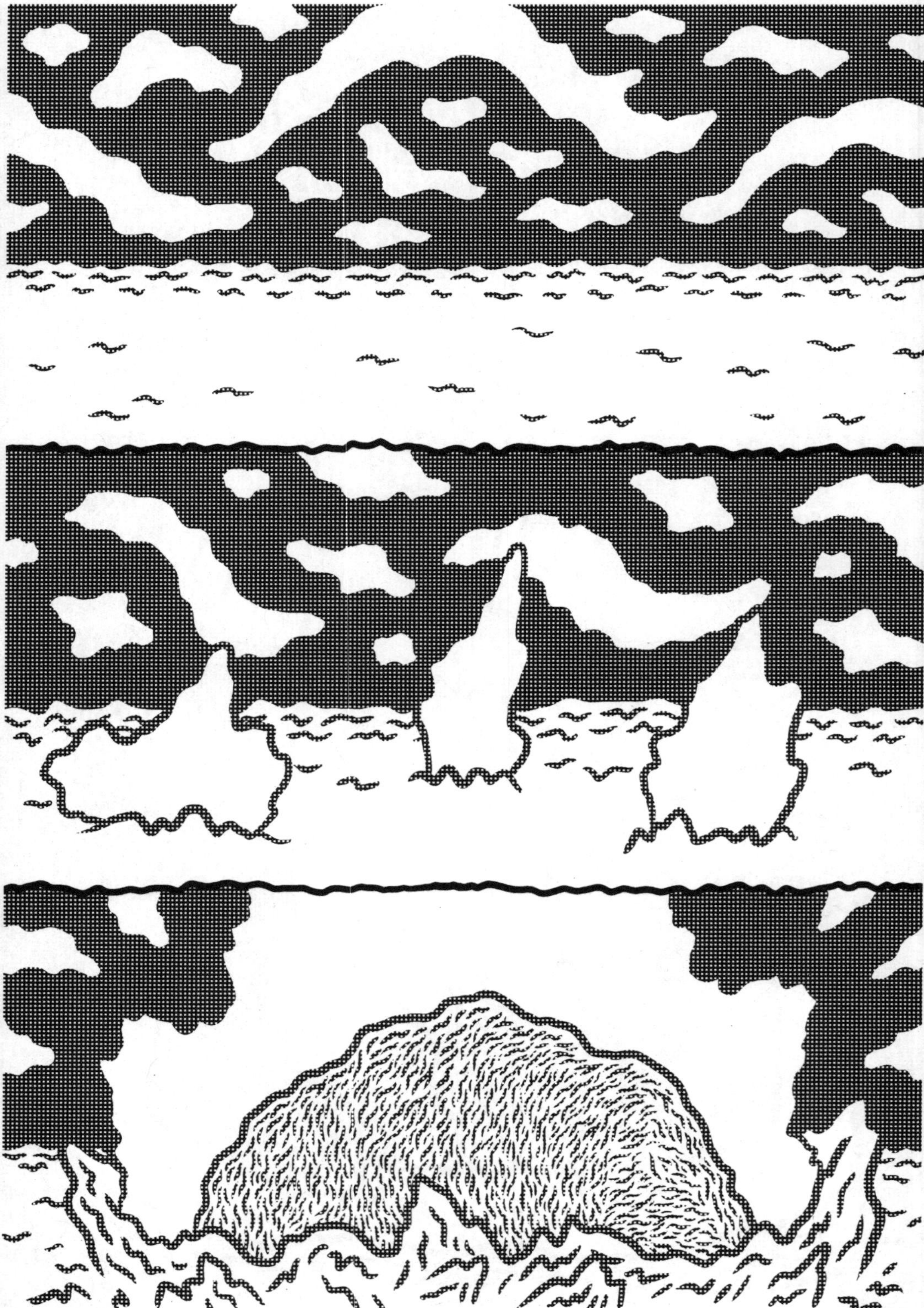

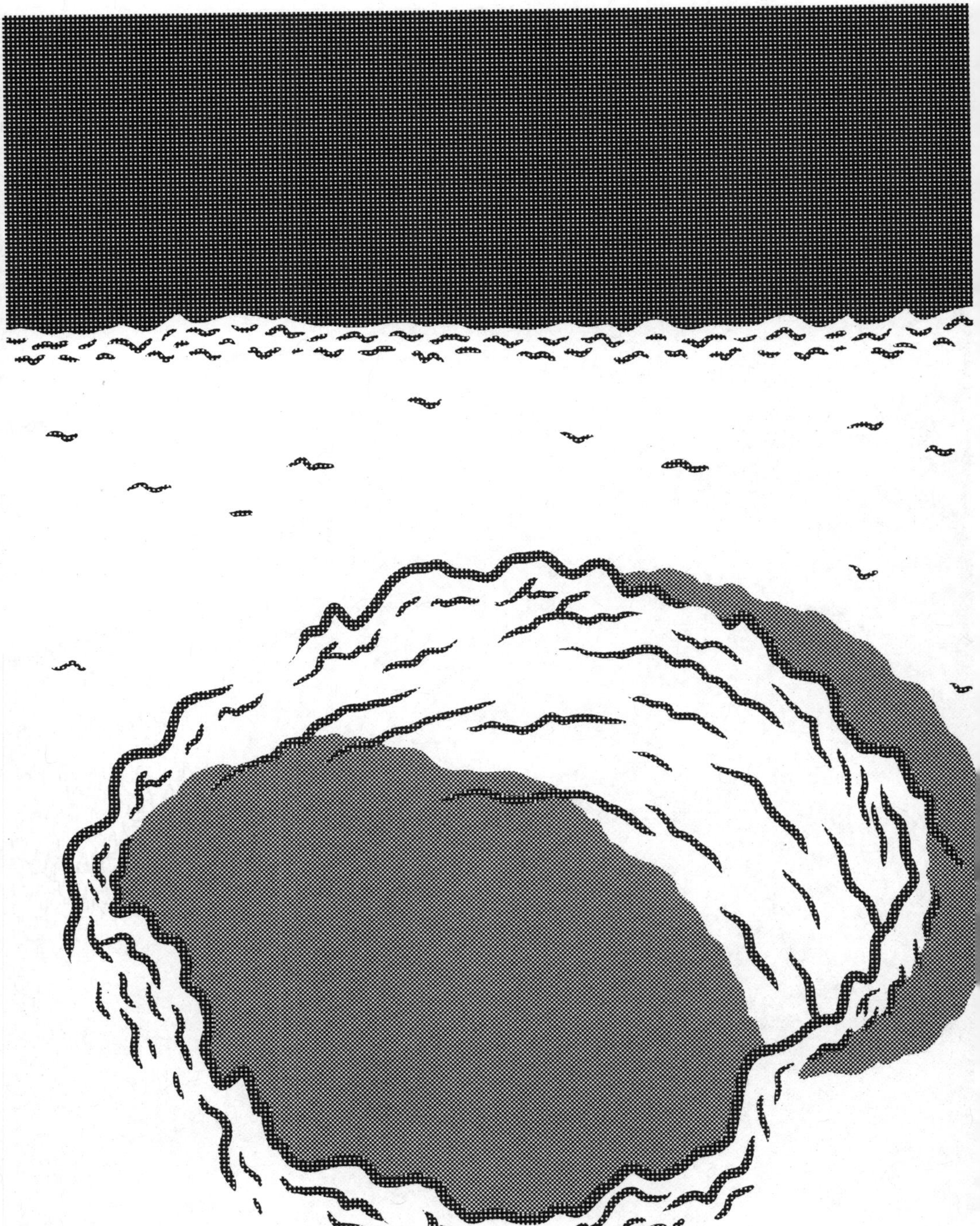

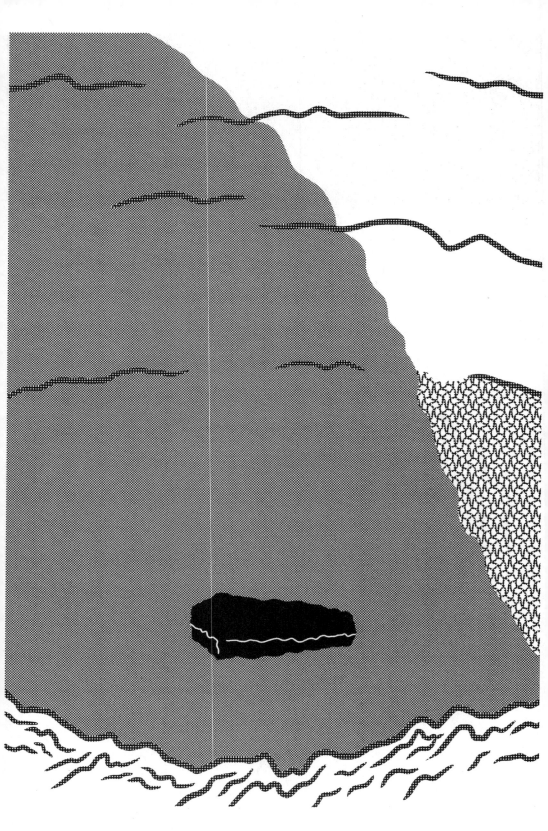

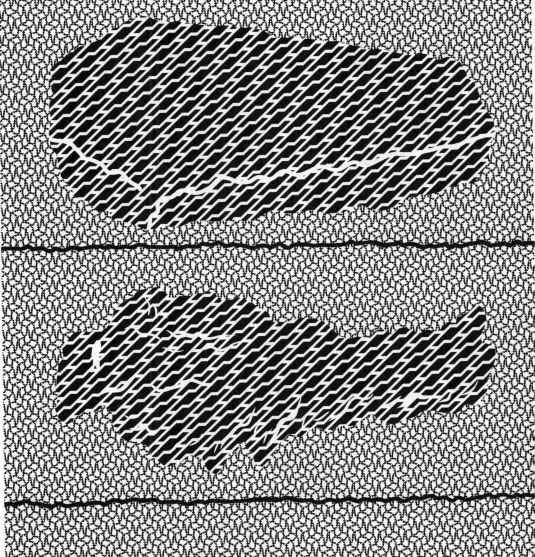

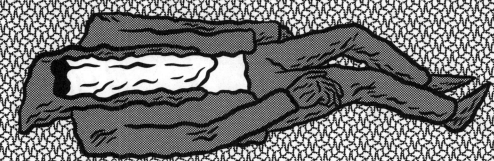

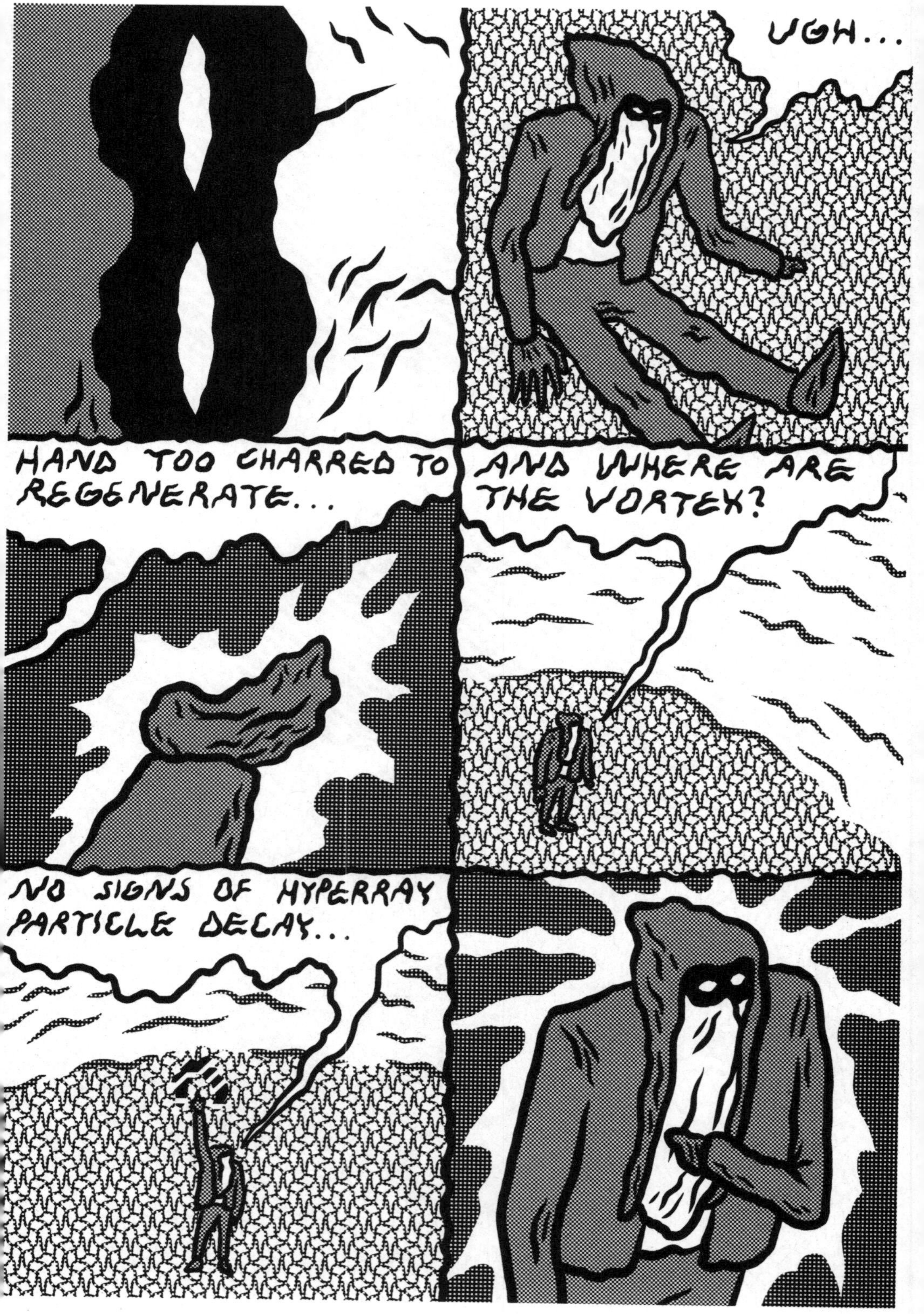
UGH...
HAND TOO CHARRED TO REGENERATE...
AND WHERE ARE THE VORTEX?
NO SIGNS OF HYPERRAY PARTICLE DECAY...

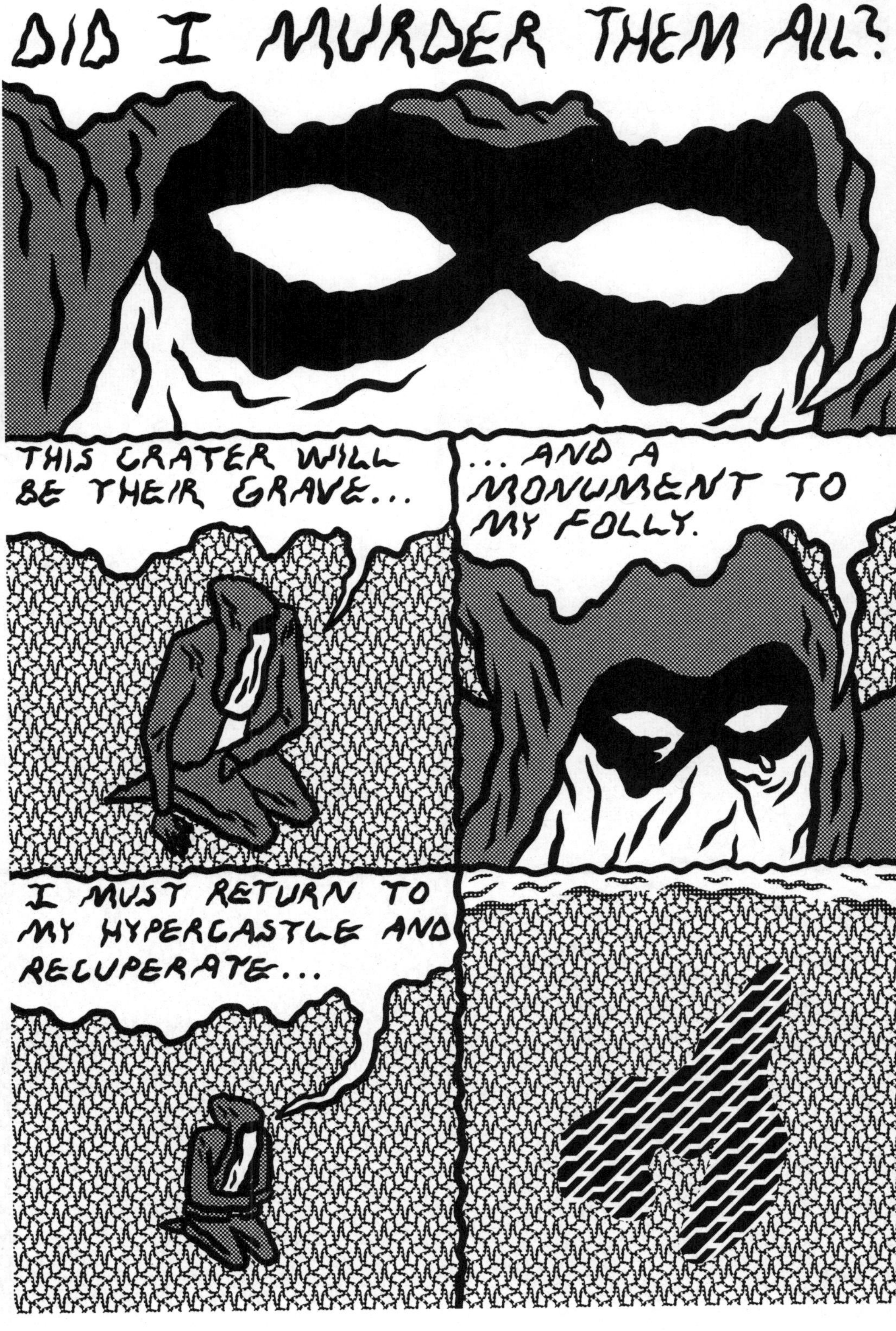
DID I MURDER THEM ALL?
THIS CRATER WILL BE THEIR GRAVE...
... AND A MONUMENT TO MY FOLLY.
I MUST RETURN TO MY HYPERCASTLE AND RECUPERATE...

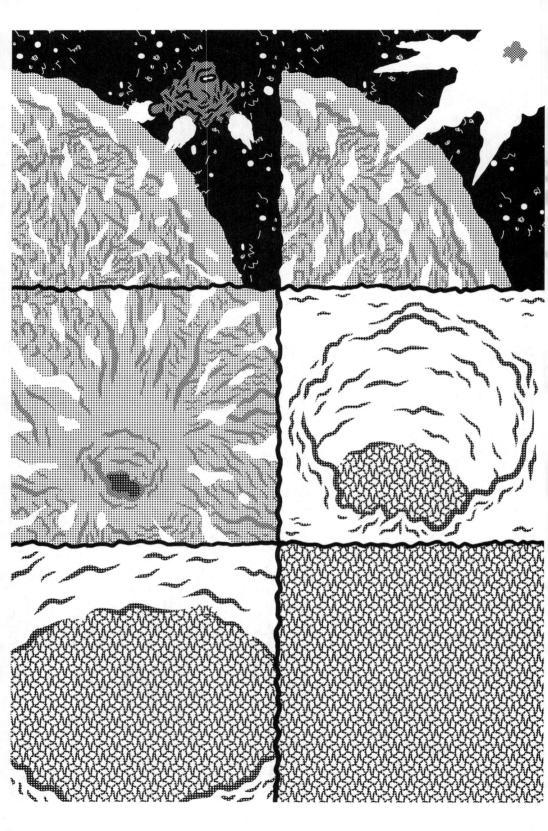

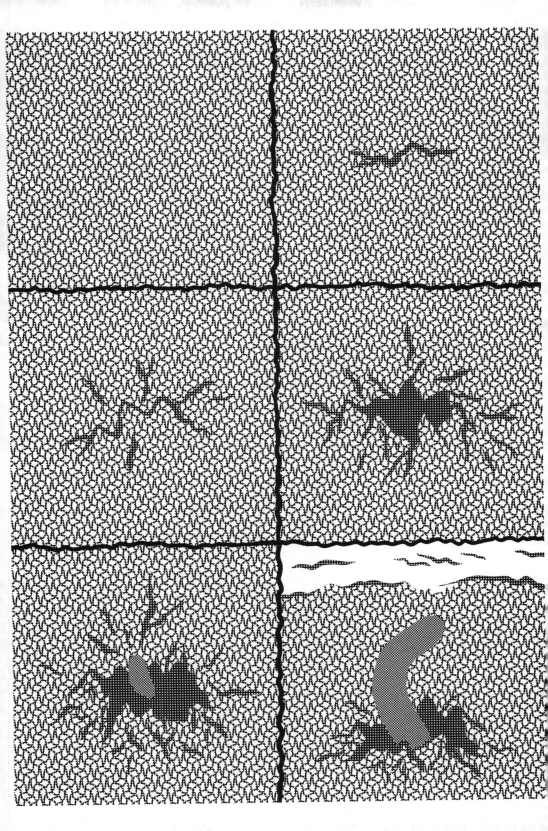

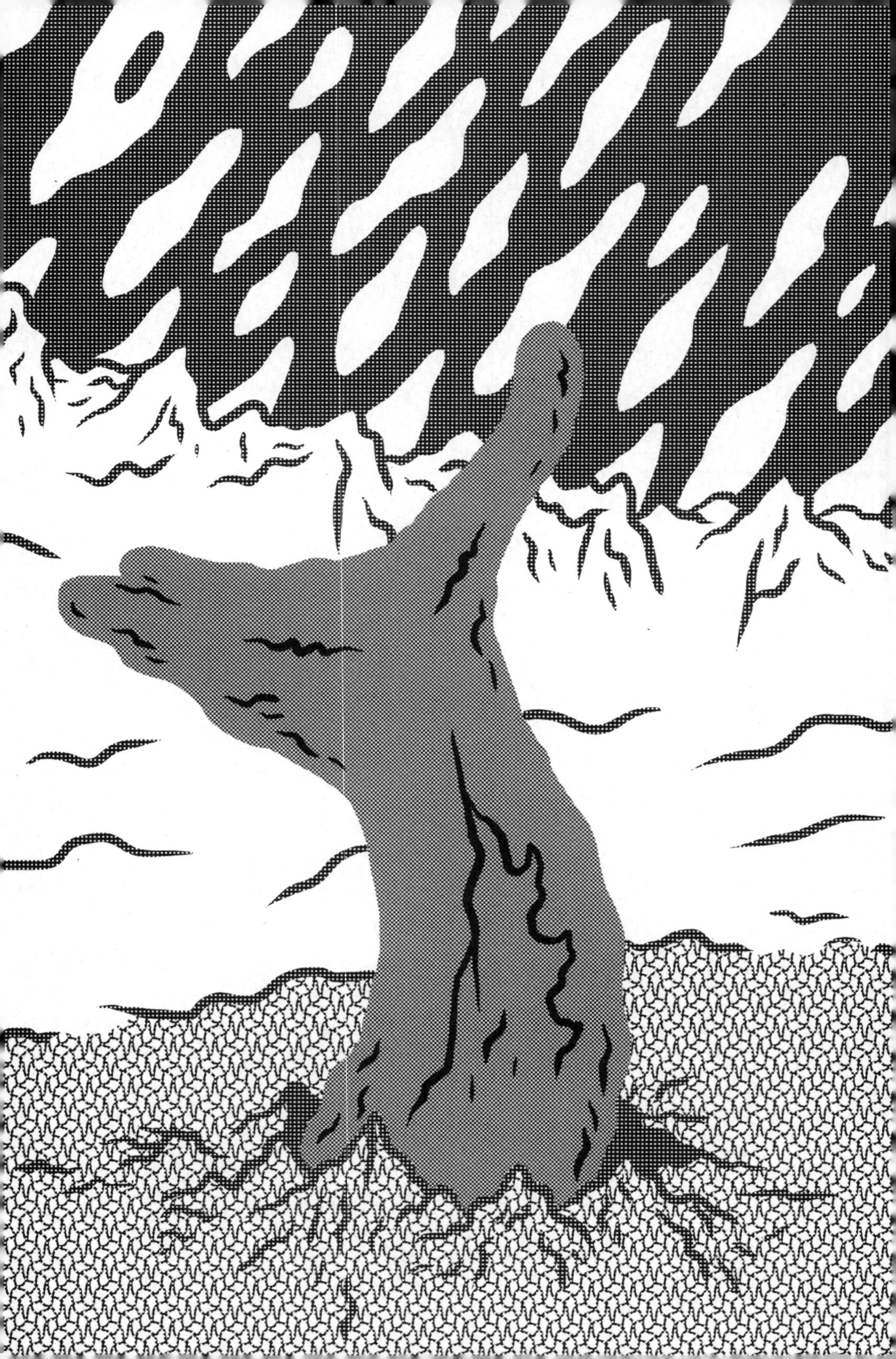

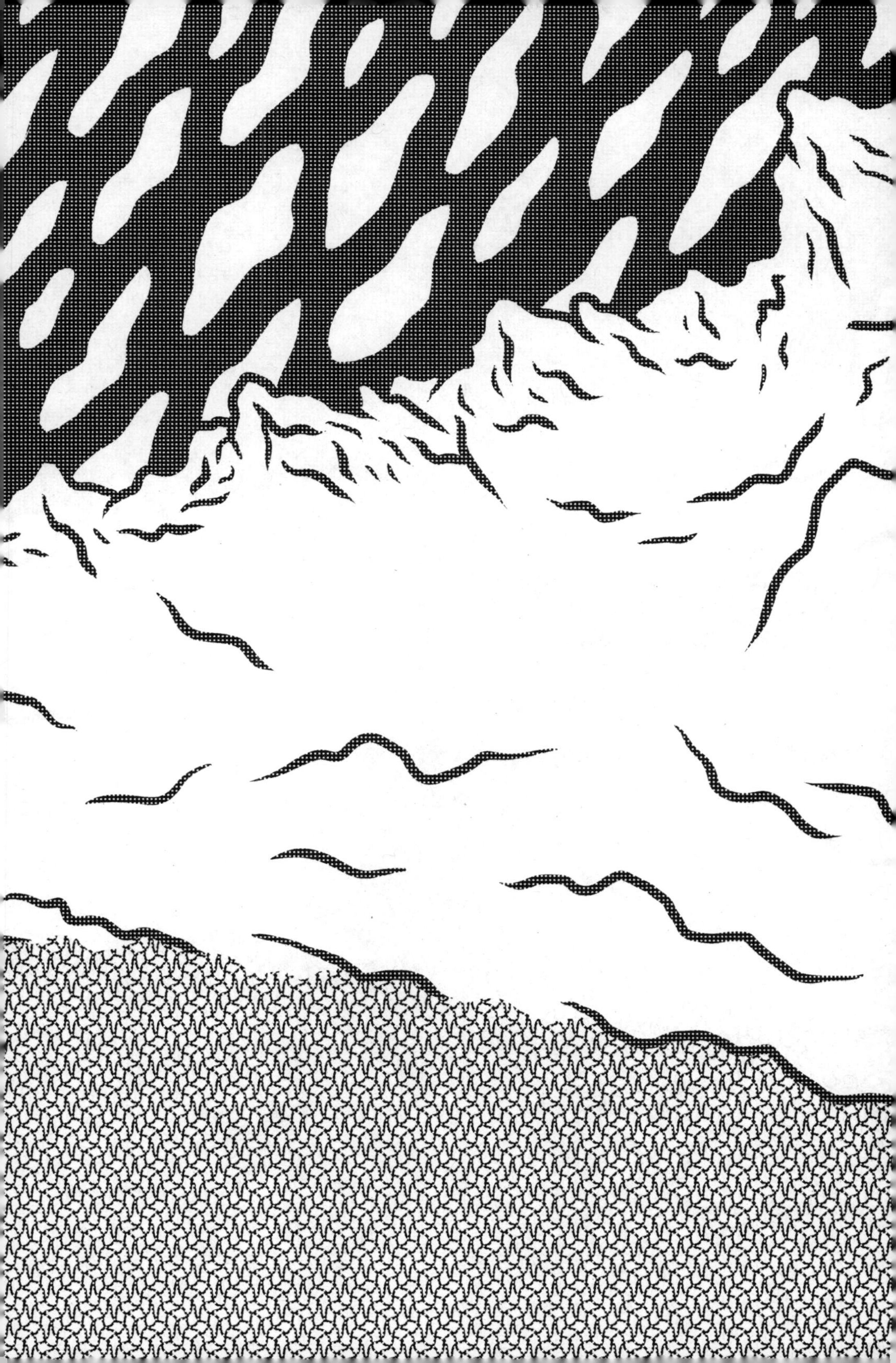

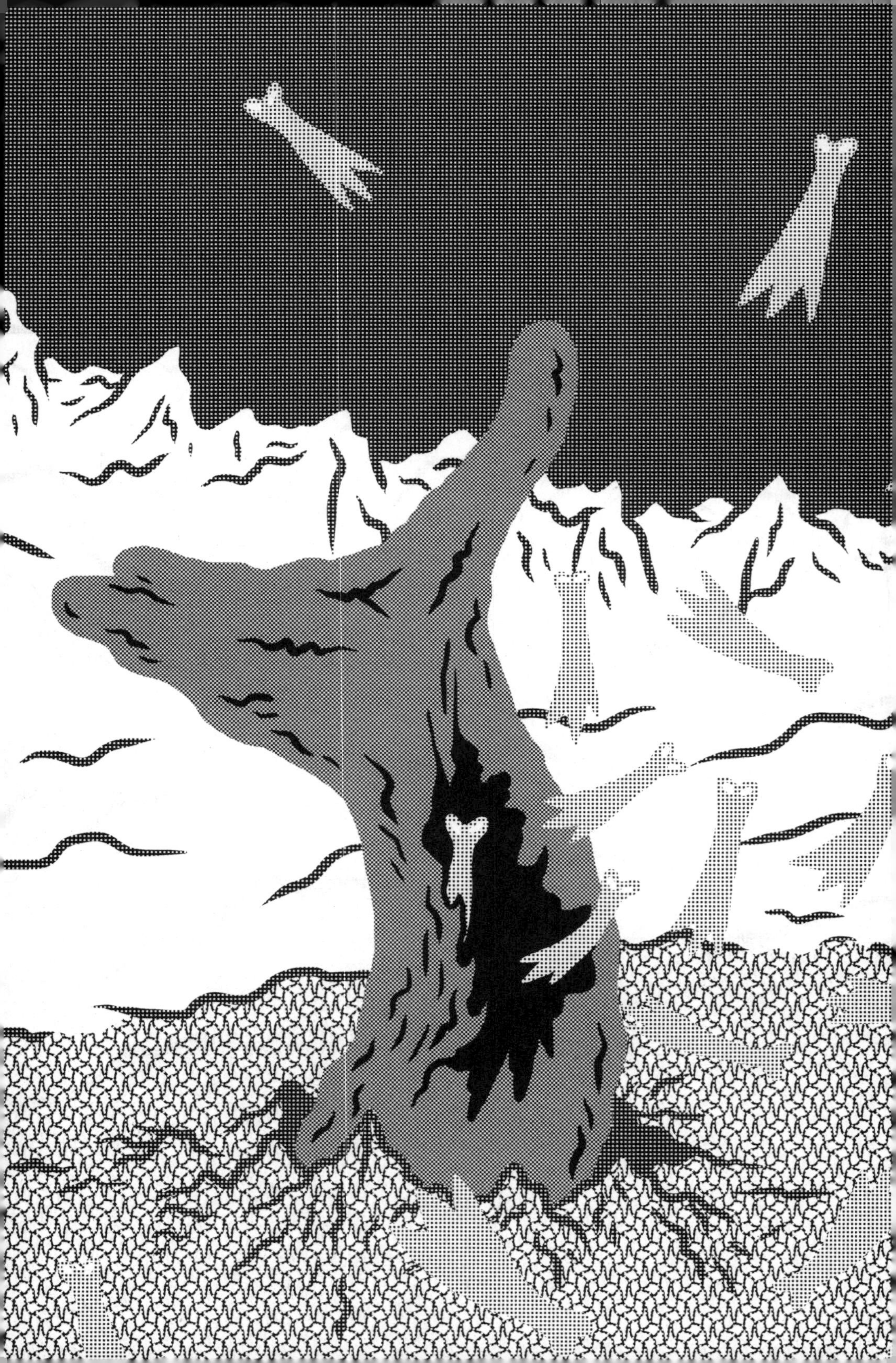

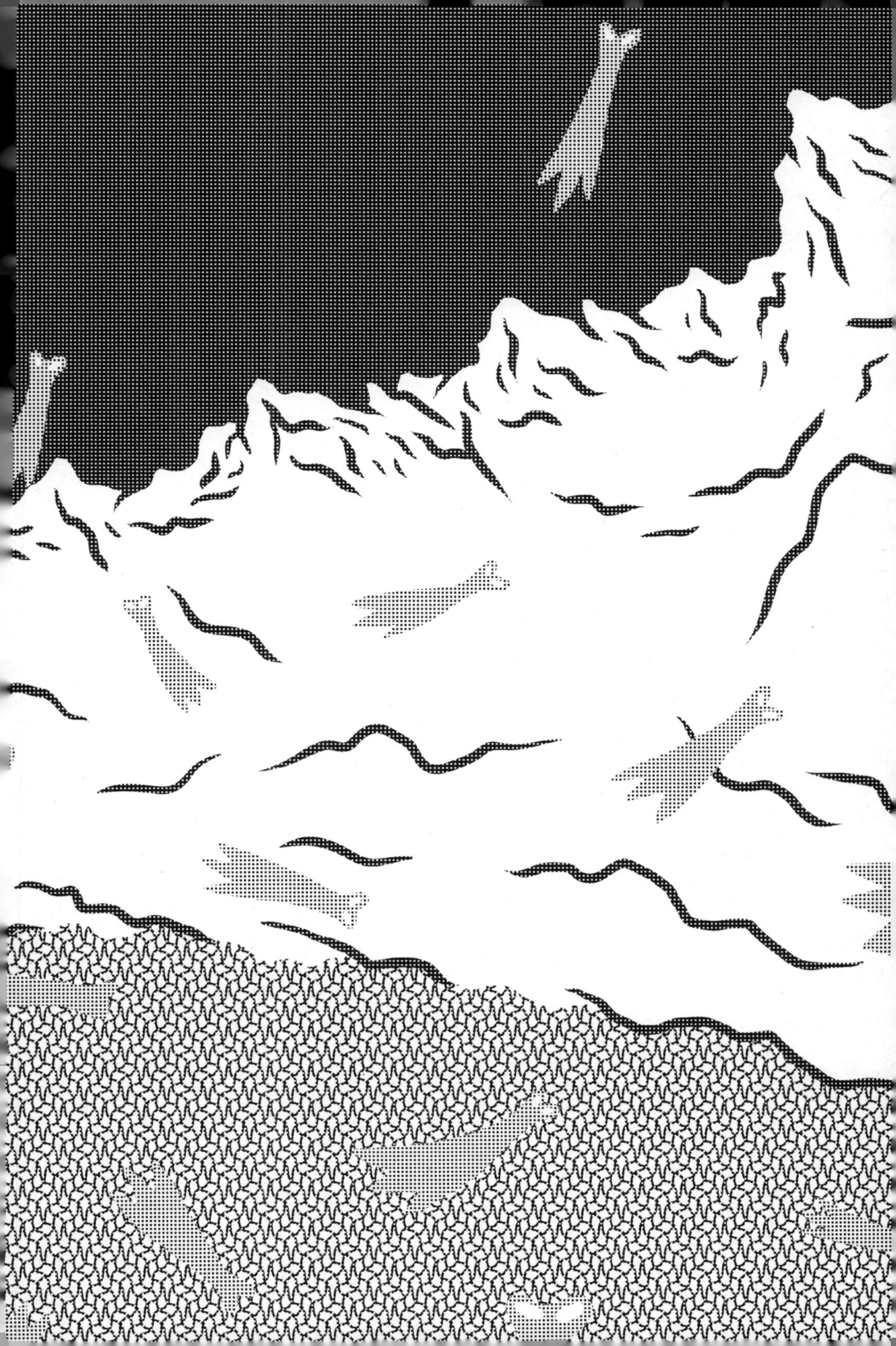

DRAWN IN AUSTIN, TEXAS,
JUNE 2011 TO AUGUST 2013 AND
REVISED MAY TO OCTOBER 2014.
ORIGINALLY SELF-PUBLISHED
AS VORTEX #1-4.

THANKS TO VIRGINIA PAINE AND EVERYONE
ELSE AT SPARKPLUG; MY BETA READERS
JOSH BURGGRAF, JASON POLAND, GRANT
DAVIS, ALLISON MURPHY, AND MARTIN
THOMAS — WITHOUT Y'ALL THIS BOOK
WOULD MAKE EVEN LESS SENSE;
FRANK SANTORO FOR TEACHING ME TO
DRAW IN LAYERS LIKE A PRINTMAKER;
MY PARENTS FOR INSTILLING AND
SUBSIDIZING MY LOVE OF ART AND BOOKS;
MY BROTHER FOR LENDING ME HIS
COMICS AND SHARING MY ENTHUSIASM;
MY DAUGHTER FOR THE ROARS AND
LAUGHS; MY WIFE FOR HER FEEDBACK,
PRAGMATISM, AND COVER; AND
THE SUPPORT OF MY FAMILY, FRIENDS,
DISTRIBUTORS, AND READERS.

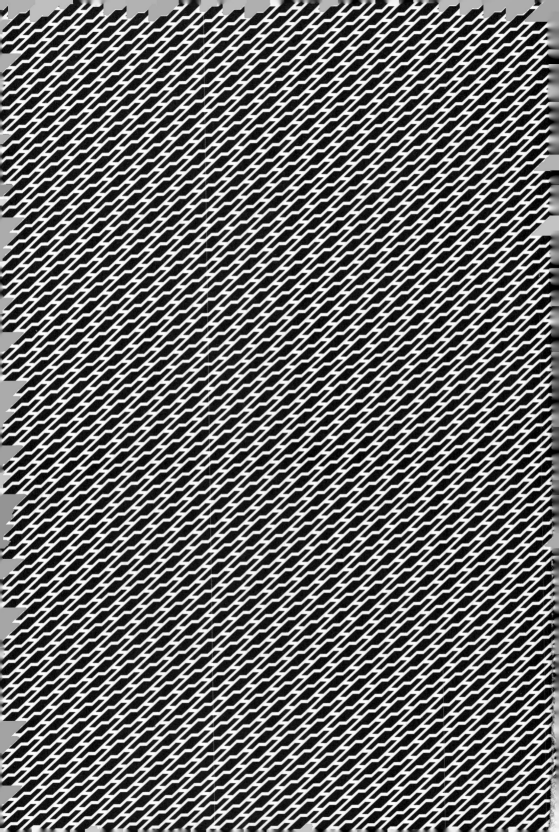